University of London Historical Studies

XVI

UNIVERSITY OF LONDON HISTORICAL STUDIES

THE SINGLE DUTY PROJECT

THE SYSTEM OF BARRIERS AND GUARDS
maintained by the General Farm of Taxes

Key

yellow line = customs (*les traites*)
green line = salt tax or monopoly (*la gabelle*)
red line = tobacco tax or monopoly (*le tabac*)

A map taken from Mahy de Cormeré, *Recherches et Considérations nouvelles sur les Finances*, London 1789, vol. II. Cormeré adds, 'Les droits de subvention par doublement, de marque des fers, de fabrication des huiles, exigent d'autres barrières et beaucoup de bureaux dans l'intérieur: leur multiplicité ne permet pas de les indiquer.'

J. F. BOSHER

The Single Duty Project

A Study of the Movement for a
French Customs Union in the
Eighteenth Century

UNIVERSITY OF LONDON
THE ATHLONE PRESS
1964

Published by
THE ATHLONE PRESS
UNIVERSITY OF LONDON
at 2 *Gower Street, London* WCI

Distributed by Constable & Co. Ltd
12 *Orange Street, London* WC2

Canada
Oxford University Press
Toronto

U.S.A.
Oxford University Press Inc
New York

Printed in Great Britain by
THE ALDEN PRESS, OXFORD

TO MARGA

PREFACE

THE modern French customs system was established in 1790 and 1791 by the *Assemblée constituante*, but it was planned much earlier by the men of a reform movement which began in the reign of Louis XIV. Officials of the Crown and the General Farm of Taxes led this movement. Drawing their inspiration from the tariff policy of Colbert, they planned to abolish all the internal customs duties in favour of a single rational tariff imposed at the frontiers of the kingdom. Their efforts to perfect and to implement their project, which they usually called *le projet du droit unique*, are the subject of this book. The project had several different aspects: the transformation of the customs from a mere hodge-podge of taxes to a system for enforcing an economic policy; the replacement of the General Farm of Taxes by a *régie* or Crown administration in order to increase government control of the customs; the creation of a national free trade area protected from foreign competition; and the defeat of powerful vested interests which defended the internal duties. This is one of those reform projects characteristic of the 'Age of Reform' which Professor Alfred Cobban has described. Like many other projects of that time it had to wait until the Revolution had provided the occasion and the force needed to put it into effect. It was by wielding the power of national authority over private, provincial and local privilege that the *Assemblée constituante* enabled its committees, in co-operation with Crown officials, to create a French customs union.

This study began as an inquiry into the French free trade movement to see how far it was concerned with internal free trade, and it was submitted in an early form as a thesis for the Ph.D degree of London University. The original idea I owe to Professor Alfred Cobban of University College, London, who supervised both the writing of the thesis and the revision of it for the book. I wish to thank him here for his painstaking labour on my many drafts, for his continuous scholarly guidance, and for the stimulation of his friendship. I also wish to express gratitude to Professor S. T. Bindoff of Queen Mary College, London, for his generous help and encouragement, and to Dr. D. Dakin of Birkbeck College, London, for reading and criticizing the manuscript. For the shortcomings of the book I am entirely responsible.

The research for it was made possible by grants from the Canada Council, the French Government, Queen Mary College, London, and the Central Research Fund of London University. Acknowledgments are also owing to the staffs of many libraries and archives, notably those at the *Archives nationales*, the *Ecole des Ponts et Chaussées* and the archives of the *Département du Loir et Cher* who went out of their way to assist. Mrs. Joan Kennard and Miss Janette Fulker typed the manuscript. Finally, for help at various stages I wish to thank Professor Jean Meuvret, who found some useful manuscripts for me, and my friends, Hubert Mondor, Geoffrey Mead and John Norris.

J. F. B.

University of British Columbia

CONTENTS

ABBREVIATIONS

The titles and the names of the authors of nearly all printed works cited in the footnotes have been abbreviated. Full names, titles, etc. are listed in the Bibliography. In addition, the following abbreviations have been used:

A.N.	Archives nationales
Arch. Ass. Pub.	Archives de l'Assistance Publique
B.N.	Bibliothèque nationale
G.L.	Goldsmiths Library, University of London
B.M.	British Museum
L.S.E.	Library of the London School of Economics
P. et C.	Ecole nationale des Ponts et Chaussées
Rev. d'éc. pol.	*Revue d'économie politique*
Rev. hist.	*Revue historique*
R.h.d.e.s.	*Revue d'histoire des doctrines économiques et sociales*

CHAPTER I

The Customs Duties of the *Ancien Régime*

TOLLS on trade were collected throughout Europe in medieval times, and although many more were added in the sixteenth and seventeenth centuries it was long before the toll system lost its medieval character. Tolls were established in the first place because they were among the simplest and most effective of taxes. It was possible to collect them without preparing tax rolls, with only the most rudimentary kind oɪ assessment, and with the greatest possible certainty, because travelling merchants were obliged to use roads, rivers and sea-ports, and if they could not or would not pay as directed, their goods could be confiscated. If the taxing authorities took proper precautions against smuggling most of the tax payers did not have to be sought out but came themselves to the collec-tion bureaux. And these bureaux might consist of nothing more than teams of officials—guards, assessors, collectors and accoun-tants—at strategic points on trade routes. Because of their advantages as a method of taxation, tolls had come to be col-lected by many different authorities: governments of towns and provinces, feudal barons on their estates, rulers at the frontiers of their domains and principalities. In France, the tolls established by such authorities in medieval and early modern times remained unchanged in many respects until the French Revolution. As the Valois and Bourbon Kings extended royal power over France, they gradually acquired the tolls, whether of medieval or modern origin, and added them to the revenue system of the Crown. This process continued through the eighteenth century and was completed by the governments of the Revolution. Not until then did the congeries of tolls give way to a unified customs system of the kind we know today. But the work of the Revolution in this sphere, far from being revolutionary, was the culmination of a long development. By the eighteenth century it was possible to distinguish at least five kinds of tolls: the *péages*, the *octrois*, the tolls collected as adjuncts to the excise duties (*aides* and *droits de marque*) and to the crown monopolies of salt and tobacco (*gabelle* and *tabac*), and the customs duties (*traites* or *douanes*). The *péages*, or tolls proper, were commonly collected at convenient points on roads and rivers. Although originally instituted to pay for the maintenance of a bridge, ferry or road, most *péages* were justified in the eighteenth century only by legal titles. They were still largely in private hands, being in most cases attached to private estates, but the crown made spasmodic attempts to acquire them, partly in response to complaints from those who paid them and partly because of its own natural desire to increase its revenues. In 1724 a royal *Commission des péages* began systematically to confiscate *péages* for which there were no proper titles, abolishing some and adding others to the tax farms of the customs as *péages royaux*. The Commission claimed to have reduced the number in private hands from 5,688 to 2,054 during the reign of Louis XV. By 1789, just before their total abolition, they had been still further reduced to about 1,600.[1]

The *octrois*, collected on goods entering and leaving certain cities, were an important source of municipal revenue until the twentieth century. Their characteristic use was to provide funds for the maintenance of town councils, gilds, hospitals and the like. Under the *ancien régime* the crown did not endeavour to confiscate them, as it did the *péages*, but rather to burden them with the payment of the Chambers of Commerce and the royal Inspectors of Manufactures. At the gates of Paris, however, the royal tax farmers collected tolls of this type, the *entrées de Paris*, which yielded substantial returns.[2]

[1] Jeanne Bouteil, *Le Rachat*, p. 77. Cf. G.-F. Mahy de Cormeré, *Rech. fin.*, i, 461 and vol. ii, *passim*.

[2] In the 1780s there were reported to be 1,500 *octrois* belonging to 793 cities, hospitals, gilds and other organizations (A.N., H 1448. Papers from Calonne's office). A statement of the *octrois* of Rouen, sent by the syndics of the city to the Controller General of Finance in 1764, reports an annual payment to the Chamber of Commerce of 16,000 *livres* authorized by a law of 19 June 1730, and by 1774 this had risen to 17,800 *livres*. An annual salary of 8,000 *livres* for John Holker, General Inspector of Manufactures, was also charged to the *octrois* of Rouen by Holker's commission of 4 April 1755 (A.N., F12 831). The Inspectors of Manufactures in

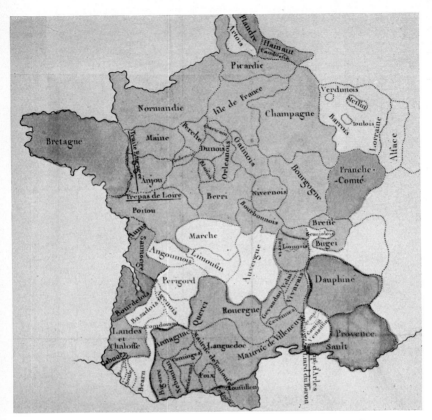

THE PROVINCES AND CUSTOMS AREAS IN 1762

A map taken from J. Michau de Montaran, *Mémoire sur les tarifs* . . ., Paris 1762. In the original map the customs areas are variously coloured, with an explanatory key, here summarized.

Light grey area extending from Picardie to Aunis and from Normandie to Bourgogne and Bourbonnois: *Cinq Grosses Fermes, tarif de* 1664. The central white area extending south to Béarn: *Provinces réputées Etrangères dans l'Intérieur*. North eastern white area: *Provinces réputées Etrangères Frontières*. The remaining areas are designated as: Bretagne: *Prévosté de Nantes, Brieux, Ports et Havres, Traitte Domaniale*. Saintonge: *Traitte de Charente, Droits des Seigneurs, Parisis*. Bourdelois: *Comptablie*, 4*p*% *des Drogueries, Convoi, Courtage*. Landes et Chalosse: *Traitte d'Arsac*. Labour et Bayonne: *Coûtume de Bayonne*. Flandre, Hainaut, Cambresis: *Tarifs de* 1671. Franche Comté: *Droits Uniformes*. Lionnois et Foresic: *Douane de Lyon, Douane de Valence*, 4*p*% *des Drogueries, Foraine de Lyon*. Dauphiné: *Douane de Lyon, Douane de Valence*. Provence: *Douane de Lyon*, 4*p*% *des Drogueries, Table de Mer, Foraine Domaniale*. Languedoc et partie de Guienne: *Douane de Lyon*, 4*p*% *des Drogueries, Foraine Domaniale*. Cerdagne et Roussillon: *Tarif Catalan*.

Certain tolls formed part of the system of excise taxes (*aides* and *droits de marque*). The *aides* were an excise charge mainly on wine and other alcoholic drinks in certain provinces known as the *pays des aides*, and they were collected in the form of a toll on such beverages sent into the *pays des aides* from other provinces. In a similar way, the *droits de marque*—taxes on iron, oils and soaps, paper, some kinds of cloth, and leather—were also levied as tolls at the borders of the provinces in which they were imposed. All these dues, whether excise taxes or tolls, were collected for the Crown by tax farmers who from 1681 came together to form the General Farm of Taxes. But whereas the collection of the excise taxes was the function of one department of the General Farm, for reasons of convenience the tolls were usually collected by another department which dealt with the customs. Thus, tolls such as the lucrative *subvention par double-ment*[1] which were legally excise taxes, for administrative purposes became part of the customs system.

A few toll charges on the movement of salt and tobacco were collected by those branches of the General Farm which managed the two royal monopolies, the *gabelle* and the *tabac*. They were part of a system in which salt and tobacco were sold at varying prices in different provinces according to time-honoured provincial agreements with the Crown. Price variations made necessary a control of the borders between the different price zones and tolls at points where the transport of the monopoly products from one zone to another was permitted.

There was only a vague difference between all these tolls and the customs duties. In general, the tolls already described were for the most part mere taxes, whereas the customs were taxes which sometimes served to favour certain kinds of trade, or the

---

[1] Payable on all alcoholic drinks entering or leaving the *pays des aides*, except eau-de-vie for export to foreign countries. Other *aides* collected as duties were the *jauge et courtage* also on the borders of the *pays des aides*, a duty on wine leaving the *généralités* of Amiens, Soissons and Châlons, another levied in Boulogne, Calais and Etaples on wine destined for Picardy and Champagne. All these are described in Moreau de Beaumont, *Mém. con.*

Bordeaux and Lyon were also paid from the receipts of the *octrois* in their cities (A.N., F¹² 152: letters of Trudaine de Montigny of 24 May 1776 to Dupré de Saint-Maur, and of 17 June 1776 to the Commissioners of the Assembly of Notables in Lyon).

B

trade of certain merchants, or certain areas, at the expense of others. Thus, the customs tended to have an economic as well as a financial function. But there were so many customs duties which were nothing more than taxes that this generalization is of very little use. Eighteenth-century definitions of the customs do not satisfactorily distinguish them from other tolls. Thus, the terms *douanes* and *traites* were commonly supposed to refer to 'all the duties levied on all types of merchandise whether exported from the kingdom or any designated territory, or imported into it'.[1] Such definitions mark off the customs from the *péages* by showing that customs officers had to take into account the origin and destination of taxable goods, so that a consignment of goods normally had to pay a customs duty only once whereas it might have to pay a *péage* every time it passed the point of collection. Again, customs duties were supposed to be collected anywhere that a frontier was crossed rather than at a specific place on a road or river. Yet it is useless to try to prove this distinction with reference to the tolls as they were; and as for the *octrois* and tolls derived from the excise taxes and crown monopolies, the definition fits them as well as it fits the customs. The location of the customs bureaux does not distinguish them from other tolls. Though some bureaux were established in a modern manner along the foreign frontiers, others were not, and no distinction was made between the internal duties and those on the frontiers, except by the adherents of the customs reform movement, who had a precocious insight into the future role of the customs in national economic policy.

Most customs tolls were such only by usage and by law. In general, the *ancien régime* knew its customs duties from its other tolls only as a father might know his children—individually and by name.[2] They defy any but the crudest classification. They ranged in importance from the *liard du baron*, collected in a single bureau on the Rhône at Arles to the amount of about a thousand *livres* a year (in the period 1768–77) to the *douane de Lyon*, which in the same period yielded an annual 722,435 *livres* through 150 bureaux on the frontiers of Lyonnais, Forez, Dauphiné, Provence, Languedoc and at a later stage, Roussillon.

---

[1] A.N., G⁷ 1176, *Etat des directions de la ferme*, ms.   [2] See table on p. 10.

They varied in their rates from the ½ per cent *ad valorem* charge of the *table de mer* on all goods imported into Provence, to the rate of one-twelfth charged by the *foraine* on practically all goods transported in or out of Provence, Languedoc, Dauphiné, Avignon and Orange. Even their names were not standard, for the *foraine*, depending on where it was levied, was variously named *patente de Languedoc, traite foraine, foraine domainiale, foraine de Provence* or *foraine*. Some of them, such as the *tarif Catalan* of Roussillon, were purely provincial in scope, whereas others such as the *péage de Péronne* which was collected in more than forty bureaux between Reims and Abbeville, were not confined to a single province. Most of them had little in common ✔ to distinguish them from other tolls except their traditional and legal inclusion in the tax farm of the customs. This was still so when Colbert, under Louis XIV, seized the idea that they ought to play a characteristic role in the encouragement of French trade and industry, and took the first steps towards reforming them for this purpose. More than a hundred years later the Constituent Assembly completed this process of reform and thereby realized his conception of the customs as tolls with economic uses.

Colbert's plan was to unite the provinces of the kingdom into a single customs union and for this purpose he drew up a new tariff which he hoped might eventually replace all others. When this tariff was officially published on 18 September 1664 it was accepted by a group of provinces which together occupied most of the northern half of France—Brittany, Alsace, Flanders, Artois, Hainaut and Cambrésis excepted—and which were administered for customs purposes by an amalgamated company of tax farmers known as the *Cinq Grosses Fermes*.[1] He was unable to extend this union any further owing to resistance

[1] The *Cinq Grosses Fermes* had originally been separate farms charged with collecting the *rêve*, the *haut passage*, the *imposition foraine*, the *trépas de Loire* and the *traite d'Anjou*. In the eighteenth century, the provinces of the *Cinq Grosses Fermes* were: Anjou, Aunis, Beaujolais, Bourgogne, Bresse, Bourbonnais, Bugey, Champagne, Châtellenie, Chantoceaux, Dombes, Maine, Normandy, Picardy, Poiten, Thouars and their dependent territories, and within this outer ring of provinces were Ile de France, Orléanais, Nivernais, Perche and Touraine. The most reliable books on the geography and structure of the customs system are, Vivent Magnien, *Rec. alph.*; G.-F. Mahy de Cormeré, *Rech. fin.*; and Moreau de Beaumont, *Mém. con.* A useful short study is, G. T. Mathews, *Gen. Farm.* Finally, there are three con-

in the other provinces. Those remaining outside the union became known as the Provinces Reputed Foreign (*provinces réputées étrangères*) to distinguish them from the provinces of the *Cinq Grosses Fermes*.[1]

Dissatisfied with this imperfect union, Colbert decided that if the remaining duties could not be consolidated, at least the industry of the kingdom as a whole might be protected by a special new tariff. He published on 11 April 1667 a tariff of protective duties to be imposed only at the frontiers of the kingdom and only on a select list of fifty-seven important industrial products and four scarce raw materials. Though the Tariff of 1667 affected only a modest range of items at first, supplementary lists of goods subject to duties known as *nouveaux droits* were appended to it from time to time. It was estimated that by the end of the *ancien régime* from two-fifths to two-thirds of all imports and exports had been added to it in this way. Known collectively as the Uniform Duties (*droits uniformes*), the Tariff of 1667 and the *nouveaux droits* were uniform only in the sense that their rates did not vary from place to place. They were collected at different rates on different products. Although they all tended to discourage imports of foreign manufactured goods and exports of raw materials by high duties and to favour exports of French manufactures and imports of raw materials by low duties, they were not uniformly imposed even on the kingdom's frontiers, for many territories lay outside their cordon. These latter, referred to as the *provinces traitées à l'instar de l'étranger effectif* (which will henceforth be abbreviated as Foreign Provinces), fall conveniently into two groups. One, including Alsace, Trois Evêchés (Metz, Toul and Verdun) and, when it became French, Lorraine, were said to be 'free' because

---

[1] The Provinces Reputed Foreign were: Angoumois, Artois, Auvergne, lower Navarre, Béarn, Brittany, Cambrésis, Foix, Dauphiné, Flanders, Forez, Franche Comté, Gascony, Guyenne, Hainaut, Ile-de-Rhé, Ile d'Oléron, Languedoc, Limousin, Lyonnais, Marche, Provence (with the exception of Marseille and its dependent territory), Roussillon, Rouergue, Saintonge and Vivarais. Flanders, Hainaut, Cambrésis and, to some extent Artois, were subject to a special tariff of 13 June 1671 in their trade with the rest of the kingdom.

temporary coloured maps of the customs system: (1) in Cormeré, *Rech. fin.* (see frontispiece), (2) in Jacques Necker, *Compte rendu*, (3) in Michau de Montaran (*père*), *Mémoire sur les tarifs* (see p. 2).

they remained almost entirely outside the royal customs system; but Lorraine had its own system which the Crown came to control. A second group consisted of scattered small territories which were excluded for various reasons from the royal customs system: the free ports of Marseille, Dunkirk and, from 1784, Bayonne and Lorient; the county of Venaissin, often called Avignon after its chief city; and, from 1775, the territory of Gex on the Swiss frontier.[1] Thus, to sum up, as a result of Colbert's efforts, the kingdom was divided for customs purposes into three types of provinces—those of the *Cinq Grosses Fermes*, the Provinces Reputed Foreign, and the Foreign Provinces; and there were three main sets of duties, none of which applied to the whole of France: the duties of the Tariff of 1664, the Uniform Duties which included the Tariff of 1667 and the *nouveaux droits*, and the so-called 'local duties' or older duties not affected by Colbert's reforms.

From the time of Colbert until the Revolution the system remained unchanged in its main outlines, but there were various alterations in detail. Some, like the suppression of the Tariff of Roussillon in 1785,[2] and the exclusion from the customs system of Gex in 1775 and of the ports of Bayonne and Lorient, created 'free ports' in 1784, were made partly in response to local or commercial pressure.[3] But undoubtedly most changes were made in an endeavour to increase customs revenue. Thus, the various duties on French colonial trade, referred to as the *domaine d'Occident et du Canada*, were fixed at the general rate of 3 per cent in 1717, raised to 3½ per cent in 1727, became part of the General Farm in 1732, and counted as a customs duty from 1780.[4] The *péages royaux* increased in number: in 1774 the *Commission des péages* reported a total of 203.[5] Most lucrative of all was a surtax

---

[1] After much difficulty in collecting customs duties on goods passing between France and Venaissin, the Crown signed a Concordat with the Papacy on 11 March 1734 which established a limited free trade with special provisions for the important Venaissin products of wine, oil and silk (B.N., ms. fr. 8371: Orry to Fontanieu, 2 Feb. 1732; there is a copy of the Concordat in A.N., G¹ 6). For Gex, see Félix Gerlier, *Voltaire*.

[2] By an *arrêt* of 24 September 1785 to take effect on 1 January 1787. Rousselot de Surgy, *Enc. méth.*, articles 'Roussillon' and 'Tarif'.

[3] Felix Gerlier, *Voltaire*; and Boyetet des Bordes, *Précis sur la franchise*.

[4] A.N., G⁷ 1176, *Ecclaircissements préliminaires*, ms.

[5] Jeanne Bouteil, *Le Rachat*, pp. 77 ff.

on all duties, the *sols pour livre*, fixed at 20 per cent or 4 *sols pour livre* in 1715, raised to 5 *sols pour livre* in 1760, 6 in 1763, 8 in 1771 and finally to 10 in 1781; so that during the last years of the *ancien régime* there was a surtax of 50 per cent on customs duties.

Closely connected with efforts to increase revenue was the slow, halting extension of royal control over the duties. Most of them had found their way permanently into the royal tax farms before Colbert's time, but a few remained to be expropriated in the eighteenth century. The most notable of these were the *trépas de Loire* and an associated duty variously called the *traite par terre*, *traite d'Anjou*, or *foraine d'Anjou*. The first, as its name implies, was a tax on goods mounting and descending the Loire, and was payable in ten bureaux from Chantoceaux up as far as Saumur, and in two inland bureaux at Château Gontier and Laval. The *traite d'Anjou* was levied on everything which passed between Brittany on the one hand and on the other, Anjou and the *vicomtés* of Thouars and Beaumont. The tariffs of these duties contain imposing lists of items but do not indicate the principles upon which the taxes on them were calculated. Indeed, the tariff of the *traite d'Anjou* announces that all goods not listed will be taxed at the discretion of the tax officials.[1] Colbert had intended to replace both of these duties by the Tariff of 1664, but instead they found their way into private hands. There they remained for more than a century. Then in a Declaration of 1 June 1771, the Controller General claimed for the Crown all duties, whoever the owners, and seven months later issued a specific order that the *trépas de Loire* and the *traite d'Anjou* be levied for the King's profit from 1 January 1772. This did not mean, however, that they were to be confiscated but that the owners were to be bought out. The cost of this is said to have been 410,496 *livres*.[2] As an adherent of the customs reform movement remarked in 1787, to serve the

---

[1] A.N., G¹ 63, *Etat général des bureaux de la Ferme rangés alphabétiquement*, ms.; *Traite par terre et imposition foraine* (reprinted), Angers, 1765, 35 pp.; and F. Uzereau, 'Le Trépas de Loire', *Andegaviana*, 13ᵉ série, Anger and Paris, 1913, pp. 115–17.

[2] Rousselot de Surgy, *Enc. méth.*, article, 'Traite par Terre'. According to an *arrêt* of 2 August 1723 the owners were then the duc de Noirmoutier, Saron de Champigny, president of the *Enquêtes*, le Guerchois, Master of Requests, Brunet, president in the Chamber of Accounts, Goislart de Monsabert, Councillor in the Grand Chamber of the Parlement, 'and others' (*Traite par terre*, &c., p. 30; also, A.N., AD IX 488, *arrêt* of 12 December 1771).

national advantage this transaction should have resulted in the abolition of the two duties. Instead, the comte de Provence, brother of Louis XVI, asked for them and after five years, during which the Farmers General quietly went on collecting them, his request was granted on condition that he paid 30,000 *livres* a year into the Royal Treasury. His ownership was made retrospective from 1 January 1772, and it was estimated that for the five past years the receipts from the two duties had amounted to more than 800,000 *livres*.[1] Provence made a net profit of 200,000 *livres* after paying all costs including 150,000 *livres* for five years' rental to the Crown. Finally, he retroceded the two duties to the Crown and received in their place an annuity of 180,000 *livres*.[2]

The Crown also acquired the *coûtume de Bayonne* in the course of the eighteenth century. This was an import and export duty of 5 per cent collected on the borders of the little *pays de Labour* including the city of Bayonne, by the family of Gramont. In 1664 the government obtained half of it, but the division appears to have been in dispute until defined in a royal *arrêt* of 31 August 1728. The duc de Gramont defended the duty against proposals for its abolition in 1720 and 1737, but in 1784 the Crown bought it for the price of a pension of 12,000 *livres* a month in order to confer upon Bayonne the privileges of a free port.[3]

These were among the last of a long list of expropriations. One by one the duties had been added to the royal holdings and, except for Colbert and the reforming officials of the eighteenth century, most servants of the Crown continued to regard the customs as a collection of separate dues rather than a general system. And a collection it remained, for each duty retained its separate identity in the customs records and accounts of the General Farm of Taxes. Although administrative convenience would have been best served by a thorough integration of the various duties, this was prevented by the law and custom which alone justified the levy of each duty, and

---

[1] Rousselot de Surgy, *Enc. méth.*, article, 'Traite par Terre'. His estimate is supported by another that the annual product of these duties was 40 or 50 thousand écus (A.N., G¹ 1–2, *Mémoire sur la régie en générale* (ms).

[2] *Convention nationale, troisième registre des dépenses secrètes de la Cour connu sous le nom de livre rouge*, Paris, 1793, p. 53.

[3] This was paid, though erratically, until 1 January 1791.

THE INTERNAL CUSTOM DUTIES

A table of the principal customs duties collected either wholly or in part at internal bureaux

Name of customs duty	No. of bureaux in which collected[1]	Average annual yield for the period 1768–1777[2]		
		livres	*sols*	*deniers*
Uniform duties (Tariff of 1667 and the *nouveaux arrets*)	433	881,787	3	0
Duties collected within or on the borders of the territory of the Cinq Grosses Fermes				
Tariff of 1664	425	3,296,483	6	4
Trépas de Loire	12	150,000	0	0
Traite d'Anjou	?	?		
Parisis, sol, six deniers, etc.	12	90,619	4	7
Prévôté de Nantes	36	176,836	15	0
Péage de Péronne	42	16,612	3	4
Subvention par doublement	346	312,947	2	5
40 *livres*, 10 *sols* per tonneau	202	?		
9 *livres*, 18 *sols* per tonneau	3	18,834	2	6
Droit d'abord	111	4,920	13	10
Droit de consommation	125	178,200	0	9
Duties of the Provinces Reputed Foreign, commonly called 'local duties'				
Douane de Lyon	150	722,435	19	6
Douane de Valence	155	554,778	15	9
Foraine	235	539,481	14	2
Denier Saint André	16	6,278	11	11
2 per cent d'Arles	1	26,371	0	7
Liard du Baron	1	1,086	15	3
Table de Mer	?	35,853	1	11
Ecu per quintal of alum	?	?		
4 per cent on drugs and spices	?	37,706	2	8
Péage du Paty	?	22,825	0	10
Duties of Roussillon (tarif Catalan)	23	23,801	11	2
Traite d'Arzac	33	22,059	16	10
Coûtume de Bayonne	18	32,793	16	10
Convoy	11	1,768,620	15	9
Comptablie	9	336,210	8	10
Courtage	4	144,462	14	6
Traite de Charente (mostly on salt)	25	665,036	10	1
Tariff of 1671	90	562,210	4	3
Sols pour livre (eight in this period, i.e. 40 per cent surtax on duties internal and external)		5,193,886	9	9

[1] A.N., G¹ 63, *Etat général des bureaux* (ms.). Usually more than one duty was collected in each bureau. Many were collected at certain frontier bureaux as well as in the interior of the country. For another table of duties, see Rousselot de Surgy, *Enc. méth.*, vol. iii, p. 683.

[2] Arch. Ass. Pub., papers of Auget de Montyon, *Etat général du produit des droits de traites et toiles peintes des neuf années composées de six du Bail d'Alaterre et des trois premières de celuy de David et de l'année commune desdites neuf années.*

THE INTERNAL DUTIES IN 1784

The annual products by regions and provinces of the internal duties to be suppressed according to the single duty project of Mahy de Cormeré[1]

Regions or provinces	Internal customs duties	Marque des huiles	Marque des fers	Subvention, par doublement, jauge et courage	18ˢ per tonneau, 5ˢ and 15ˢ per muid	13 livres 10ˢ per muid	Totals
Cinq Grosses Fermes	1,372,066	249,911	730,229	56,336	26,508		2,435,120
Flanders, Artois, Hainaut and Cambrésis	262,549	417,544			3,276	280,141	963,510
Brittany	1,037,798		90,000	6,052			1,133,850
Saintonge	69,116						69,116
Sénéch. de Bordeaux	242,887	5,846					248,733
Languedoc, Roussillon, Landes and adjacent provinces	670,587	258,283	89,925				1,018,795
Provence	300,856	478,192	26,570				779,048
Dauphiné	233,020	12,052		9,486			271,642
Lyonnais, Forez and Beaujolais	266,890	15,695		4,224			292,071
Franche Comté	33,023	10,434				446	48,127
Totals	4,488,792	1,447,957	936,794	76,098	29,784	280,587	7,260,102

[1] Arch. Ass. Pub., papers of Auget de Montyon, *Extraits du mémoire sur la réforme des Traites par Monsieur de Cormeré* (1786). The figures are of 1784.

11

THE CUSTOMS DUTIES IN 1784

The annual products by regions and provinces of the customs duties compared with the products expected after the execution of the single duty project of Mahy de Cormeré[1]

Regions or provinces	Internal duties	Import duties	Export duties	Deductions	Actual totals	Anticipated totals
Cinq Grosses Fermes	2,435,120	5,434,490	1,325,941	418,800	8,766,251	7,468,108
Flanders, Artois, Hainaut and Cambrésis	963,510	1,000,855	131,220		2,095,585	1,246,553
Brittany	1,133,850	257,593	146,699		1,538,142	654,947
Saintonge	69,116	71,933	57,327		198,376	86,052
Sénéch. de Bordeaux	248,733	900,650	2,405,430	191,500	3,363,313	2,844,530
Languedoc, Roussillon, Landes and adjacent provinces	1,018,795	624,457	558,508	70,000	2,131,760	1,326,790
Provence	779,048	1,224,291	554,039	281,700	2,275,671	2,072,043
Dauphiné	271,642	135,606	55,636		462,884	297,948
Lyonnais, Forez and Beaujolais	292,071	1,501,564	47,209	200,000	1,640,844	1,404,950
Franche Comté	48,127	244,066	54,777		346,970	415,087
Totals	7,260,012	11,395,505	5,336,779	1,162,000	22,831,296	17,817,008

[1] *Loc. cit.*

by the provincial forces which opposed any change in them. Each duty existed in law only through an early document proving royal recognition of it or through an agreement of the Crown with provincial estates, municipal government or other local authority whereby the Crown had acquired the right to collect it. In either case, the duty had been mentioned by name or described, if not precisely defined, in a contract which amounted to a tax agreement based on the consent of the taxpayers in so far as they were represented by the local or provincial authority. Any changes by the Crown were likely to meet with the resistance of that authority and of the provincial *parlement, cour des aides,* or other high court. The last government of the *ancien régime* which made a determined attempt to overcome this resistance and to unify the customs duties was that of Louis XIV and Colbert. But Colbert's tariffs of 1664 and 1667, though intended as steps towards unification, were themselves added to—without replacing—the general congeries of dues; and for more than a century the collection of duties, old and new, was leased at regular intervals to the tax farmers. The tax leases, which contained lists of the duties by name, thus helped to preserve their separate identity and to show that the tax farmers had no authority to change them, even if they wished to do so.

If the companies of tax farmers could not unify the duties they could at least increase the efficiency of the collection system. And they had every reason for doing this because they were profit-making companies which paid the Crown fixed sums, according to the terms of their leases, and recovered these sums and their own profits by working the tax farms. In 1681 the major farms merged to form the monopolistic Company of the General Farm. The fortunes of this Company fluctuated during the next forty years but during the reign of Louis XV it improved its position to such an extent that in the later years of the *ancien régime* the Controller General found it desirable to include in the leases a formal claim on a proportion of the profits. By eighteenth-century standards, the General Farm had become extraordinarily efficient. Dividing the country systematically into a number of Directions (26 in mid-century; 42 later on—the number varied) it had organized a hierarchical administration with effective subordination, control and inspection. Within each Direction customs bureaux had been amalgamated, so that each bureau normally served to collect several different duties. The regional Directors, responsible to the Farmers General in Paris, supervised the work of teams of controllers, collectors and clerks in more than a thousand customs bureaux and of many thousands of guards organized in military fashion into brigades. Increasing efficiency, together with a growing volume of trade, additional *sous pour livres* (surtax) and other factors produced more and more revenue. The net annual yield of the customs rose throughout the century from 7 or 8 million *livres* in the years 1715–18 to over 14 millions in 1768, 22 millions in 1784, and perhaps 28 millions in 1788.[1] But however favourable its effect on revenues, efficiency had a damaging effect on trade. Trade suffered not only from taxes that were rising and becoming more difficult to evade, but also from the more exacting administration of a system of unfathomable complexity. The methods of collection had been reformed without reforming the system of duties. The more stringent enforcement of the organization which the Farmers General had built up around these duties, and the extension of bureaucratic controls, only increased the harm which they did to French trade.

The most striking feature of the system was that it imposed costs, delays, paperwork and risks on internal as well as foreign trade. Surviving records convey no accurate idea of the relative importance of the internal and the frontier duties, mainly because the General Farm did not distinguish between them, but we shall not go far wrong in estimating that during the later decades of the century about 500 bureaux, or approximately half of the total number, were placed on internal borders and in 1784 produced about one-third of the total customs revenue or approximately 7 million livres.[2] The General Farm deployed

---

[1] Bib. P. et C., ms. 1046. *Tarif général du droit unique,* vol. xiv, p. 7732; Arch. Ass. Pub., papers of Auget de Montyon, *Etat général du produit des droits de traites . . . ; Ibid., Extraits du mémoire sur la réforme des traites par Monsieur de Cormeré;* and Loménie de Brienne, *Compte rendu au Roi au mois de mars 1788,* Paris, 1788, p. 1.

[2] The list of bureaux which I used is the ms. A.N., G¹ 63, *Etat général des bureaux des fermes rangés alphabétiquement avec la Direction et les droits qui s'y perçoivent;* it shows a total of 1070 bureaux. See table on p. 12. It will hereafter be abbreviated as *Etat gén.*

its brigades of guards, about 15,000 strong, in a network across the country in order to prevent evasion of the tobacco and salt taxes as well as the customs; thus, in 1787, some 770 men patrolled the vicinity of Amiens, Angers had 857, Châteauroux 567, Langres 230, Moulins 721, Toulouse 481 and so on.[1] The brigades could stop anyone with a load of goods in order to inspect his papers and, if they thought necessary, his goods also. Even supposing that a driver or boatman were fortunate enough to avoid any such casual inspection, a great deal was required of him merely to cross an internal customs barrier such as that of the *Cinq Grosses Fermes* which separated Brittany from the rest of the kingdom and divided France in half on a line running roughly east and west almost through Lyon and a point a few miles south of La Rochelle. When he arrived at the first bureau on his route, he had to go in and declare his goods, giving an exhaustive description of his merchandise. This declaration was written in a register on a printed form which he had to sign. The declaration was then given to the Visitor, who inspected the goods and, having verified the declaration, signed it on the back. A maximum error of 5 per cent was allowed in the declaration of weight; value being more difficult to assess, an error of up to 10 per cent was not treated as a false declaration. Thus certified, the declaration was returned to the bureau where the duties were computed and paid. The receipt was finally issued only after the Receiver and the Controller had checked the operation.[2]

There were four kinds of receipts, one or other of which was issued for every load of goods at the first bureau of the journey, whether or not the goods were subject to duties.[3] The *acquit de paiement*, though intended to be a simple receipt, bore an astonishing amount of information. Besides the quality,

[1] A.N., G¹ 63, 70, 71, 73.

[2] B.N., nouv. acq. fr. 4701, *Traites*, a manuscript manual for inspecting officers containing a detailed account of the operations of a bureau. Also, Moreau de Beaumont, *Mem. con.*, p. 407, and Pierre Roux, *Les Fermes*.

[3] For copies of some of these documents see Appendix I, *infra*, p. 173. The formalities of the customs service are explained in detail in B.N., ms. fr. 11166–11178, *Dictionnaire alphabétique des traites*, 13 vols. in ms. This work was prepared by an employee of the General Farm between 1726 and 1738 (A.N., G¹ 79, *Mémoire—projet d'un dictionnaire pour la partie des traites* (sic.) *par le Sieur Duclos, secrétaire de Monsieur de la Borde, Fermier Général*, 14 fols.).

quantity, weight and value, number of boxes with their marks and seals, and the amount of duties paid, it recorded the name of the merchant who owned the goods, their destination and the route which they were expected to follow. This route was generally marked out with the names of the principal bureaux along it, for the merchant had to present the *acquit* at each one and have it countersigned by the clerks. It was finally delivered to the last bureau on the route, where the goods were re-examined, the assessment of duties reviewed and any error in the amount made good. Finally a *brevet de contrôle* was issued in place of the *acquit de paiement*.

A second form of receipt, the *acquit à caution*, was an even more elaborate document. It allowed the recipient to pay all duties in the place where the goods were to be delivered. Because this convenience entailed greater risk of fraud, the *acquit à caution* contained, in addition to all the usual information, a formal oath or *soumission* of an inhabitant of the place where it was issued, who guaranteed that the carter or merchant would deliver the goods at the specified destination and within a certain limited time (usually three months). The guarantor also had to undertake that the *acquit à caution* would be signed on the back by the customs clerk or other local officials at the stated destination, and that he would receive the document from the merchant and return it to the issuing office. This was not all. At the beginning of the journey the clerks in the first bureau on the route examined the merchandise, and when it was re-packed bound the boxes or packages with cord and sealed them with lead seals that were not to be broken except by the officials of the bureau at the destination specified on the *acquit à caution*. Because it permitted a delay in the payment of duties, this method was frequently used for merchandise to be sold in Paris, or for goods shipped from any fair-sized town to another across the barrier of the *Cinq Grosses Fermes* or any of the local barriers. Yet even at its most useful the *acquit à caution* was costly in time and effort, and there were a great many required uses in which it served only to check fraud. For instance, goods listed in the tariff of the *Cinq Grosses Fermes* were legally required to have an *acquit à caution* if they were to be transported within four leagues of the *Cinq Grosses Fermes* barrier. Again, consignments of merchandise which by virtue of their origin or destination were exempt from paying any of the main duties of the General Farm had nevertheless to be accompanied by this document.

Thirdly, there was the *acquit à caution de transit*. This was intended to accompany goods which, by virtue of a privilege accorded to their owner, enjoyed the right of *transit*; that is, the right to pass freely across an area without paying the usual duties. The privilege of *transit* had been generally suppressed by a law of 1688, but it remained in certain small territories where it was essential to economic life. Thus, Artois was permitted to trade across the barrier of the Tariff of 1671; and Venaissin long enjoyed the privilege of trading between her two parts. A similar document used to control the free movement of goods to and from the free fairs, was called an *acquit* or *certificat de franchise*.

Finally, there was the *passavant* used to identify goods transported within the territory of the *Cinq Grosses Fermes*, and the *passe-debout* for the internal trade of the Provinces Reputed Foreign.

The law required everyone transporting goods to carry the appropriate papers ready for inspection. When the clerks at a bureau or the patrolling brigades found a merchant who was carrying goods not properly documented they subjected him to a process known as declaring seizure. The Farmers General furnished their employees with detailed instructions on how to declare seizure, and especially on how to prepare a *procès-verbal*, a full record of all the circumstances of the case, which was the most difficult part of the seizure. In the employees' guide of 1751[1] for the Direction of Amiens, the brigades were instructed not to unpack wagons and boxes for inspection in the highway, but to take them to the nearest bureau where the whole case could be examined and the *procès-verbal* drawn up. The *procès-verbal* had to be prepared by two employees, to mention the date and the time, and to furnish a complete description of the merchant and his goods. The merchant could then be ordered to appear in court before a judge maintained especially for this purpose and called a *juge des traites*, though other judges might be called upon if there were no *juges des traites* in the vicinity. Appeals from these courts were heard by the *Cour des aides* and

---

[1] *Le Guide des employés*, pp. 160 ff.

where no such court existed by the Parlement or other high court.

Penalties were laid down in an Ordinance of 1687:[1]

For transporting goods from a place where there is a bureau without first taking them to the bureau for inspection before loading or packing them,   300 *livres* fine and confiscation

For loading goods on a vessel without permission from the General Farm, and for putting out to sea or into a river without an *acquit de paiement* or *à caution*,   200 *livres* fine and confiscation

For making a false declaration of either the quality or the quantity of merchandise,   300 *livres* fine and confiscation

For taking goods by other routes and to other bureaux than those marked on the *acquit*,   100 *livres* fine and confiscation

For conveying goods into the area of the *Cinq Grosses Fermes*, and passing a bureau without declaring them,
                                       300 *livres* fine and confiscation

For conveying goods in the area of the *fermes* within the four-league border strip and taking oblique or unauthorized roads, even though carrying *acquits* or *passavans*,   300 *livres* fine and confiscation

For carrying goods within the border strip without an *acquit à caution*,
                                       300 *livres* fine and confiscation

For failing to declare goods within twenty-four hours of arrival in a harbour,   300 *livres* fine and confiscation

The case of a merchant, Claude Perillat, shows how these penalties were applied.[2] Early in April 1771, a brigade stopped him and found that he had broken three regulations. First, he was driving a load of 450 pounds of silk goods, 400 pounds of hosiery and 800 pounds of mercery, all without identification of weight or quality. Secondly, he was travelling through Clermontois without authorization. Lastly, whereas his *acquit à caution* indicated that he was travelling from Vendress to Vouziers, he was found on a side road and not on his direct route. Having seized his goods, the brigade had him summoned before the *juge des traites* in Saint-Menehould, who sentenced him to pay 300 *livres* fine and expenses and to suffer confiscation of goods,

---

[1] *Loc. cit.*

[2] A.N., AD IX 488, decision of the *Conseil supérieur* in an *arrêt* of 1 January 1772.

horses and wagons. When he appealed to the *Conseil supérieur* of Chalon, it confirmed the sentence of the *juge des traites*.

Contemporary reports show how burdensome the merchants found this system. One of the best is by an official, Louis Blanchet, who was instructed by the council of the duc d'Orleans and the proprietors of the Canal de Briare to transport some wine down the Allier, the Loire and the Seine for the express purpose of finding out just what duties, *péages* and *octrois* were levied on those rivers. Late in September 1763, Blanchet and an employee of the canal company left Paris and travelled as far as a little town on the Allier, where they bought two barrels of wine and loaded them in a boat. Coming down the Allier, they were first stopped in the village of Vialle, a *bureau de conserve*[1] in the Direction of Moulins and on the frontier of the *Cinq Grosses Fermes* where it ran along the border of Auvergne and Bourbonnais. Blanchet writes:

The clerks stationed at this bureau inspect the goods in conveyances and oblige those in charge of them to make a declaration undertaking to pay the import duties in Vichy. This was done in our presence. Having moored our boat, the sieur Faucher, mariner, entered the bureau and there made his declaration on a register and the sieur Frottier, receiving clerk, gave him a printed *acquit à caution* which we filled out. This declaration duly made and delivered, the clerks came to make their inspection of our boat, which lasted about an hour, because there was some straw on board and they suspected they might find other goods hidden in it.[2]

They arrived in Vichy towards evening but, as Blanchet says, would have had to stop there for the night no matter what time of day they had arrived because the town was for customs purposes 'a port of entry into the kingdom' (it is in fact almost in the centre of France) and the customs formalities took several hours. The following morning, after they had made their declaration they had to wait from 7 to 11 while the customs clerks inspected their boat and cargo. If there had been any boats ahead of them they might not have been visited at all that

---

[1] The *bureaux de conserve* were smaller bureaux used mainly for controlling local movements of goods. There were 23 of them in a total of 1,070 bureaux listed in A.N., G¹ 63, *Etat gén.*

[2] 'Detail historique des droits . . . ', *Les nouvelles ephémérides économiques*, 1775, tome v, pp. 1–92 (B.N., Z. 21949), p. 10.

day for there were only enough clerks to visit one boat at a time. Blanchet paid, in all, the duties of the Tariff of 1664, along with the *subvention par doublement,* the *boëte,* the *courtiers jaugeurs* and the *jauge et courtage,* the latter three being paid in a separate office because they were *aides* and administered as such. For the rest of the journey they were charged only with a series of *péages* and *octrois,* which we need not describe in detail.

The burden of customs duties was heaviest on the major rivers. One well-informed contemporary claims that from the town of Gray in Franche-Comté, situated on the Saône at the point where it began to be navigable, down to the city of Arles near the mouth of the Rhône, there were six duties of the General Farm to be paid at different bureaux along the way as well as thirty *péages,* many of which belonged to the Crown.[1] Another relates that between Lyon and Marseille, a distance of 54 leagues, the Farmers General levied nine different duties, in addition to *péages,* each with a separate tariff and different formalities.[2] It was said that as a result iron produced in Franche Comté cost about 35 per cent of its value to transport to Marseille, whereas Russian iron could be shipped there at a cost of less than 20 per cent.[3] A boatman taking a load of cask staves down from Lorraine to Sète in Languedoc had to stop twenty-two times to pay thirty-eight different duties and *péages.*[4] Again, one merchant, applying to the *Contrôle général* to reimburse him, stated that he had paid duties totalling more than 91 *livres,* about 24 per cent of the value of 400 pounds of cloth which he had sent from Amiens to Marseille by way of Lyon in wartime when the ocean was not safe. He claimed that if he had sent it by sea it would have cost him only 7 *livres* in duties; and an official commented that it would have cost him no more than 5 *sols* to have exported such a cargo from Holland and nothing at all from England.[5]

---

[1] Rousselot de Surgy, *Enc. méth.,* article, 'Droits'. Cf. A.N., G⁷ 1704, *Mémoire sur les péages du Rhône* which describes 63 péages from Lyon to the river's mouth.

[2] A.N., F¹² 827, *Mémoire pour le droit unique,* by Jean Anisson de Hauteroche. Another edition in A.N., F¹² 693.

[3] A.N. (Marine), B³ 348, fol. 394.

[4] A.N., H⁴ 2967¹. Cf. Dutil, *L'Etat économique, livre* 4; and Cormeré, *Rech. fin.,* vol. i, p. 462.

[5] Jean Anisson, Deputy of Commerce, *Mémoire pour le droit unique,* A.N., F¹² 693.

Duties on other rivers were nearly as troublesome as those on the Rhône. One writer tells of twenty-five bottles of eau-de-vie which he bought in 1787 in Bayonne for 30 *livres* and shipped to Paris by way of the Atlantic coast and the Loire. According to his records, he paid a total of more than 41 *livres* in duties, of which 6½ *livres* were charged at various points on the Loire.[1] A worse case is that of a Toulousain who in 1749 dispatched a barrel of wine worth about 36 *livres* from his vineyard down the Garonne to Bordeaux, round by sea to Rouen, and up the Seine to Paris. It was finally sold there for 500 *livres* which, although almost fourteen times the original value represented a loss, for the total cost of transportation, consisting mainly of duties payable, had been 501 *livres*, 7 *sols*, and 7 *deniers*.[2]

The internal duties cost a great deal in delay, inconvenience and risk as well as in money. Goods travelling overland from Brittany to Provence, it was said in a report of 1790, were subject to eight inspections calling for eight declarations and the payment of seven different duties; the goods had to be loaded twice into different vehicles and the driver had to return two *acquits à caution*. Besides the cost and inevitable waste of time, there was a great risk of the goods being confiscated and those responsible for them brought into court.[3] The fate of a gauze manufacturer in 1786 shows how easily this could happen. The mere loss of two lead seals from a load of gauze, he alleged, cost him a great deal of litigation in Lyon, many visits to the *Hôtel des fermes* in Paris, and eventually, when the case was judged, the payment of the duties and a fine of much more than the goods were worth.[4]

Most of the above testimony comes from merchants. It is confirmed by the complaints of officials. An Intendant of Commerce, Isaac de Bacalan, wrote in his *Observations faites par ... voyage en Picardie, Haynaut, et Flandre l'an 1768*,[5] that industry ought to flourish in the town of Amiens. Its situation on the

---

[1] Grouber de Groubenthall, *Théorie générale*, vol. ii, p. 25. Cf. complaints of the Intendant Bégon in 1707 against the duty at Ingrande (Roger Dion, *Histoire de la Vigne*, p. 451).

[2] Dutil, *L'Etat éc.*, p. 738.

[3] Goudard, Fontenay and Roussillou, *Rapport fait*, p. 15.

[4] Renouard (fabricant de gazes), *Réflexions*.

[5] A.N., F¹² 650, cited in full in *R.h.d.e.s.*, 1908, pp. 367–424.

Somme and near the sea, the many canals and mills in the area, the abundance of foodstuffs, the low cost of labour were all favourable to industry, but these advantages were offset by the situation of the city relative to the customs barriers:

Amiens being on the frontier between Artois and Flanders, both Provinces Reputed Foreign, the customs authorities have a very strict system of inspection. The gates of the city are closed at nightfall which severely constricts trade and prevents it from expanding into the suburbs.

The customs officials in Amiens collected the Uniform Duties, the Tariff of 1664, the *péage de Péronne*, and four aides: the *subvention par doublement*, the *droits d'abord*, and the *consommation*, and the duty of 40 *livres*, 10 *sols* per *tonneau* of wine leaving the Generalities of Amiens, Soissons and Chalon.[1]

The customs system, with its network of internal bureaux, was widely acknowledged to be cumbersome, but few of those who criticized it explained, or perhaps realized, that it had faults arising from the manner in which the Crown was endeavouring to use it to implement an economic policy. That policy was to encourage the exportation of French products and to protect French industry from the competition of foreign manufactures on the domestic market. The protective Uniform Duties, first imposed on the kingdom's frontiers by Colbert, were the principal means of enforcing this policy. These duties were set so high that they provided a strong incentive for smugglers who never ceased to import large quantities of contraband goods into France. The government was unable to stamp out smuggling which remained a threat to French industry.

There was a further danger. Following Colbert's example the Crown had continued to add to the small list of imports and exports selected for payment of the Uniform Duties. Imports which were so designated—and this is the crux of the matter— were exempted from paying internal duties for a period of three months or until they reached the destination specified at the port of entry.[2] Similarly, exports subject to the Uniform

---

[1] A.N., G¹ 63, *Etat gén.*
[2] Vivent Magnien, *Recueil alph.*, p. xii.

Duties, provided they carried the proper documents, were allowed to cross and quit the country without paying any other customs duties. The arrangement was intended to favour foreign trade and indeed its effect was that imports and exports could often be shipped more easily and quickly, and even more cheaply, than goods intended for domestic sale. Internal trade had to bear a burden of internal duties which affected foreign trade less and less. As long as the Uniform Duties on imports remained high and the system was buttressed with outright prohibition of many foreign manufactures, the stifling effect of the internal duties on domestic trade and industrial production was offset and French manufactures could at least compete against foreign goods on the domestic market. But any substantial reduction of the Uniform Duties and any removal of the ban on, for example, British textiles, such as was threatened by the abortive Anglo-French Trade Treaty of 1713 and put into effect by that of 1786, was bound to affect French industry adversely. If, for example, British hosiery and hardware were admitted into France on payment of a 12 per cent duty, how could a French manufacturer survive when the internal duties often amounted to 12 per cent on his raw materials as well as on his products? As one observer wrote, after the Trade Treaty of 1786 had drawn attention to the situation:

Although English merchandise is subject to duties of 10 per cent or 12 per cent, England can supply nearly all the provinces of the kingdom more cheaply than can our own industry. Our goods are subject to customs duties which prevent them from meeting English competition. It costs from 10 per cent to 12 per cent to send silk gauze, cotton cloth and velveteen from Lyon to Brittany, and it costs as much to send Flemish products into the interior of the kingdom. Woollen goods manufactured in Lille pay 7½ per cent at the bureau in Peronne alone. The cloth of Languedoc arrives in Paris and in Brittany only after having paid 15 per cent or 16 per cent in duties and expenses.[1]

This cumbersome and disorderly system of duties aroused opposition in many quarters. Merchants, who naturally disliked paying duties, were doubly resentful of a system which could not prevent smuggling. Writers protested against the

[1] A.N. (Marine), B⁷ 546, dossier, *Observations sur le Traité de Commerce* (ms.).

system and against the Farmers General who operated it. By the middle of the century some of them felt so strongly that they could extol the virtues of smuggling. 'Do not interfere with contraband trading', wrote Dupont de Nemours in 1765, 'for what you call smuggling is very profitable commerce.'[1] Again, in a book attributed to the economist, Ange de Goudar, one of the characters writes an imaginary letter to a celebrated master-smuggler, Louis Mandrin: 'I have all the means necessary to become a famous smuggler. I have not yet killed anyone, but have weapons enough to dispose of half the tax farmers, including fourteen double-barrelled muskets, six carbines, twenty pistols and fifty bayonets. Furthermore, I can shoot so well that I flatter myself I could kill a clerk of the General Farm at eight hundred paces.'[2] Lines like these amused a public whose sympathy lay with the *contrebandiers* rather than the Farmers General. And popular feeling against the customs and other obstacles to trade found expression during the second half of the eighteenth century in the writings of the Physiocrats, who urged the total abolition of all duties. The most serious and effective protest, however, was made by men who led a movement for reform rather than abolition, and who looked back to Jean-Baptiste Colbert, the reforming minister of Louis XIV, for their inspiration.

[1] *Journal de l'agriculture*, Nov. 1765, p. 196 note.
[2] *Testament politique de Louis Mandrin, Généralissime des Troupes de Contrebandiers écrit par lui-même dans sa prison*, Geneva, 1755, 67 pp., p. 49.

CHAPTER II

The Men and Politics of the Single Duty Project (1700-1776)

I

'WE clearly saw,' wrote Colbert, 'that it was absolutely necessary for the restoration of trade both within and without, which is our goal, to reduce all the customs duties to a single import and a single export duty, and even to lower these considerably.'[1] He was not the first to think of unifying the customs—it had been proposed in the reign of Henri II (1547–59) and again in 1614 at the meeting of the Estates General[2] but he was the only minister before the French Revolution to have any success in putting his plans into effect. If his Tariffs of 1664, 1667 and 1671, and his *nouveaux droits* left the country still riddled with internal trade barriers, they stood nevertheless as an impressive example of reform for others to follow. Yet little was done in the remaining years of the seventeenth century. In 1688, it is true, the Controller General sent a senior official, Henri Daguesseau, into the south-eastern provinces to study the local duties and to hear the complaints of the merchants. Daguesseau's report contains a remarkably detailed study of the local duties in the south-east. But it makes no recommendation for a general reform[3] and if such a reform was being planned nothing came of it.

[1] In the *arrêt* introducing the Tariff of 1664. I consulted an edition published in Paris in 1748 (B.N. F40820).

[2] S. Elzinger, 'Le Tarif de Colbert de 1664 et celui de 1667 et leur signification', *Economisch-Historisch-Jaarboek*, vol. xv, 1929.

[3] *Mémoire de Monsieur Daguesseau sur la douane de Lyon et la douane de Valence*, 252 fols. Bib. de l'Arsenal, ms. 4029; and other copies in Lyon, Bib. Publique, ms. 6737, and Aix-en-Provence, Bib. Publique, ms. 48–R.14. There are important comments on this work in Rousselot de Surgy, *Enc. méth.*, articles, 'Droits' and 'Douane de Lyon', and in Véron de Fortbonnais, *Rech. et cons.*, vol. i, pp. 73 ff.

At the turn of the century, however, the first reform project of the eighteenth century appeared under Daguesseau's direction. He and other officials, particularly the Controller General of Finance, Chamillart, and the Secretary of State for the Navy, Pontchartrain, were disturbed during the negotiations leading to the commercial treaty with the United Provinces in 1699 by the 'confused and disadvantageous' character of the French customs.[1] They took the view that the customs ought to be made to assist French trade and industry and in the years following the Peace of Ryswick they were eager to promote the economic welfare of the country. Daguesseau, who had been in charge of commercial affairs since 1691, seemed the most appropriate official to direct a programme of reform, and when in June 1700 the government decided to set up an advisory Council of Commerce it asked Daguesseau to preside over it. At the same time, the day-to-day administration of the Council's affairs devolved upon his nephew, Michel Amelot de Gournay, a *conseiller d'Etat* who had assisted him since September 1699.[2] But months before this Council of Commerce was called—as early as 1699, according to Daguesseau—'it was decided to draw up a new tariff project in which all the duties, old and new, would be combined in a single tariff. The Farmers General and some of the chief merchants of Paris held various conferences to discuss the project . . . ',[3] and senior officials of the General Farm went out to the provinces to prepare revisions of major groups of tariffs in collaboration with the Intendants. In Guyenne, two Directors of the Farms, Louis Chevalier and Melchior de Blair, aided by other Farm officials, notably de Baritault and Donmé, began in 1699 to revise the tariffs of the

---

[1] A.N., F[12] 51, meeting of 4 Feb. 1705. Henri Daguesseau (1636–1716), former Intendant of Languedoc, widely respected for his ability and honesty, succeeded Pellisson in 1693 as administrator of the confiscated property of Huguenot fugitives, and was appointed to the Royal Council of Finances in 1695. Michel Chamillart (1652–1721) was Controller General of Finances 1699–1708. Jérôme Pontchartrain, comte de Maurepas (1674–1747) inherited the post of Secretary of State for the Navy in 1693 when, as Saint-Simon writes, he was not yet twenty.

[2] Michel-Jean Amelot de Gournay, Baron de Brunelles (1654–1724) served as *conseiller au parlement* and *maître des requêtes*, ambassador to Venice (1682), Portugal (1685), Switzerland (1688), Spain (1705) and Rome (1715), and was made *conseiller d'Etat* in 1695.

[3] A.N., F[12] 51, *Procès Verbaux du Conseil de Commerce*, meeting of 4 Feb. 1705.

traite d'Arzac, the *comptablie*, the *convoy*, the *coûtume de Bayonne*, and other duties of the south-western provinces.[1] They worked closely with the Intendants, de Bezons and (from September 1700) de la Bourdonnaye. To the east there was a similar co-operation of Intendants and Farm officials in revising such tariffs as the *douane de Lyon*, the *douane de Valence* and the *patente de Languedoc*. The Intendant of Languedoc, Basville,[2] was enthusiastic and even undertook to revise the *patente* himself, but the principal agent in his province and in Lyonnais, Dauphiné and Provence was a Director of the General Farm, Le Febvre, whom Amelot dispatched in October 1700 with instructions to begin with the revision of the *douane de Lyon*. There is evidence that other Farm officials were working concurrently on a new tariff for the *Cinq Grosses Fermes*.[3]

Although these officials were instructed to consult the principal merchants in the towns which they visited, it is clear that the Crown was leaning heavily upon the General Farm for the preparation of the reforms. Not unnaturally, therefore, the reform project as a whole reflected an overriding concern for the maintenance of customs revenue. No barriers were to be moved nor any duties abolished. The men sent to the provinces were to do little more than compile an alphabetical list or tariff of taxable commodities together with the rates to be charged for each duty, and in doing so to make adjustments in the current rates, bearing in mind the advice of the local merchants and the principle that the export of French manufactures and the import of raw materials were to be promoted whereas the import of foreign manufactures and the export of raw materials were to be discouraged. The reformers in Paris appear to have had some intention of combining the tariffs of small duties wherever possible, but they certainly envisaged no major changes and no sacrifice of revenue. When, therefore, the Council of Commerce discussed the new tariffs, beginning with that for the *Cinq Grosses Fermes*, first presented at the meeting of

[1] A.N., F^{12} 114, Amelot to the Intendants, 4 Sept., 1700; and A.N., F^{12} 114 and 115, *passim*, Amelot's correspondence with all these officials; also, A.-M. de Boislisle, *Corresp.*, vol. ii, de Blair to Amelot, 26 Dec., 1701.

[2] Nicolas de Lamoignon de Basville (1648–1724) replaced Henri Daguesseau as Intendant of Languedoc in 1685 and held the office for 33 years.

[3] A.N., F^{12} 115, Amelot to the *procureur du roi des traites* at Reims, 17 Feb. 1701.

27 January 1702, some members received them very coldly. Among them were certain Deputies of Commerce who soon became bitterly critical of what they called 'the Farmers General's tariffs' and proposed plans of their own.

These Deputies of Commerce were appointed as part of the general scheme for the revival of trade. By the *arrêt* of 29 June 1700 which established the Council of Commerce, twelve Deputies were appointed as auxiliaries in the Council to represent the towns of Paris, Lyon, Rouen, Marseille, Saint Malo, La Rochelle, Bordeaux, Lille, Nantes, Dunkirk and Bayonne, and the province of Languedoc. Later, Deputies were invited from Amiens (1761), Martinique (1761), Saint Domingo (1761) and Guadeloupe (1766). In later years, and increasingly until their suppression in 1790, the Deputies of Commerce tended to break free of their allegiance to their towns, which claimed them as delegates, and to become officials of the Crown with the duty of expressing their collective opinion on any matter that was put before them.[1] Even in these early years, when they were still mainly concerned with advancing local interests, they held their own formal meetings in which they often recorded common views in memoranda to be read to the Council of Commerce or sent to the Controller General. Their function, in brief, was to represent trade and industry; while *finance*, by which was meant the Farmers General, had two spokesmen in the persons of Charles de Poiret de Grandval and Jean-Rémy Hénault. These and the Deputies of Commerce were auxiliaries who could not speak in the meetings of the Council and they passed their opinions on the questions raised to the commissioners in writing. Although silenced in the Council meetings by the minor place which rank and procedure assigned to them, the Deputies of Commerce and the representatives of the Farmers General carried on a debate outside the Council for the edification of the senior councillors, Daguesseau and Amelot in particular, who endeavoured to take into account the views of both sides in framing recommendations to the Crown. But it was difficult to satisfy both sides at the same time.

[1] For the commercial administration see, Léon Biollay, *L'Admin.*, pp. 325 ff.; and also Pierre Bonnassieux, *Cons. de comm.* Both must lead, for serious work, to a study of the A.N. F¹² series.

The question of customs reform was to come before the Council several times a year until August 1710, without any substantial agreement being reached.[1] Reform was prevented during those years by the fundamental opposition between the views of the Farmers General and of the Deputies of Commerce, but this does not mean that the Council recommended no changes at all in the customs. On the contrary, it was a minor though not unimportant adjustment in the Tariff of 1664 which first provoked some of the Deputies of Commerce to draw up their own reform project.

At first the Deputies had no very precise views on the customs. The memoirs which they each delivered to the Council of Commerce after its first meeting on 24 November 1700 made few concrete proposals and showed that the Deputies were as yet agreed on nothing more precise than the need for some kind of reform. But they all declared customs reform to be one of the most necessary steps for the revival of French trade and industry, and Nicolas Mesnager, Deputy for Rouen, expressed the opinion of many when he wrote: 'To begin with, taxes on our own export products should be reduced and import duties on foreign manufactures raised.'[2] Accordingly, at its meeting of 10 June 1701 the Council of Commerce proposed to alter the Tariff of 1664 in some such manner, and appointed a committee of three—Jean Anisson, Deputy for Lyon, Peletyer, Deputy for Paris and Nicolas Mesnager himself—to study and report on this proposal. This committee suggested a reform in two parts, of which one, the raising of import duties on a variety of English manufactures and the prohibition of others, aroused little opposition, being worked out in detail and enacted by an *arrêt* of 6 September 1701.[3] The other part, however, was challenged by the representatives of the Farmers General because it involved a reduction of the duties on six kinds of goods: silk; cloth of wool, wool and silk, and hair; linen cloth; paper; hats (especially beaver hats); and cotton cloth. Hénault and

---

[1] The Council discussed the question at five meetings in 1701, two in 1702, eight in 1703, one in 1704, twenty in 1705, five in 1706, six in 1707, seven in 1709, eight in 1710 (A.N. F^{12} 51).

[2] Boislisle, *Corresp.*, vol. ii, pp. 477–9. Some of these memoirs are printed in Boislisle, *Corresp.*, but most of them must still be read as manuscripts. Two manuscript volumes of them are: B.N., ms. fr. 8083, and B. Ars., mss. 4395 and 4396.

[3] A copy of this important *arrêt* is in A.N., F^{12} 694.

Grandval argued that the General Farm could accept no such loss, but after considerable debate and during the absence of Grandval, the Council approved this part of the reform also. An *arrêt du Council* of 24 December 1701 confirmed this decision.[1] The Farmers General, indignant at this *arrêt*, hinted to the Controller General that they would not put it into effect unless compensated for a loss which they estimated at more than 713,000 *livres*.[2] Faced with such a determined opposition, the Crown compromised and published on 2 April 1702 a second *arrêt* more acceptable to the Farmers General. This law permitted only a modest reduction of the duties on a very few exports, but it is important because of the dispute which arose between the Farmers General and the Deputies of Commerce over the interpretation of it. It states 'that in conformity with the said *arrêt* of 24 December 1701 the merchandise hereinafter mentioned will be charged, on being exported from the territory of the *Cinq Grosses Fermes* (*à la sortie de l'étendue des Cinq Grosses Fermes*) only the duties specified . . .'.[3] The Farmers General and their employees understood that this referred only to exports directly to foreign countries, whereas a number of merchants and Intendants, and the Deputies of Commerce, interpreted it more literally to include exports from the *Cinq Grosses Fermes* whatever their destination, even if it were only Rennes or Toulouse. Why, they asked, should not the government reduce the duties of the *Cinq Grosses Fermes* for the benefit of domestic as well as foreign trade?[4] But the Farmers General insisted that 'there is not a single word in these two *arrêts* which changes the nature of the duties or the organization of the tax farms, so that the goods transported within the kingdom from one province to another, even *en route* to a port from which they may be sent abroad, whether by land or sea, must remain subject to the local duties . . .'.[5] The Crown ruled in favour of this

---

[1] A copy of the *arrêt* of 24 Dec. 1701 (5 pp.) is in A.N., F12 1910.

[2] A.N., F12 1903, 'Etat des Droits que S. Templier prétend que perdra . . .'; A.N., F12 1910, 'La Vérification a été fait par M. de la Vigne . . .'.

[3] A.N., F12 1910, *arrêt* of 2 April 1702.

[4] A.N., F12 1910, 'Extrait d'une lettre écrite à M de Grandval par M. le Riche . . .'; 'A Mr. Amelot. Les marchands de Tours ayant prétendu . . .'; 'Mémoire des Députés . . .', dated 31 May 1702, etc.

[5] A.N., F12 1910, 'Réponse des Fermiers Généraux à deux mémoires', dated 15 July 1702.

interpretation by a third *arrêt* of 3 October 1702, and there, so far as the law was concerned, the matter rested. But in the eyes of the Deputies of Commerce the Crown, by refusing to reduce the internal customs duties, had emasculated not only the *arrêts* of 24 December 1701 and 2 April 1702, but also the new reform projects which in the meantime had come before the Council of Commerce on 27 January 1702 and made public in the *arrêt* of 2 April. During the controversy the Deputies of Commerce became impatient with these limited reform plans and some of them drew up a 'grand plan' for the suppression of all the internal customs duties and the substitution of a single duty on the frontiers of the kingdom.

This plan was inspired by Jean Anisson de Hauteroche, the Deputy of Commerce for Lyon, who was to bring it to the notice of the Council of Commerce and the Controller General repeatedly over the next twenty years, and was to be the leading figure in the agitation for the abolition of the internal duties. Jean Anisson was born in 1644 into a family of Lyon printers. He became a printer and bookseller himself and early in his career moved with his business to Paris. On 15 January 1691 he was appointed director of the *Imprimerie royale*, a post which remained in his family after he died; and on 25 September 1700 he was elected Deputy of Commerce for Lyon. Anisson may very well have formulated his ideas on customs reform before this appointment, but this seems unlikely because in his first memoir for the Council of Commerce he makes only the general type of complaint about the internal duties which is to be found in the early memoirs of every Deputy. What appears to be the earliest statement of his ideas is dated 11 August 1702 and entitled, *Mémoire donné par Monsieur le Député de Lyon pour la réduction des droits qui se payent dans l'intérieur du Royaume sur les marchandises en un seul droit d'entrée et de sortie, et pour mettre tous les Bureaux sur les frontières*.[1] He wrote at least five other versions of it, four of them before 1707 and the last one in the summer of 1720, a year before his death.[2]

Anisson began by acknowledging that the Council of Com-

---

[1] A.N., F12 693, 13 fols. ms.

[2] B.N., ms. fr. 14294, fols. 10–15; A.N., F12 693 (5 copies); A.N., F12 827, written in summer 1720 (the Archives nationales dates it 1724 in error).

merce, sincerely desiring a revival of trade, had passed some wise laws; but all of these, he held, were inadequate. The extreme evil wrought by thirty years of war required an exteme remedy. Almost all the Deputies, he said, had agreed upon such a remedy 'which [was] to reduce all the duties on merchandise, paid inside the kingdom, to a single import and export duty, and to put all the customs bureaux on the frontiers'.[1] The chief advantage of this plan, in his view, was that the French merchants would be better able to compete in foreign markets. Only if the products of French industry could be offered abroad at prices lower than those of their competitors would trade and industry revive. The existing internal customs barriers raised the price of French goods by at least 6 per cent and often by as much as 15 per cent, an extra cost which was one of the chief obstacles to their sale abroad. If a single duty were imposed at the frontiers, Anisson wrote, prices could be reduced by even more than the amount of the internal duties by the simple expedient of imposing the single duty in such a way that it would not tax exports of manufactured goods and imports of raw materials for industry. The second advantage of the reform, he continued, was that French manufacturers could sell their products much more cheaply on the domestic market, thus driving out foreign goods which were being sold in large quantities in the Provinces Reputed Foreign. Thirdly, by stimulating internal trade the abolition of the internal duties would strengthen the political unity of France and demonstrate to all the provinces the value of their union. Fourthly, goods would no longer be spoiled by being opened too often in transit, and merchants would not be annoyed by the delays and complications of the bureaucratic controls. Finally, a single duty payable in one ring of bureaux on the frontiers of the country, would make it possible to compile an exact account of French imports and exports. And until it was possible to calculate the balance of trade, how could measures be taken which might change it to the advantage of France?

Anisson also tried to meet several objections which had been made against the project. It had been argued that the project was a novelty and therefore dangerous; that it would cause a

[1] A.N., F¹² 693, *Mémoire donné par Mr. le Député de Lyon . . .*, 11 August 1702.

reduction of the King's revenues; that it would put a great number of employees out of work; that the Provinces Reputed Foreign were against the plan; and that it was nothing more than an impracticable theory. To the first objection he had a solid and unimpeachable answer: the great Colbert himself had been in favour of the plan, as the *déclaration* attached to the Tariff of 1664 proved. Here Anisson adduced personal knowledge of Colbert's intentions. In 1673, he went on to explain, he had gone on a special mission as the representative of Lyon to beg Colbert not to extend the stamp tax to books and other products. In the course of an interview Colbert had asked him why the book merchants and paper sellers of Lyon and the southern provinces did not take the Spanish market away from the Genoese. Anisson had replied that the *douane de Lyon*, the *douane de Valence*, the *foraine* and other duties amounted to 15 per cent or 16 per cent of the value of the merchandise, thus putting the Spanish market out of reach of all the provinces whose goods travelled on the Rhône. Colbert had then given Anisson reason to hope that after the war all the internal duties would be suppressed so that French merchants might compete successfully in foreign markets.[1] To the objection that the project would reduce revenues, Anisson replied in his early memoirs that what was lost would be more than made up by the extension of the *gabelle* and the *tabac* equally over the kingdom. He abandoned this idea at least as early as 1713,[2] but continued to insist that in the long run increased trade and general prosperity would repay any immediate sacrifices. He met the third objection—that the single duty would throw many employees out of work—with the argument that the ensuing prosperity would give employment in trade and industry to those who were not retained to man the extra bureaux on the frontiers. The fourth objection, concerning the opposition of the Provinces Reputed Foreign, was more serious than Anisson realized, at least in the early versions of his memoir. This was not, of course, an argument against the single duty so

---

[1] *Mémoire sur la réformation du tarif des Cinq Grosses Fermes*, 20 May 1705, submitted to the Council by some of the Deputies. There are copies in A.N., G⁷ 1687 and F¹² 1910.
[2] A.N., G⁷ 1699, Anisson to the Controller General, 29 March 1713.

much an obstacle which would have to be surmounted. Anisson believed—wrongly, as it turned out—that these provinces would come to see the reasonableness of the project. Reason, as the history of the single duty project was to show, could make little impression on private or regional interest. In reply to the final objection, that the project was only an impracticable idea, Anisson offered a vigorous plan of action. If the Council of Commerce, he said, would appoint two Councillors as an executive commission, they would find willing helpers among the Deputies of Commerce and with their aid could transfer all internal bureaux to the frontiers and carry out all the necessary incidental operations in six months.

The idea of a single duty, which Anisson defended so assiduously, enjoyed much support during the first decade of the century, but it is not easy to assess either the strength or the extent of this support. A number of economic writers recommended it, though in somewhat general terms, as a means of ridding the country of the troublesome internal duties. Such were Pierre le Pesant Boisguillebert, Lieutenant-général in Rouen; Jean Lepelletier, a merchant, and Jean-Charles Anquetin, a priest and sometime financial official, both of Rouen; comte Henri de Boulainvilliers; and maréchal Vauban, the great military engineer of Louis XIV.[1] Henri Daguesseau, in the Contrôle Général, was later regarded as an early champion of the idea;[2] and in 1720 Amelot claimed to have believed in it for many years,[3] but there is no evidence that they did any more during this period than give it a sympathetic hearing in the Council of Commerce. The only continuous and active support was that of Jean Anisson and his colleagues, Nicolas Mesnager (Deputy for Rouen), Claude Villain (Deputy for Paris) and his successors, and the frequently changed Deputies of Commerce for Languedoc. In time they won over several of the other Deputies of Commerce, particularly Jean-Baptiste

---

[1] Boisguillebert, *La France ruinée* (1696), pp. 87 and 175. Boisguillebert, *Le Détail de la France* (1707), vol. i, p. 171 and vol. ii, p. 100. J. Lepelletier, *Mémoires pour* (1701), p. 26. J.-C. Anquetin, ms. of 1709 published in the *R.h.d.e.s.*, 1910. Vauban, *Le Dîme royal* (1707), pp. 26 and 31. Boulainvilliers, *Mémoires présentés*, tome ii, pp. 5 ff.

[2] Rousselot de Surgy, *Enc. méth.*, articles 'Droits' and 'Douane de Lyon'.

[3] A.N., F[12] 119, Amelot to the maréchal d'Estrées, 22 Sept. 1720.

Fenellon of Bordeaux, and were then able to urge their idea upon the Farmers General and the Council of Commerce without fear of serious challenge in their own group.

The Deputies from the seaports, whatever their personal convictions, were influenced by the knowledge that the coastal provinces would resist any change in the customs system which threatened to restrict their foreign trade and force them to look for markets inside France. The Deputies from Bordeaux, Nantes, La Rochelle and Saint Malo made this quite clear as early as 25 March 1703.[1] Yet the Council of Commerce did not regard this as an insurmountable difficulty because on 28 July it resolved that the Deputies of Commerce should prepare a memoir on 'the means of establishing a single duty at all the frontiers of the kingdom and finding a financial substitute in order not to diminish the King's revenues'.[2] Again, when the Council heard one of Anisson's memoirs on the single duty read at the meeting of 30 January 1704[3] the members discussed the projected reform at some length and eventually decided that certain aspects of it needed clarifying: the problem of making up for the revenue that would be lost by suppressing the internal duties; the need for an analysis of the customs registers in order to establish statistics of imports and exports; the effect of war on customs revenue; and the opposition which the Provinces Reputed Foreign were certain to raise. Clearly, the Council's principal concern was to avoid loss of revenue. It was hoping to work out some way of reforming the tariffs for the benefit of trade without risking this consequence. The Controller General, Chamillart, categorically refused to reduce duties in any way during the war.[4] The Council therefore recognized that it would have to treat the single duty as a desirable long-term objective —'le grand plan'—which in the immediate future would have to take second place to 'le petit plan', the more limited but practicable tariff revisions which officials of the General Farm

---

[1] A.N., F¹² 693, *Mémoire sur le rétablissement du commerce avec les étrangers et sur les difficultes de l'établissement du droit unique*, 26 fols; and A.N., F¹² 1910, memoirs 'A' and 'C' of 25 March 1703.

[2] A.N., F¹² 51, entry for 28 July 1703.

[3] A.N., F¹² 51, entry for 30 Jan. 1704.

[4] The War of the Spanish Succession (1701–13). A.N., G⁷ 1687, *Mémoire sur la réformation du tarif des Cinq Grosses Fermes*, 20 May 1705.

D

had prepared. These revised tariffs remained the basis of official discussions throughout the entire ten-year period of the Council's interest in customs reform. Yet to the irritation of the Council, Anisson and his group never ceased to put forward their radical counter-plan for a single duty. Their persistence is reflected as early as 1705 in a memoir in which they wrote:

. . . the Deputies beg the members of the Council not to become discouraged at seeing the question of the tariff put before them so often. They hope that this repetition will not tire them and that perhaps it will serve to show them that the Deputies are resisting the Farmers General for the good of commerce rather than the detriment of the tax farm.[1]

The Council, however, would not adopt the principle of the single duty as the basis for its reform projects and the deadlock continued through twenty Council meetings in 1705 and five meetings in 1706. On 7 January 1707, Anisson, Mesnager and Fenellon, although they had just made a vigorous restatement of the case for a single duty, came to an agreement with de Grandval and Hénault on a compromise plan for three new tariffs to replace those in force in the *Cinq Grosses Fermes*, the south-eastern region, and the south-western region.[2] Yet when it came to working this plan out in detail, the agreement broke down. Banished once more to the realm of mere debate, the tariff question took its former permanent position on the agenda of the Council meetings until, after the meeting of 2 August 1710, it disappeared abruptly and without a word of explanation in the *procès-verbaux*.

II

When in 1716 the tariff question was revived, and a second project for reform took shape, it was in different circumstances. Nicolas Mesnager was no longer a Deputy of Commerce, having been replaced in 1712 when he was sent as one of the French representatives to the peace conference at Utrecht.

[1] *Loc. cit.*
[2] A.N., F¹² 1910, note beginning 'Vendredi, Février 2, 1707. Principes à établir pour le nouveau tarif', and also that headed, 'Du Jeudy, Février 3, 1707'; also A.N., F¹² 54.

Anisson and Fenellon had recently returned from England where they had been sent in 1713 to assist in the negotiations for what in 1715 proved to be an abortive Anglo-French commercial treaty. Most important of all, Michel Amelot had become *de facto* head of the Council of Commerce. His appointment, and the reform of this Council in January 1716, were part of the administrative change which followed the death of Louis XIV. At first Amelot received only a subordinate post because, according to Saint-Simon, he had been so successful in directing Spanish economic affairs while posted there as French ambassador from 1705 to 1712 that when he returned to France some of the French ministers regarded him as a dangerous rival.[1] He was excluded from the chief councils, such as those for finance and marine affairs; but when the executive direction of commerce and industry was divided into five departments within the Council of Commerce, he was given the second department. The first, including the regulation of tariffs, went to Henri Daguesseau, who was also appointed to preside over the Council as a whole. But as Daguesseau was more than eighty years old and in bad health, the five heads of departments planned to hold their meetings at Amelot's house and under his leadership. Then, in April 1716, Daguesseau died. As two of the other heads of departments, de Nointel and d'Argenson, for various reasons did not attend Council meetings, and the remaining Councillor, de Machault, was distinctly subordinate, Amelot assumed the control of affairs.[2] From the spring of 1716 he had what amounted to a portfolio of trade and industry.

Under Amelot's direction the question of customs reform came to the fore once again and this time the Deputies' idea of a single duty had more success. In March 1716 the Deputies wrote to Amelot saying that they felt they could not 'abandon their old plan for a single import and export duty for all the King's subjects with no distinction between the provinces of the tax farms and those Reputed Foreign ... '.[3] In May 1716 the

[1] Saint-Simon, *Mémoires*, vol. iii, p. 249.

[2] Léon Biollay, *L'Admin.*, pp. 330–2. An *ordonnance* of 25 Oct. 1718 gave Amelot 'entrée, séance, et voix délibérative' in the Regency Council for the affairs of trade.

[3] A.N., F¹² 693, *Avis des Députés* on a request of the *Etats de Lille* for a reduction of the entry duties of the *Cinq Grosses Fermes* on goods from French Flanders.

Council of Commerce received two memoirs recommending a single duty and passed them on to the Deputies for their opinion. The Deputies reported on them at some length, concluding that the ideas expressed were very common ones which had been thoroughly examined a long time before. They themselves were ready to submit a much more detailed exposition of them.[1] Meanwhile, Amelot appears to have been already preparing plans for a single duty. Exactly when he decided upon the necessity for it is not clear, but in 1720 he referred to the plan for a single duty as 'the work which we have all long regarded as the most important necessity for the trade of the kingdom'.[2] Most probably he had believed in this reform for many years but had hitherto not thought it feasible. The first clear evidence of his plans is a letter of 17 January 1718 to Le Febvre, by then a Director of the General Farm in the Direction of La Rochelle, asking for some memoirs which Le Febvre had written years before on the subject of the losses which the Farmers General would sustain in the Provinces Reputed Foreign if the government abolished the internal duties in favour of a single duty on the frontiers.[3]

These plans proceeded slowly until the summer of 1720 when suddenly the Regent himself began to take an intense interest in them and instructed Amelot and the Council of Commerce to prepare them with all possible speed. The cause of this sudden interest is not at all certain. There is, however, strong circumstantial evidence to suggest that John Law may have been responsible for drawing the attention of the duc d'Orléans to the single tariff project. Law became Controller General on 5 January 1720 and though his financial system was beginning to crumble he was endeavouring to promote trade and industry by a series of economic measures of a scope unprecedented since the time of Colbert. He concentrated his attention on ways of freeing and encouraging the exchange of goods, and some of his most important reforms reduced and abolished customs duties of many kinds.[4] Although the Regent

---

[1] *Loc. cit.*
[2] A.N., F¹² 119, Amelot to the maréchal d'Estrées, 22 Sept. 1720.
[3] A.N., F¹² 117, Amelot to Le Febvre, 1 Jan. 1718.
[4] Dom H. Leclercq, *Histoire de la Régence*, vol. ii, pp. 430 ff.

discharged Law from the post of Controller General on 29 May, and momentarily disgraced him, he quickly received Law back into favour and did not finally banish him until December. It was in December that the project which Amelot was called upon to prepare virtually came to an end, interrupted by a series of administrative changes. Thus, the interest of the Regent in the single duty project subsided with the disappearance of Law from the French scene.

On 13 August 1720, acting on orders from the Regent, Amelot had quickly scribbled out a plan of action. We have several pages of rough notes which he jotted down under the heading, *Droit unique avec la suppression des bureaux intérieurs*,[1] but probably the best short description of the stage which the project had reached by this time is the letter which he wrote on the same day to the Intendant at Bordeaux, de Courson:

The Council of Commerce, Monsieur, is at work following the orders of Monseigneur le duc d'Orléans, on the execution of a project proposed a long time ago, a project which His Royal Highness would dearly like to see finished. It concerns the suppression of all the internal bureaux in which duties are paid on goods passing from one province to another, even those in the Provinces Reputed Foreign, and the subsequent imposition of a single duty at all ports of entry into the kingdom. The Council is not ignorant of the difficulties in the way of this undertaking, the majority of provinces enjoying privileges and exemptions having hitherto regarded subjection to the regulations of the *Cinq Grosses Fermes* as a form of servitude. Some provinces, however, have begun to think otherwise, and to see the advantages of the change in question. Languedoc, Provence, and Dauphiné are to be found among these, and a Council regulation will, at the earliest opportunity, include them in the scope of the new plan. Guyenne is very important and we know that the traditions and the situation of Bordeaux will raise difficulties. The Council thinks that while you are still on the spot it is desirable to have the benefit of your knowledge in the discussion of the more difficult points and in the search for an appropriate compromise between the interests of the region and the proposed new establishment. We are therefore sending sieur Bilatte, Deputy of Commerce for Bordeaux, to explain to you in greater detail the Council's intentions and to work under your orders, as soon as

---

[1] A.N., F12 827. See Appendix II, *infra*, p. 177.

possible, on the task that is required of you. You will see well enough that there is no time to lose.[1]

The plan for the province of Guyenne was to replace local duties, particularly the *convoy* and *comptablie* which weighed heavily on the wine trade, with a new uniform duty along the coast. The chief problem was that two annual fairs, each lasting fifteen days, carried privileges of exemption from the *comptablie* and it was feared that if the Crown allowed them a similar freedom from the single duty the whole Bordeaux trade in wine and eaux-de-vie, which Amelot estimated to be worth 3,500,000 *livres* for an average peacetime year, would be carried on untaxed during the time of the free fairs. Amelot believed that the Crown would have to abolish the privileges of the fairs, but as this would be a very unpopular measure he was willing to consider a suggestion of the Deputy of Commerce for Bordeaux that these privileges be preserved roughly in proportion to the benefit which would accrue from the stimulation of trade resulting from the free fairs. In other words, the tax farm in Guyenne would have to maintain the existing level of customs revenue, but could dispose of any increase in the form of exemptions for goods travelling to and from the fairs of Bordeaux.

Though Amelot expected Guyenne to be the chief centre of resistance in the south-west, he expected other parts of the region to offer difficulties also. The duc de Gramont, owner of half the *coûtume de Bayonne*, would have to be indemnified for the loss of it and was certain to protest. The *bourgeois* of Bayonne enjoyed privileges which rendered their city a free port for most purposes and Amelot thought that the customs barriers should probably be established on the landward side and the city officially confirmed as a free port. The town of Saint-Jean-de-Luz, south of Bayonne, should be treated in the same way. On the other hand, the inhabitants of the *pays de Labour* might be asked to sacrifice their foreign trade privileges in return for freedom to trade with the rest of France. The people in the Pyrenees, accustomed to passing freely in and out of Spain, were sure to resent the new line of bureaux and brigades

[1] A.N., F12 119, Amelot to de Courson, 13 August 1720. De Courson was soon to be sent to another Intendance, which was one reason for haste.

along the Spanish border and it would be extremely difficult to prevent smuggling in such mountainous territory.

Amelot anticipated powerful resistance in the provinces of three other frontier regions: Alsace and the Trois Evêchés; Hainaut, Artois and Flanders; and Brittany. The first were so closely intermingled with Lorraine, and with Clermontois which belonged to the duc de Lorraine, that Amelot planned to avoid the difficulty and expense of maintaining the single duty on their outer borders by leaving them outside the new ring of customs barriers, which would therefore pass merely along the outer border of Champagne. This decision also had the advantage of avoiding the resistance in that region. Secondly, the inhabitants of Hainaut, Artois and Flanders, who enjoyed the rare privilege of growing, manufacturing and selling tobacco freely, suspected that if they accepted a uniform customs system the Crown would soon force them to submit to the monopoly of the *tabac* as well—a reasonable suspicion, because the internal customs barriers also served as the limit of the tobacco monopoly's area of jurisdiction. Another problem in that region was posed by the privilege of *transit* which the city of Lille had secured to facilitate its foreign trade. The Crown would have to suppress this privilege unless the General Farm could be certain of controlling trade between Lille and the rest of France strictly enough to prevent smuggling. Thirdly, the most difficult province to deal with, in Amelot's view, was Brittany, because the Bretons were exempt from the *gabelle* and ready to believe that the single duty project concealed a plot to subject them to this hated tax. Amelot toyed briefly with the idea of replacing the *gabelle* altogether by a tax on production at the salt marshes, but this in itself would have been so formidable a task as to offer no real solution.

In view of the difficult problems which the single duty project entailed, Jean Anisson, who by 1720 had long been the senior Deputy of Commerce, all his original colleagues having been replaced, suggested that the best course might be to implement the project first of all in a region where neither the provinces nor the Farmers General could reasonably object to it. His *Proposition subsidiaire sur la suppression des bureaux intérieurs dans les provinces de Lyon, de Dauphiné, de Languedoc, d'Auvergne et de*

Provence recommended, in effect, that the south-eastern region be joined to the territory of the *Cinq Grosses Fermes*. He believed that the benefits of internal free trade in this region, especially on the Rhône, would soon convince the resisting provinces that they too would gain by joining this customs union. Any loss of revenue, he thought, could be made up by setting higher duties on the frontiers of the region and by suppressing the privilege of *transit* enjoyed by certain merchants of Marseille for their trade with Geneva. In his view, the administration, with the assistance of the Deputies of Commerce, could put this plan into effect in less than six months.[1]

Amelot was certainly willing to receive Anisson's ideas, but he also had to listen to the Farmers General, who held very different views.[2] As they saw it, there were three main problems to be solved in planning a single uniform duty: first, to maintain customs revenue undiminished; secondly, to preserve a just economic balance between the different provinces of the kingdom; and finally, to do justice to each particular branch of trade in setting the duties of the new single tariff. They proposed to undertake a vast and detailed study to see whether a single tariff could be devised which would damage neither royal revenues nor the interests of trade. They hoped thereby to be in a position 'to show the Council whether it should pursue or forever reject the idea of establishing a single duty'.[3] This definitive study was shortly to be undertaken by a Farmer General, Lallemant de Betz, who was to work on it for nearly twenty years, but in the summer and autumn months of 1720 the Council of Commerce, engrossed in its immediate plans, wanted nothing more of the Farmers General than a three-man committee to consist of Bertholet de Saint Laurent, Le Gendre and Desvieux who would meet weekly like the Deputies of Commerce to give advice as required.[4]

[1] A.N., F12 827.

[2] B.N., nouv. acq. fr. 22253, fols. 276–301, *Projet du travail nécessaire pour parvenir a l'établissement d'un droit unique sur toutes les marchandises qui entrent dans le Royaume et qui en sortent.* Amelot sent this memoir to Le Febvre for his comments (A.N., F12 119, Amelot to Le Febvre, 31 August 1720).

[3] *Loc. cit.*

[4] A.N., F12 119, Amelot to Desforts, 9 Sept. 1720. The Farmers General were at this time called Directors of the Indies Company.

The planners now proceeded to work out the various phases of the project as rapidly as possible. Vaulthier, an official of the General Farm, found it necessary to consult Amelot from time to time in preparing the reform of the duties in Flanders.[1] The plans for Brittany, it was hoped, would be sufficiently advanced to permit an announcement at the biennial meeting of the Estates of Brittany in September. Although this turned out to be impossible, the Estates got wind of the project and assailed the Governor of the province, d'Estrées, with protests and demands for information about the intentions of the Crown. Acting on Amelot's advice that it was not yet time 'to put the irons in the fire', d'Estrées made evasive replies.[2] Meanwhile, the duc de Gramont heard rumours that the *coûtume de Bayonne* was to be abolished and on 15 September wrote a letter of protest to Amelot. Amelot hastened to assure him that although plans were being made to suppress all the internal duties, the Council had always intended to leave the privileges of Bayonne and the *coûtume* undisturbed.[3] In Bordeaux, the Intendant and the Deputy of Commerce met with uncompromising opposition to their efforts to reconcile the project with the privileges of the Bordeaux fairs.[4] On the other hand, the Chamber of Commerce of Toulouse became so enthusiastic over the project that in 1721 it made repeated efforts to have it put into effect in Languedoc, if not in the whole kingdom.[5] But by then the project had been abandoned.

It was not provincial resistance, formidable though it was, which undermined the project, but 'various changes in the administration of finance'.[6] When John Law fled, his 'system' in ruins, there was an administrative shuffle in which the Council of Commerce lost much of its power to the new Controller General of Finances, Le Pelletier de la Houssaye, who was

[1] A.N., F¹² 119, Amelot to Desforts, 13 Sept. 1720; and A.N., F¹² 171, fol. 4; Vaulthier was first employed in government commercial affairs in 1713, and on 19 Dec. 1729 a bundle of *Mémoires généraux sur les tarifs par rapport au project d'un droit unique* found in his office was turned over to Louis Fagon by a certain Petit.

[2] A.N., F¹² 119, Amelot to d'Estrées, 22 Sept. 1720.

[3] A.N., F¹² 119, Amelot to the duc de Gramont, 23 Sept. 1720.

[4] A.N., F¹² 119, Amelot to de la Houssaye, 19 Jan. 1722.

[5] Jules Chinault, *La Chambre de Commerce*, p. 77; and F¹² 119, Amelot to the Chamber of Commerce of Toulouse, 28 Jan. 1722.

[6] *Loc. cit.*

appointed on 2 January 1721. De la Houssaye was not interested in the project. A little later an *arrêt* confirmed the new subordinate role of the Council by reducing it to a mere *bureau*.[1] Moreover, although Amelot had hopes of reviving the project, he was preoccupied with other matters and was also in bad health. He had gout in both feet which rendered him incapable of walking and it is probable, to judge from his handwriting, that his hands were similarly crippled.[2] By May 1724 his health prevented him from attending the meetings of the Bureau of Commerce and he died on 20 June 1724. Jean Anisson had died on 13 November 1721. With their deaths, the second stage of the struggle for a single uniform duty came to an end.

III

Already the third stage had begun, but on a completely different basis. Thus far the single duty project had been the creature of officials associated with the administration of trade and industry, the financiers of the tax farms opposing it at least until 1720. During the second quarter of the century it continued to enjoy the support of officials such as de Fondières, a General Inspector of Manufactures (1734–44),[3] Gaspard Moise de Fontanieu, Intendant of Dauphiné (1724–40),[4] and Louis Fagon, President of the Bureau of Commerce (1730–44),[5] but this and all other official and commercial support was now overshadowed by a new and surprising enthusiasm for the project in the General Farm itself. Claude Dupin, a Farmer General (1727–62), gave it his unqualified approval,[6] and Jean-François Melon, a Director in the Farm, wrote:' . . . many memoirs, printed and

---

[1] *Arrêt* of 22 June 1722: Léon Biollay, *L'Admin.*, p. 334.

[2] A.N., F12 119, Amelot to Saint Contest, 16 April 1721.

[3] See a manuscript memoir by de Fondières, B.N., ms. fr. 7771, fols. 239 to 326, dated 1747.

[4] De Fontanieu, *Mémoires généraux sur toutes les fermes en Dauphiné* (about 1732), B.N., ms. fr. 8360, fol. 137.

[5] 'Suite des considérations sur les finances et le commerce de France', *Journal de Commerce*, Brussels, October 1761, reprinted in Michau de Montaran, *Mémoire sur les tarifs*, p. 8; and also, de Fondières, *op. cit.*

[6] Claude Dupin, *Œconomiques*, vol. i, p. 119.

manuscript, are crying out against the internal customs bureaux. Our internal trade is continually weakened by these bureaux which prevent freedom of transport from one province to another ... their yield is inconsiderable and could be made up by a slight increase in the duties collected by the import and export bureaux on the frontiers of the kingdom.'[1] On this question, Dupin and Melon were expressing not only their own private opinions but also the official attitude of the Company of the General Farm. During this period and until the War of the Austrian Succession had given rise to heavier financial requirements, the Farmers General themselves sponsored a single duty project.

It is not clear exactly why they did so, but part of the explanation evidently lies in the outstanding personal efforts of one of their number, Michel-Joseph Hyacinth Lallemant de Betz, seigneur de Nanteau. Born in Paris on 15 March 1694, the son of a Farmer General, Lallemant de Betz was sent out at an early age into the provinces where he served for a time as a Receiver General of Finances at Soissons and as a Controller General of the tax farm.[2] In 1719 he became a Director of the *Compagnie des Indes*; in 1721 Lepelletier de la Houssaye appointed him Farmer General, and in the following year invited him to be one of the three Farmers General who customarily represented the interests of the whole company in the meetings of the Bureau of Commerce. This last appointment, renewed by an *arrêt* of 20 December 1735, he continued to hold until 21 September 1762. A contemporary alleged that he obtained from Cardinal Fleury a post of Farmer General for his brother, Lallemant de Nantouillet, over the heads of four other candidates who were supported respectively by the Queen, the king of Spain, the duc d'Orléans, and the duc de la Trémoïlle. The same writer judged him 'insufferably proud and haughty with his inferiors. He is a great courtier', he continued, 'and makes many promises which he scarcely ever keeps'.[3] Whatever the defects of his personality, Lallemant de Betz appears to have been extraordinarily interested and competent not only in

---

[1] J.-F. Melon, *Essai politique* (1734), p. 151.
[2] Ferdinand Courtoy, *Inventaire*, table, p. 102.
[3] B. Ars., ms. 4905; and Pierre Bonnassieux, *Cons. de Com.*, biographical appendix.

matters relating to his job as Farmer General but in the whole
field of political economy. He does not seem to have published
anything: his numerous writings, many of which are listed by a
contemporary in a manuscript bibliography, have for the most
part either been lost or are unidentified.[1] But two which have
survived, the *Mémoire sur les finances pour servir d'introduction au
travail du projet du droit unique*,[2] and the *Tarif général du droit unique*,[3]
provide detailed information on the single duty project of the
Farmers General up to 1737. 'This work', writes an official of
the reign of Louis XVI, Auget de Montyon, 'undertaken at
great expense by Monsieur de Betz, who was not reimbursed
for it, had as its object, 1° to favour commerce by simplifying
the collection of the duties imposed on it, 2° to assimilate the
Provinces Reputed Foreign with those of the *Cinq Grosses Fermes*
by suppressing the tariffs and the local duties which hamper the
movement of goods in the interior of the kingdom.'[4] Lallemant
de Betz was the instigator, the director and the principal ex-
ponent of this project, and as such he was probably mainly
responsible for its adoption by the Company.

The sustained interest of the General Farm may also be
partly explained by the way in which de Betz approached the
reform. He set out mainly to discover whether it could be put
into effect in such a way as to avoid loss of customs revenue.
The Farmers General had hitherto assumed that a substantial
loss was inevitable but, although this was their principal reason
for opposing the project for a single duty, they had never before
attempted to calculate the cost of the reform, nor to work out
any of its other implications. They had never, indeed, had any
reason to do so as long as they could obstruct the reform by the
mere threat of financial loss to the Crown, or by their own
political power. But during the regency they had been unable
to keep their control of the financial system, even under the
powerful leadership of Joseph Pâris-Duverney. In 1719 the tax

[1] Arch. Ass. Pub., papers of Auget de Montyon (unclassified boxes).

[2] B.N., ms. fr. 7771, fols. 204–17.

[3] Bib. de l'Ecole nationale des ponts et chaussees, ms. 1046, 15 tomes in 16
vols., continuous pagination with 8185 pp. Proof that Lallemant de Betz is the
author of these two manuscripts is contained in Arch. Ass. Pub., papers of Auget de
Montyon; and see Appendix III.

[4] Arch. Ass. Pub., papers of Auget de Montyon.

farms had become part of John Law's great 'system' and the Farmers General mere directors of the *Compagnie des Indes*.[1] For a time it had looked as though the *système* would produce enough revenue to free the Crown from its dependence on the tax farms and, brief though that period was, it had seen a momentary revival of the single duty project under the direction of Michel Amelot. In their new subordinate role the Farmers General had been consulted, but no more. This had shown them what might happen to the customs in such circumstances. Impressed with the force of the reform movement at that time, the Farmers General supported de Betz's investigations not only in order to discover what the reform might cost but also to be in a position to control and execute it themselves should it prove to be feasible. If there was ever to be a new tariff for a single duty, it had better be one of their own making.

In 1728, after Lallemant de Betz had made long preparatory studies, the Farmers General met to examine the whole undertaking. Struck by its magnitude, they were fearful that it might take too long—had not the Dutch adopted a new tariff in 1725 after only five years of planning?—and to speed up the work, they considered dividing it between two committees. In view of the integrated nature of the project, however, they adopted the more obvious plan of confirming Lallemant de Betz as sole director. To preserve a semblance of collective control they drew up on 9 July 1728 an official statement of policy in the form of a *Délibération* of twenty-eight articles which seven Farmers General, including de Betz himself, signed.[2] De Betz had already spent several years working on the project, and from the time the Company gave it official recognition he took nearly ten more years to complete it. But time mattered less to the Company when they found that he had sufficient personal interest in the work to pay for most of it himself. Besides, although his main purpose appeared so simple as hardly to require such a long period, it was obvious to anyone

[1] G. T. Mathews, *Gén. Farm.*, p. 66.

[2] Copied in full in B.N., ms. fr 7771, fol. 209; signed by Jean-François de la Porte, Louis-Denis de Lalive de Bellegarde, François-Paul le Normant de Townshent, Louis Chevalier (who as a Director of the Farm had worked on the project of 1699–1710; see *supra*, p. 26), André-Guillaume Darlus and Charles Savalette.

who cared to examine the incidental operations that some of
them had to be worked out slowly by trial and error with much
unavoidable repetition.

Reduced to its essentials, the project had three phases. The
first was an analysis of the customs registers kept during the
three years of the lease Paul Manis (1715–18). De Betz chose
this as the most recent period of normal tax farming and by the
time it had received approval in the *Délibération* of 1728 he had
already gone some way in his analysis. The purpose of the
analysis was to establish a list of every type of goods traded
during those years and for each type to draw up tables showing
the amount of duties paid on the various quantities imported,
exported, shipped in and out of the territory of the *Cinq Grosses
Fermes*, shipped across the Provinces Reputed Foreign, sent from
one port to another in different provinces and from one port to
another in the same province—to have, in short, a detailed
picture of French trade. This proved to be extremely difficult,
partly because of the confusion of the customs system. De Betz
attempted to draw maps of the system, and of the trade routes,
to assist in correlating the registers of the different customs
bureaux, but was forced by insurmountable difficulties to
abandon the attempt and to establish instead what he called
'la scholastique des droits locaux',[1] a descriptive list of the
various duties for the assistance of the clerks engaged in analys-
ing the customs registers. Then, because these registers used an
infinity of local weights and measures, and local terms for many
types of goods, he undertook a vast study to establish con-
cordances and to reduce the entries in the registers to a common standard.[2] In the course of this first phase with all its un-
foreseen problems, his clerks were forced to repeat their analysis
of the registers three times; not until 1732 were they able to
move on to the second phase of the project.

It was at this stage that de Betz compiled the new general
tariff. He commenced by writing a brief memoir on the customs
history of each type of merchandise, on the basis of 'five or six
thousand edicts, declarations, *arrêts*, orders and decisions of the

[1] Lallemant de Betz, ms. B.N., ms. fr. 7771, fol. 207.
[2] This study of weights and measures forms tome vii (pp. 2975–3792) of the
manuscript *Tarif gén.*, Bib. Ponts et Chaussées, ms. 1045.

Council gathered from everywhere and for which even the cupboards of the Louvre were searched.'[1] But the duties levied in the past, as shown in these memoirs, were only one consideration in calculating the duties to be charged in the new tariff. In order to calculate the anticipated yield of the new duties, he had to evaluate the quantities of imports and exports for the base period 1715–18 in terms of standard prices. Although article 14 of the *Délibération* of 1728 laid down that prices must be standardized in accordance with reports from the Chambers of Commerce and the merchant gilds of Paris, the Controller General, Le Peletier Desforts, when consulted thought that it would be too difficult for the merchants of 120 gilds to reach any agreement on prices. Accordingly, a copy of the list of goods established for the new tariff was sent only to the eight Chambers of Commerce in Bayonne, Bordeaux, La Rochelle, Lille, Lyon, Marseille, Nantes and Rouen, and the price returns for each item in the list, though often very different, were reduced to an arithmetic mean or average.[2] De Betz now knew the quantities of goods which, if the years 1715–18 were indeed normal years, would be subject to the new single duty, and he knew their value. It remained to set the *ad valorem* duties on these goods at figures which would yield a total customs revenue no less than would be produced by the customs system as it stood. The new duties would have to produce as much revenue from imports and exports alone as the existing duties produced from the various kinds of internal trade as well as imports and exports. Furthermore, according to the policy expressed in the *Délibération* of 1728, the commonly accepted Colbertist policy embodied in the Tariff of 1667 and the *nouveaux droits*, the import duties had to be high on foreign manufactures and low on raw materials, whereas the export duties were to be high on raw materials and low on French manufactures. When Lallemant de Betz, taking these and other factors into account, had drawn up the new tariff of duties, little remained to be done.

In the third and final phase, de Betz prepared a table of merchandise in alphabetical order comparing the revenue from

---

[1] B.N., ms. fr. 7771, fol. 211. They occupy tome v of the *Tarif gén.*

[2] The price lists sent in by the Chambers of Commerce, together with the averages worked out by Lallemant de Betz, are contained in tome vi of the *Tarif gén.*

the duties collected during 1715–18 with what would have been produced in those years by the new tariff of duties, had it been imposed on imports and exports alone. The result of his calculations was this:[1]

	livres	sous	deniers
The annual product of the duties actually levied in 1715–18 was	7,378,532	14	5
The annual product of the single duty would have been	7,555,055	7	10
Thus, the annual increase due to the project would have been	176,522	13	5

This high hypothetical yield of the single duty was partly the result of systematically adding all industrial products and raw materials to the list of goods subject to special duties in favour of French industry. Except for the goods listed in the Tariff of 1667 and the *nouveaux droits*, few had been taxed more than 5 per cent to 10 per cent in any tariff. But in the new tariff, while few duties were reduced to less than 2½ per cent, many were raised to 20 per cent and higher. Thus, much more revenue was gained on the increases than was lost on the reductions. Another way in which de Betz increased the hypothetical earnings of the single duty was by including in the tariff certain goods such as English tin, lead, coal and glassware which the Crown had hitherto officially prohibited while allowing importers to handle them under special permits. De Betz argued that these should not be prohibited but heavily taxed instead. The Crown does not appear to have rejected these two means of compensating for the loss of the revenue from the internal duties.[2] But had the new tariff been put into effect it might well have produced either far less revenue, or far more, than de Betz predicted because it was based on the assumption that the change in duties would not affect trade but leave it much as it had been in the period 1715–18.

[1] Contained in tome xiv of the *Tarif gén.*

[2] A.N., G¹ 79, *Etat des droits du projet du nouveau tarif sur lesquels le Conseil du Commerce a fait des changements avec un précis des motifs qui ont déterminé à fixer ou proposer lesdits droits et de ceux qui ont engagé le Conseil à les changer* (ms.), 22 fols., double spread in the form of a table, drawn up soon after May 1738. It is described in the *Inventaire raisonné* (A.N., G¹ 3–5). See Appendix III, *infra*, p 183.

Whatever the defects of the proposed tariff and the investigation on which it was based, it met with the approval of the Deputies of Commerce and the *Conseil royal du commerce*.[1] True, the three Deputies of Commerce to whom the General Farm submitted it for examination in 1737 had a certain sympathy with the interests of the Farm, which was almost a guarantee of their approval. François de Laborde, Deputy for Bayonne, became a Farmer General in 1739 and was appointed to represent the Farmers General in the Bureau of Commerce along with Lallemant de Betz and others; Louis Pasquier, Deputy for Rouen, was the nephew of his predecessor, Godeheu, who had given up the post of Deputy to become a Farmer General and who represented the Farmers General in the Bureau of Commerce from 1720 to 1735; Nicolas Claessen, Deputy for La Rochelle, became a Director of the *Compagnie des Indes* in 1746.[2] It is therefore not surprising that, as de Betz reported, 'these Deputies thought at first that to fulfil their mission they ought to raise some objections, but their studies only served to convince them that in this work the Company had sacrificed the interests of the Adjudicator to those of the merchants'.[3] The approval of the *Conseil Royal du Commerce*, however, was not a foregone conclusion. This Council, in which Louis Fagon, charged with the direction of commerce (1730–44), played a leading part, received the new tariff with all the incidental calculations late in 1737 in fifteen folio-size volumes entitled *Le Tarif général du droit unique*.[4] After examining it, the Council made changes affecting fifty-six products, but nearly all of them had the effect of emphasizing the protectionist tendency of the tariff in accordance with the terms of the *Délibération* of 9 July 1728. Moreover, the Crown showed its agreement with the terms of de Betz's work by immediately implementing some of it in laws such as the *arrêt* of 20 May

---

[1] The *Conseil royal du Commerce*, created on 29 March 1730, did not replace the Bureau of Commerce but dealt with certain important commercial subjects, such as the single duty project, until the early 1740's when it ceased meeting. (Biollay, *L'Admin.*, p. 343.)

[2] Pierre Bonnassieux, *Cons. de Com.*, biographical appendix; Léon Biollay, *L'Admin.*, p. 539.

[3] Lallemant de Betz, *Mém.* (B.N., ms. fr. 7771), fol. 214.

[4] Bib. Ponts et Chaussées, ms. 1046.

E

1738 permitting the importation of English tin and lead, 'without waiting', as the Farmers General remarked, 'for the execution of the new project'.[1]

Official approval notwithstanding, the project was abandoned in the early 1740's, but only after a struggle to foist it on the unwilling Provinces Reputed Foreign. De Betz and other officials wrote memoirs to prove its usefulness to these provinces, and they considered various means of implementing it.[2] Thoroughly alarmed, the Estates of Brittany, the Bayonne Chamber of Commerce and other agencies raised a vociferous protest.[3] Yet these were not the only reason for the abandonment of the project. A Breton contributor to the *Journal de Commerce*, who stated in 1761 that de Betz's project had been dropped because 'it was agreed that its establishment would inevitably cause the ruin of our foreign trade ... ',[4] was not so correct as de Fondières, General Inspector of Manufactures, who wrote that 'the greatest obstacle which the late Monsieur Fagon found in the way of bringing into force the new tariff of customs duties was the treaty of commerce made with Holland in 1738'.[5] True, the outbreak of the War of Austrian Succession in 1740 cancelled this treaty, but then, as de Fondières observed, 'that was not an appropriate time for the authorities to strike blows against powerful provinces'.[6] In war time the contributions of these provinces were needed, and—equally important—so was the revenue from the internal duties.[7] Consequently, de Betz's project was put aside. It was scarcely ever mentioned again.

---

[1] A.N., G¹ 79, *Etat des droits du projet du nouveau tarif*, article 'Etain'.

[2] A.N., G¹ 3–5, *Inventaire raisonné des opérations concernant le tarif du droit unique*, 20 fols. References here given to paragraphs nos. 29–35. See Appendix III, *infra*, p. 185.

[3] A.N., F¹² 2427, *Mémoire concernant le droit unique nouveau droit d'entrée et de sortie par mer que les Fermiers généraux proposent de faire établir dans tous les ports et havres de la province de Bretagne* (1770), which makes reference to the project of the 1720–40 period. Cf. Claude Dupin, *Œconomiques*, vol. i, pp. 118–19, which refers to Brittany as the worst enemy of the project.

[4] *Journal de Commerce*, Oct. 1761, reprinted in Montaran, *Mémoire sur les tarifs*, p. 8.

[5] B.N., ms. fr. 7771, fols. 239 to 326 (1747), fol. 253.

[6] *Ibid.*, fol. 255.

[7] Rousselot de Surgy, *Encyc. Méth.*, article, 'Droit'; Lallemant de Betz, *Mem.*, B.N., ms. fr. 7771, fol. 209 and 215; and Claude Dupin, *Observations sur*, p. 105.

IV

For the next twenty years the government took no great interest in customs reform. Why this was so it is not easy to see because there was no lack of interest in certain official circles, especially during the 1750's when attacks on the internal duties appeared in books by J.-B. Naveau, an employee of the General Farm,[1] Jean-Charles de Lavie, a member of the Parlement of Bordeaux,[2] Claude Dupin, a Farmer General,[3] François Veron de Fortbonnais, a well-known writer on financial matters,[4] Simon Cliquot-Blervache, a General Inspector of Manufactures, and the celebrated Vincent de Gournay, Intendant of Commerce,[5] to mention only a few. Why, then, was the next customs reform project not begun until 1759? Furthermore, why did Daniel Trudaine, an Intendant of Finances charged with the administration of commerce from 1749, neglect customs reform during the first ten years of his administration and then proceed to give it such whole-hearted support that in later years he was sometimes named as its creator? The answer is given by Trudaine's son, Trudaine de Montigny, who writes, 'This project was conceived by Monsieur Bertin'.[6] Henri Bertin, Controller General from 1759 to 1763 appears to have been personally responsible for launching the fourth of the single duty projects, which began in 1759, and until his time no one, not even Trudaine, seems to have been willing to take the matter up again.

[1] J.-B. Naveau, *Le Financier citoyen*, 2 vols., 1757, vol. i, p. 214.

[2] J.-C. de Lavie, *Abrégé de la république de Bodin*, 2 vols., London, 1755, vol. ii, p. 82.

[3] Claude Dupin, *Observations*, vol. iii, p. 83.

[4] Veron de Fortbonnais, *Rech. et cons.*, vol. i, pp. 144 and 524. This work is said by the publishers to have been written in 1754 (see *l'avertissement*). In Nov. 1756 Fortbonnais applied for the post of Deputy of Commerce for Nantes, which suggests that he was intent upon doing something about the problems of commerce (see two autographed letters of Fortbonnais dated 17 Nov. 1756, to Trudaine, and 19 Nov. 1756, together with related papers in A.N., F12 726B). His application was supported by Le Couteulx de la Noraye who worked on the single duty project. Unsuccessful in this application, Fortbonnais was soon afterwards appointed as a financial assistant to Silhouette. A critic of the Physiocrats, Fortbonnais was a staunch supporter of internal free trade and it is unfortunate that his *Mémoire sur les traites* has disappeared with most of his other papers. (Gabriel Fleury, *François Veron de Fortbonnais*, Le Mans, 1915, appendix 8.)

[5] They were joint authors of a book, *Considérations sur le commerce*, p. 55. Also Clicquot-Blervache, *Le Réformateur*, tome i, p. 24.

[6] A.N., F12 2427, Montigny to Terray, 20 Nov. 1770.

Bertin appointed a committee of officials to prepare a plan. This committee included two Intendants of Finances, Daniel Trudaine and Barberie de Courteilles; two Intendants of Commerce, Jacques-Marie Jerôme Michau de Montaran and Trudaine de Montigny; three Deputies of Commerce, Le Couteulx de la Noraye, Deputy for Paris, Joseph Marion, Deputy for Saint-Malo and then Paris, and Parent, Deputy for Amiens; and a Farmer General, Gigault des Marches de Crisenoy, who in September 1762 was appointed as representative of the General Farm in the Bureau of Commerce.[1] But the real task of preparing the project in detail fell to de Montaran and de Montigny, who were assisted by de Crisenoy and the three Deputies of Commerce, and a number of minor officials of whom one, a chief clerk in the *contrôle général* named Dureau de Blancourt, appears to have taken more than a perfunctory interest in the project.[2] All the members of the committee represented the Crown rather than special interests. The composition of the working party might suggest, it is true, that in planning the reform the officials of the Crown negotiated with the trade representatives from certain cities and a representative of financial interests, but this was not the case. The Deputies of Commerce had been appointed to their posts not to defend the views of the cities they represented but because the administration—Daniel Trudaine in particular—believed that they would represent the interests of commerce in general. De Crisenoy appears to have been selected for the planning committee as an able Farmer General and a pleasant colleague rather than as a delegate of the General Farm. Certainly it was Bertin rather than the Farmers General who chose him to sit in the Bureau of Commerce.[3] Moreover, it is difficult to see how either de Crisenoy himself or the Farmers

---

[1] *Loc. cit.*

[2] Dureau de Blancourt, who figures in the Almanach Royal from 1762 to 1776 as a clerk in the department of Trudaine de Montigny, worked for years on the single duty project. Among the papers of Auget de Montyon, Bib. Ass. Pub. are extensive notes entitled, *Extrait d'un livre fait par Monsieur Dureau (manuscrit et projet) intitulé tarif des droits d'entrée et de sortie substituer à tous les anciens droits des traites,* which appears to be an account of the project of these years. He died either in 1783 or 1784.

[3] A.N., F¹² 2427, Montigny to Terray, 20 Nov. 1770; and Léon Biollay, *L'Admin.,* p. 400.

General can have regarded him as a representative of the General Farm. He clearly had neither the authority to speak for the Company nor the duty to act as a liaison with it, for after receiving the finished reform project the General Farm pronounced it invalid on the grounds that it would cause too great a loss of revenue.[1] An official project in every way, it was planned by a team working together in the closest harmony.

The planners appear to have consulted no unofficial agency until the spring of 1761 when the new tariff project had already reached an advanced stage. They had prepared a comprehensive list of merchandise, and had it printed in the form of a table which filled two thick folio volumes. In a column beside each item they had recorded the amount charged on it in the Tariff of 1664, the Tariff of 1667 or the *nouveaux droits*, as the case might be, for the purpose of comparison with the amount of the new duty which was to be recorded in another column. The most difficult task was to calculate the new duty. The planners intended to express that duty as a percentage of the price of each item, and therefore they had to decide two things about each type of goods in the list: first, the rate at which it ought to be taxed according to its function in the national economy, and this rate ranged from 1 per cent on imports of scarce raw materials and exports of French finished manufactures to 20 per cent on imports of foreign manufactures and exports of industrial raw materials.[2] Secondly, they had to fix a price for each item, and for this purpose they decided to consult the Chambers of Commerce. On 8 April 1761, Bertin dispatched a dozen copies of the model tariff to the Intendant of Brittany, and copies to several other Intendants, instructing them to distribute them among the Chambers of Commerce in their intendancies with a request that they mark the price of each item in the appropriate column and make any comments they wished on the tariff.[3] A copy returned by the Chamber of

---

[1] *Collection des mémoires présentés à l'Assemblée des notables*, Versailles, 1787, 'Mémoire sur la reformation des droits de traites . . . ', p. 10.

[2] Jacques-Marie-Jérôme Michau de Montaran, *Mémoire sur les tarifs*, p. 88.

[3] Bertin to Le Bret, Intendant of Brittany, quoted in Coquelin and Guillaumin, *Dictionnaire*, vol. i, p. 584. Bertin says he is sending twelve copies of the model tariff for distribution. On the same date, 8 April 1761, Bertin wrote about the project to the Intendant of Metz (see Roederer mss., A.N., AP 29 68).

Commerce of Rouen, duly filled out with prices and much comment, bears witness that this Chamber 'was persuaded of the
advantages for national trade which would result from the
execution of the Project. . . . '.[1] But approval was only to be
expected in Rouen, situated as it was in the territory of the
Cinq Grosses Fermes. In the Province Reputed Foreign the model
general tariff appeared as the harbinger of another tyrannical
attack on their provincial rights and privileges.

Opposition from these provinces was not unexpected. In a
long covering letter sent with the tariff to the Intendant of
Brittany, Bertin had written, 'I am not ignorant of the fact that
Brittany, very attached to its privileges and ancient usages, will
perhaps have some difficulty in accommodating itself to the
new tariff, which will replace the harbour duties, the *brieux*, the
traites domainiales, and all the others now being collected . . . I
feel that the Chambers of Commerce of Nantes and Saint Malo
will help you a great deal in this work.'[2] He was perhaps too
optimistic. A ship-owner of Nantes, probably Jean-Gabriel
Montaudouin de la Touche, got possession of this letter through
one of the Chambers of Commerce of Brittany and published it,
together with a great deal of critical comment on the whole
project, in the *Journal de Commerce* of October 1761.[3] He warned
his readers that the Farmers General, intent upon consolidat-
ing their grip on the country, were behind this scheme and
would not only ruin French trade for their own financial ends
but would also eventually extend the *tailles*, *aides* and *gabelle*
over the free provinces, including Brittany. Early in 1762 a
reply to this article, published in Paris, suggested that the
author objected to the reform project because he feared that it
might damage his own shipping business and went on to demonstrate at great length that the project was not a sinister plot of

---

[1] Bib. Mazarine, mss. 2778 and 2779, *Projet de tarif pour servir a la perception des
droits de traites à l'importation des marchandises de l'étranger dans le Royaume, et à l'exportation des marchandises du Royaume à l'étranger*, written in 1762 or Jan. 1763, vol. ii, fol.
21, ms. notes.

[2] Bertin to Le Bret, 8 April 1761, Guillaumin and Coquelin, *Dictionnaire*, p. 584.

[3] 'Suite des considérations sur les finances et le commerce de la France', *Journal
de Commerce*, October 1761. This article, containing Bertin's letter, was reprinted
with Michau de Montaran, *Memoire sur les tarifs*. Montaudouin de la Touche
(1722–80) was a member of the Society of Agriculture of Brittany, and contributor
to various economic journals.

the Farmers General, but a genuine endeavour to favour French trade and industry.[1] But the Estates of Brittany, only too willing to see the project as a threat, maintained a steadfast opposition to it. A similar resistance arose in Alsace, Lorraine and the Trois Evêchés where the most outspoken champion of the *status quo*, Joseph-François Coster, also put forward the damaging argument that the project was a conspiracy of financiers to batten on the foreign trade of these provinces.[2] Coster's book, and others in the same vein published about the same time, drew rejoinders in defence of the project from Louis Bresson, *Lieutenant-Général* in the *bailliage* of Darney, and abbé André Morellet, a fairly prominent writer on economic subjects.[3] Finally, in view of all this publicity, one of the planners of the project, Michau de Montaran, wrote a careful exposition of it and of the political and economic principles behind it, arguing that apart from the logical necessity for uniting the kingdom economically as it was united politically, a national customs union would be of great benefit to all the provinces including even those Reputed Foreign and the Foreign Provinces. He believed that in the unlikely event of certain provinces refusing to accept the reform, they could be left outside the new ring of customs bureaux and simply ignored.[4] 'The only real obstacle', de Montaran wrote, 'which appears capable of preventing the execution of the project is too great a diminution of revenue, incompatible with the present state of finances.'[5] Although a greater industrial and commercial activity would eventually more than make up for the losses of the moment, he could see no way of avoiding these and could only express faith in Bertin's ability to solve this problem.

Little more than a year later Bertin resigned his post. The Controllers General of the next few years, de Laverdy (December 1763 to October 1768) and Maynon d'Invault (October 1768 to December 1769), did not take any steps toward the execution of the project because, as Trudaine de Montigny explained in 1770 to the Controller General, Terray, 'They thought that the

---

[1] *Lettre sur un article.*   [2] J.-F. Coster, *Lettres d'un citoyen.*
[3] Louis Bresson, *Réponse*; and André Morellet, *Mémoire des fabriquants.*
[4] Michau de Montaran, *Mémoire sur les tarifs.*
[5] *Ibid.*, p. 128.

circumstances were not appropriate to begin an operation which, although fundamentally very useful, might somewhat reduce the King's revenue, especially in the earlier years.'[1] But de Montigny also reported that these Controllers General had given great encouragement to the partisans of the project and, indeed, there is evidence that customs reform was regarded as certain and imminent at least until summer 1767. From January 1762 the Deputies of Commerce mentioned the project from time to time in their records of proceedings as though they were taking for granted its speedy execution, but on 23 August 1767 they reluctantly admitted that it might be deferred for a long time.[2]

In the autumn of 1770, however, the single duty question was brought up again, this time in Brittany by the bishop of Rennes, François Bareau de Girac.[3] Appointed president of the session of the Estates of Brittany held from 25 September to 30 December 1770, Bareau de Girac spoke of the project to some members of the Estates, and in October he received and forwarded to Trudaine de Montigny a hostile memoir from Nantes entitled, *Mémoire concernant le droit unique, nouveau droit d'entrée et de sortie par mer que les Fermiers généraux proposent de faire établir dans tous les ports et havres de la Province de Bretagne.*[4] He asked Trudaine de Montigny to furnish him with a reply to this memoir so that he could answer all the objections raised in it, and de Montigny seems to have been only too glad to take advantage of the occasion to bring the whole matter to a climax.[5] Not only did he

[1] A.N., F[12] 2427, Montigny to Terray, 20 Nov. 1770.

[2] A.N., F[12] 713, *Avis* of 22 April 1763 on a request from Didelot, director of manufactures in Bruyere, Lorraine; *avis* of 16 Sept. 1763 on the manufactures of La Chaudeau; *avis* of 12 August 1763 on a request from the Chatellenie of Chantoceaux; A.N., F[12] 714, *avis* of 23 August 1767 on an application from a wire manufacturer of Lorraine; *avis* of 5 Sept. 1768 on a question of duties on cinders; and A.N., F[12] 716 on a request of the Etats de Bretagne for a lowering of the duties of the *Cinq Grosses Fermes* in favour of the sugar refineries of Nantes.

[3] Born in Angoulême in 1732; bishop of Saint-Brieux on 31 August 1766; bishop of Rennes late in 1769 (Henri Fréville, *L'Intendance de Bretagne*, pp. 310 and 315.) By a note of 15 July 1770 the King granted him 40,000 *livres* for expenses to be incurred during the forthcoming meeting of the Breton estates (H. 1428, *Minute des bons du roi . . . 1760 à 1781*).

[4] A.N., F[12] 2427, 25 fols. in ms.

[5] A.N., F[12] 2427, Montigny to Terray, 20 November 1770.

arrange for the drafting of a reply to the memoir from Nantes;[1] he also wrote to the Controller General asking permission to instruct the Estates of Brittany through Bareau de Girac to have their *Député-en-Cour* present officially all the Breton objections to the single duty project so that they could be discussed. In accordance with this plan, de Montigny enclosed a draft letter to Bareau de Girac which, whether or not Terray ever approved it, reveals much of de Montigny's mind on the single duty project:

You have raised the question in the Estates, and thus they know that the establishment of the Tariff may take place at any moment. They have not been consulted on this matter by the administration and are doubtless well aware that the king may change the customs barriers of his kingdom without any such preliminaries, that of all possible changes the removal of the barriers to the extreme frontiers of His Majesty's realm is the simplest because it seems to be dictated by the very nature of things, and that in consequence this of all public undertakings need take the least account of private interests. In this state of affairs it seems to me that your province must foresee a strong possibility that the establishment of the Tariff will be ordered and carried out in the interval between the present meeting of the Estates and the following one.[2]

Since the King had no obligation to consult the Estates, de Montigny continued, the reform could be put into effect without warning. Therefore the Estates would be well advised to have their *Députés-en-cour* bring the matter up in Paris. He was sure that the tariff question could be resolved in discussion with the *Députés-en-cour* who, on returning to Brittany, would have no difficulty in persuading the province of the benefits of removing the barriers which separated them from the rest of the kingdom with respect to trade.

Trudaine de Montigny was in Montigny at this time, and therefore did not see Bareau de Girac when he went to Paris not long afterwards. One of his subordinates, however, probably

---

[1] A.N., F12 2427, *Eclaircissements sur un mémoire attribué au commerce de Nantes et envoyé au mois d'8br 1770 aux Etats de Bretagne intitulé; Mémoire concernant le droit unique, nouveau droit d'entree et de sortie par mer que les Fermiers . . .*, 71. fol.

[2] A.N., F12 2427, Montigny to Bareau de Girac, November 1770, sent in draft form to Terray.

Louis-Paul Abeille,[1] had a long conversation about the project with him before he returned to Rennes to attend the meeting of the Estates at the beginning of December. 'The bishop of Rennes told me', Abeille writes, 'that the Controller General had said he would be pleased (il serait fort aise) if this question were discussed in the Estates. I am very much afraid that some private interest may have intervened and presented this matter to him in a new light.'[2] Obviously, if the new Controller General were content to have the project discussed in Rennes, where it was sure to be rejected, it could only be because he had decided, at least for the time being, to drop it. As de Montigny realized, Terray had no more interest than his two predecessors in expensive reforms of this kind.[3]

Although this attempt at reform failed like the earlier ones, it differed from them in two respects: it enjoyed wide publicity, especially among officials, and the plans drawn up for it were passed on to serve as a point of departure for the next group of reformers. Even before the public controversy which Bertin's letters of spring 1761 had touched off, many writers had condemned the internal duties and some had recommended the substitution of a single duty on the frontiers, though very few appear to have known of the efforts which had been made since the time of Colbert to carry out this reform. Possibly the only published references to them were the brief allusions of Claude Dupin, whose books are said to have been privately printed in editions of hardly more than a score of copies.[4] But after the controversy of 1761–2, it was a matter of general knowledge that

[1] The writer of two letters to Montigny dated 'Samedi, le Xbre 1770' and 'Lundi, 3 Xbre 1770' (F[12] 2427) is obviously, according to the contents of the letters, the author of the reply to the memoir from Nantes. Louis-Paul Abeille, a Breton, the secretary to the Bureau of Commerce since 1768 and the Secretary of the Society of Agriculture of Brittany, seems to be a logical person to write the reply to the memoir from Nantes. The matter seems to be proved by the handwriting of the letters which is the same as that of five autographed letters of Abeille in B.N., ms. fr. 12305, fols. 2 to 9. Abeille was a member of the physiocratic group until he left after a quarrel in 1769.

[2] A.N., F[12] 2427, Abeille to Montigny, 3 Dec. 1770.

[3] A.N., F[12] 2427, Montigny to Terray, 20 Nov. 1770. Terray was intent on persuading the Farmers General to raise the price of their lease from 132 million *livres* to 135 millions, an endeavour quite incompatible with the single duty project. (Douglas Dakin, *Turgot*, p. 158.)

[4] Dupin, *Œconomiques*, vol. i, ed. Marc Aucuy, Paris, Rivière, 1913, introduction.

the Crown desired this reform. 'We are assured', wrote Fleureau a sometime tax farmer, in 1775, 'that the Ministry is busy once again with the preparation of this interesting project'.[1] Though this was only a rumour it reflected the attention which the project had attracted at every level of the administration. An Inspector of Manufactures in Alsace, a self-appointed advocate of the project, wrote to his superior in Paris, 'People say with the greatest enthusiasm, "The Great Colbert!" because he made the tariffs of 1664 and 1667. What would they not say of Monsieur l'abbé Terray if under his ministry the General Tariff were introduced and the customs barriers removed to the frontiers?'[2] An official royal historian, Jacob-Nicolas Moreau, two Intendants of Commerce, Pottier and Isaac de Bacalan, and two Intendants of Finance, Bouvard de Fourqueux and Moreau de Beaumont, all supported the project.[3] In 1769, Moreau de Beaumont described it in detail in a financial treatise which soon became, as the preface to a later edition remarks, a manual for the Intendants.[4] It was even said that the dauphin Louis had made plans 'to destroy all the indirect taxes, and render internal trade entirely free from one end of the kingdom to the other'.[5] The comte de Lamerville, who put forward this claim, continued to urge the execution of the Dauphin's alleged plans in a memoir to the government on 19 May 1778, in three letters of 1782 to Louis XVI, and again in a book published in 1788.[6] It is therefore not surprising that the project of the 1760's,

---

[1] Fleureau, *Essai sur les moyens*, p. 39. Fleureau is named as the author of this pamphlet in Hardy, *Mes Loisirs*, vol. iii, B.N., ms. fr. 6682, p. 84, 24 March 1775. Cf. François Métra, *Correspondance secrète*, vol. i, p. 68, entry for 12 Sept. 1774.

[2] A.N., F¹² 827, D'Aigrefeuille to Saint-Prest (sic), 2 Jan. 1772; d'Aigrefeuille to Trudaine de Montigny, 27 May 1773, 1 June 1773, 29 June 1773; ms. pamphlet entitled *Recullement de la Barrière des Cinq Grosses Fermes et établissement du nouveau Tarif général aux extrémités du Royaume*, 1773 which d'Aigrefeuille sent to Montigny in May 1773.

[3] B.N., Collection Moreau, ms. 1088, fols. 196–209; for Jacques Pottier, see d'Aigrefeuille ms., *loc. cit.*; for Bacalan see 'Observations faites par Monsieur de Bacalan . . . ', *R.h.d.e.s.*, 1908.

[4] Jean-Louis Moreau de Beaumont, *Mém.*, *con.*, vol. iii, p. 411.

[5] J.-L.-T. Heurtault de Lamerville (le comte), *De l'impôt territorial*, p. vii.

[6] B.N., ms. fr. 7772, fols. 2 to 12, *Plan d'une nouvelle administration des finances qui opérera infailliblement leur restauration*, signed by Lamerville and dated 19 May 1778; A.N., K 885, three undated letters to the King signed, 'Lamerville' seem from their contents to have been composed in 1782, the year in which he claims in his book that he wrote to the King.

unlike the earlier ones, was not only used in the preparation of later projects but even remembered and acknowledged in the Assembly of Notables and the Constituent Assembly.[1] Henceforth the movement has a continuous history.

Already, without taking this history any further, we can see the primary characteristic of the movement: its component reform projects were entirely planned and largely supported by officials. The Deputies of Commerce were not at first officials, it is true, and it might be argued that Anisson was thinking of Lyon rather than France when he put forward the idea of a single duty in the early years of the century. Yet Anisson was established in Paris as King's Printer, with an honorary position of *Secrétaire du Roi*, so that serving as Deputy of Commerce for Lyon was only a secondary occupation. In any event, before his death the Deputies of Commerce were beginning to serve the Crown, especially in customs matters, rather than the cities they were supposed to represent. As early as 1720, Amelot sent the Deputy for Bordeaux to help in official efforts to win support for the single duty project among the commercial interests of Bordeaux. The Farmers Generals, too, could hardly be called officials in any strict sense. Yet their relations with the Crown were not unlike those of the Receivers General who managed the collection of the *taille* and other taxes, and the *Trésoriers* who managed the spending of Crown moneys. They were listed in the *Almanach royal*. As the process of calling for tenders for the tax farms became a mere formality, the members of the General Farm became very much a part of the official world. This was especially true during the 720's and 1730's, the heyday of political control by financiers. Lallemant de Betz was officially chosen by the Crown to represent the General Farm in the Bureau of Commerce. It is therefore not misleading to think of him as an official. We may conclude that although the official world was by no means unanimous in its support of the customs reform movement, the movement was largely promoted by officials.

---

[1] *Collection des mémoires présentés à l'Assemblée des Notables*, Versailles, 1787, 'Mémoire sur la réformation des droits de traites, &c.', p. 9; and Goudard, Fontenay and Roussillou, *Rapport fait*, p. 13.

CHAPTER III

The Reforming Officials and the Physiocrats

THE history of the movement for customs reform does not end with the reign of Louis XV, but any discussion of its later phases must begin with a study of the relation of the movement to the famous Physiocrats. This school of thinkers has been generally regarded as the inspiration of almost all movements for economic and financial reform during the thirty years which preceded the French Revolution. The movement for customs reform is no exception. Historians, from the middle of the last century to the present day—to name a few, Pierre Clément,[1] René Stourm,[2] Charles Gomel,[3] Auguste Arnauné,[4] Germain Martin,[5] Henri Sée,[6] René Gonnard,[7] and Philippe Sagnac[8]—have tended to see it as part of the physiocratic free trade movement. As a result, they have either distorted it or ignored it altogether. A typical statement is that by Emile Levasseur:

The second half of the eighteenth century was a time of struggle between the spirit of commercial liberty, championed by the Physiocrats, and the spirit of restrictive regulation which was the tradition of Colbertism sustained by private interests and popular prejudice.[9]

Consequently, historians have concentrated their attention on the second half of the century, when the Physiocrats were

[1] *Histoire du système protecteur*, 1854, pp. 88 ff.
[2] *Les Finances*, 1885, vol. ii, p. 5 and p. 74.
[3] *Histoire financière*, 1896–97, vol. i, p. 90.
[4] *Le Commerce extérieur*, 1911. [5] *Hist. éc. et fin.* (tome x of *Hist. de la Nation française*, ed. G. Hanotaux), 1927, pp. 239–72.
[6] *Histoire économique*, 1939, vol. i, p. 350.
[7] *Histoire des doctrines*, 1943, pp. 189 ff.
[8] *La Formation*, 1946, vol. ii, p. 6.
[9] *Histoire du commerce*, 1911, vol. i, p. 508.

active. They have, of course, been aware of the protests against
the customs system at the beginning of the century by Boisguillebert, Vauban, the Deputies of Commerce and others, but they
have characterized the intervening years from about 1715 to
1750 as a golden age of regulation when, according to Sagnac,
'. . . the protests of the reformers are quite forgotten; the aims
of economic and political liberalism are no longer in fashion'.[1]
Yet it was during these very same years that the single duty
projects of Amelot and Lallemant de Betz were being prepared.

This indifference to the earlier history of the movement was
the necessary result of belief on the part of Levasseur and the
others that the free trade movement was the expression of a
desire for liberation from all artificial restraints upon economic
development. For them, while 'the spirit of commercial
liberty' is unrestricted in physiocratic writings, it is marred in
the literature of the customs reform movement by a readiness
to maintain protective customs duties on the national frontiers.
The Physiocrats consistently called, in unequivocal language,
for the abolition of all customs barriers, but the reforming
officials desired only *internal* free trade. The Physiocrats led
their free trade movement in the name of economic liberty,
whereas the reforming officials were motivated as much by a
desire for simplicity, efficiency and national unity as by a
desire for liberty. Indeed, some supporters of the single duty
project, such as Fondières, General Inspector of Manufactures,
envisaged it almost exclusively as a step towards greater
efficiency.[2] The customs reform movement may be called the
internal free trade movement, one of its two major aims being to
abolish internal duties, but its goal of a single uniform duty on
the frontiers disqualifies it from association with the free trade
movement of the Physiocrats. It has been identified as part of
the physiocratic movement against the tax monopolies such as
the *gabelle* and the *tabac*, the government regulation of industry,
the *jurandes* and *maîtrises*, the various indirect taxes like the
aides and *octrois*, because it has been assumed that its goal was

---

[1] Philippe Sagnac, *La formation*, vol. ii, p. 6.

[2] B.N., ms. fr. 7771, fols. 239–64, Fondières, *Mémoire sur le crédit, il y propose
d'augmenter les droits de traite, il discute les divers droits qui sont susceptibles de cette augmentation*, etc.

ultimately international free trade. Where historians have referred to the single duty projects of Trudaine, Calonne and the Constituent Assembly (the other projects have been quite unknown to them), they have made little attempt to explain them, leaving the reader to infer that these projects arose in response to the pressure of the free trade movement led by the Physiocrats. Total freedom of trade being regarded as the proper aim of the free trade movement, the adherents of the movement for internal free trade are dismissed as at best half-hearted Physiocrats, men of affairs with slight glimmerings of liberal or physiocratic ideas.

Thus, Henri Sée is aware that during the early years of the century the attacks of French merchants on the protective régime are reflected in memoirs of the Deputies of Commerce,[1] but he does not seem to notice that those memoirs protest rather against ill-placed and ill-administered duties than against the whole system of duties. He accepts the mistaken view expressed in an article by Albert Schatz and Robert Caillemar that Jean Anisson's arguments, even though they include a plea for customs protection of French industry, 'have as their logical conclusion the demand for international free trade (des réclamations libre-échangistes)'.[2] The implication is that had Anisson lived in a more enlightened age he would have supported total free trade, which is exactly what Turgot and Boesnier de l'Orme, both under the influence of physiocracy, said of Colbert.[3] For most historians, as for the Physiocrats, the logical conclusion of all arguments for the reduction of trade duties was total international free trade. Thus, René Stourm regards Necker, in respect of his views on the customs barriers, as a perverse and limited administrator whose reform plans, including the single duty project, were merely inadequate concessions to physiocratic demands.[4] Again, the *Encyclopédie*

---

[1] Henri Sée, *Hist. économique*, vol. i, p. 236.

[2] Schatz and Caillemar, 'Le Mercantilisme liberal', 1906, pp. 29, 387, 559, 630 and 791; see p. 566. *Rev. d'éc. pol.*

[3] Turgot, 'Memoire au Roi sur les douanes interieures et la douane de Lyon en particulier', *Œuvres*, vol. v, pp. 358–68; Boesnier de l'Orme, *De l'esprit*, p. 239, quoted in G. Weulersse, *La physiocratie sous les ministères de Turgot et de Necker*, Paris, 1950, p. 163.

[4] René Stourm, *Les finances*, vol. ii, p. 11.

méthodique, Finances (1784–87), edited by Rousselot de Surgy, one of the later reforming officials of the customs reform movement, is described in an important nineteenth-century *Dictionnaire d'économie politique* as a collection of regulations and laws which is weak on doctrine although showing liberal tendencies.[1] But this is misleading, because Rousselot de Surgy, far from being weak on doctrine, deliberately attacked and ridiculed the idea of total international free trade put forward by the Physiocrat, Dupont de Nemours.[2] And in a few words he made clear the difference between the ideas of the Physiocrats and those of the reforming officials: 'Why must the lure of unlimited freedom, of impossible perfection, be mingled with speculations directed towards public welfare?'[3]

Another characteristic of the free trade movement, as seen by most of its historians, is that it was essentially a struggle of the physiocratic liberal forces against the entrenched powers of Colbertist mercantilism; and in the development of this simple antithesis the men of the internal free trade movement, when they have not been totally ignored, have been assigned to one side or the other of the struggle in a most confusing way. For instance, there cannot be the slightest doubt of Michau de Montaran's active and intelligent adherence to the internal free trade movement, and yet Pierre Bonnassieux summarized his views as follows: 'Partisan of the system of regulation, and active and competent, in the Bureau of Commerce he was the adversary of the new ideas of commercial liberty which Gournay defended there.'[4] The contrast of Montaran with Gournay in this passage seems even more unfortunate when it becomes clear that, as Professor Sauvaire-Jourdan says, Gournay was thinking only of internal trade when he pronounced his famous phrase, *laissez-faire, laissez-passer*. The same writer concludes, 'It is impossible to quote a single word from Gournay in favour of the freedom of external trade'.[5] Gournay and Montaran, like

---

[1] Coquelin and Guillaumin, *Dictionnaire*, article, 'Rousselot de Surgy'.

[2] Rousselot de Surgy, *Enc. méth.*, avertissement, pp. 2, 3, 4, note.

[3] *Ibid., Discours préliminaire*, pp. lvi ff.

[4] Bonnassieux and Lelong, *Cons. de com.*, biographical appendix.

[5] 'Isaac de Bacalan', *Rev. d'éc. pol.*, tome xvii, 1903, p. 604. Georges Weulersse, too, says that Gournay probably did not want to lift rational protective barriers (see 'Le Mouvement pré-physiocratique').

all the other reforming officials, were in favour of internal free trade and the completion of Colbert's plan for a single uniform tariff.

The most glaring example of distortion in the traditional account of the customs reform movement is the exaggeration of the role played by a Physiocrat, Dupont de Nemours, in the work on the project during the second half of the century. The writings of Gustave Schelle, Auguste Arnauné and others credit Dupont de Nemours with the preparation of the project which Calonne put before the Assembly of Notables in 1787 and in some cases even suggest that Dupont had earlier been responsible for Bertin's project.[1] There is no evidence to support the latter suggestion and a good deal to show that he had little to do with Calonne's project except as a member of a committee set up in April 1786 to examine and approve the work of the director of the official *Bureau pour la refonte des traites*, Mahy de Cormeré.[2] In the first place, Talleyrand, after relating in his memoirs how Calonne called him and a number of others together for the purpose of preparing the memoirs for the Assembly of Notables, writes, 'Monsieur de Cormeray (sic) did the whole of the project on the removal of the barriers to the frontiers ... Dupont worked on whatever he wished.'[3] In 1788 Dupont himself declared that the single duty project was the work of 'a very industrious and very learned citizen',[4] by which he could only have meant Cormeré; and Dupont's colleague, Edouard Boyetet, also spoke of the 'work on the customs which had originally been done by the sieur de Cormeré ... '.[5] Finally, the provincial assembly of Trois Evêchés and that of Lorraine and Bar recorded that Calonne's

---

[1] E.g. Gustave Schelle, *Du Pont de Nemours*, pp. 265 ff.; René Stourm, *Les finances*, vol. i, p. 479; Auguste Arnauné, 'Les Tarifs douaniers de 1791', *R.h.d.e.s.*, 1911, p. 8; Wilma J. Pugh, 'Calonne's New Deal', *The Journal of Modern History*, Sept. 1939, p. 293; Pierre Jolly, *Dupont de Nemours*, p. 60. Brienne, *Journal de l'Assemblée des Notables de 1787*, ed. Pierre Chevallier, 1960, p. 65, note 5.

[2] See *infra*, p. 106.

[3] Duc de Broglie, *Mémoires du Prince de Talleyrand-Périgord*, vol. i, p. 105. It matters little for this purpose that Aulard and others have thrown doubt on the authenticity of these memoirs.

[4] Pierre-Samuel Dupont, *Lettre à la Chambre*, p. 43.

[5] Edouard Boyetet, *Compte rendu à Messieurs de Villedeuil et Lambert, et à Mgr. de Sens, sur l'objet des places de commissaires généraux de commerce*, ms. A.N., F⁴ 1032².

project was 'based on the calculations of Monsieur de Cormeré',[1] a fact that was also emphasized by Roederer.[2] This evidence and the story of Cormeré's work[3] show that he was a major figure in the movement for customs reform and Dupont was a minor one; yet even René Stourm and His de Butenval, who have given fuller accounts of the movement than most, depict Dupont as a leader and Cormeré as of no account. 'Monsieur de Cormeré', wrote de Butenval, 'assigns himself a role and an importance in the preparation of the tariffs which we are not in a position either to confirm or to deny, no official document of the time having mentioned his name'.[4] Stourm wrote, 'Cormeré explains the financial mechanism of the period very well, but he adds details regarding his own plans for reform which are of no interest today.'[5]

Why have historians exaggerated the importance of the Physiocrats and otherwise misunderstood the customs reform movement? One reason, perhaps stemming in some measure from the fascination of systems of thought, has been the tendency to exaggerate the importance of economic literature in the history of customs reform. The economic history of the *ancien régime* has been coloured by physiocratic doctrine partly because historians have been impressed by the tremendous literary activity of the Physiocrats. Industrious propagandists, the Physiocrats created an inflated impression of their own importance, which historians of the nineteenth century were all the more willing to accept because they were themselves for the most part believers in the physiocratic doctrine of international free trade. Few of their successors of the twentieth century have realized that all the ideas basic to the customs reforms that were actually executed had been thought out many years before the Physiocrats existed and were Colbertist rather than liberal in character. It is curious and ironical that the

---

[1] *Procès-verbaux des séances de l'Assemblée provinciale des Trois Evêchés et du Clermontois*, Metz, 1788, note on table on p. 245; and *Procès-verbaux des séances de l'Assemblée provinciale des duchés de Lorraine et de Bar*, Nov. 1787, Nancy, 1788, p. 353.

[2] Pierre-Louis Roederer, *Réflexions sur le rapport*, p. 15.

[3] *Infra*, p. 106.

[4] Comte His de Butenval, *Etablissement en France*, p. 45. Cormeré's name is mentioned in many official documents.

[5] René Stourm, *Bibliographie historique*, p. 28.

Colbertist doctrine of internal free trade failed to influence historical writing partly because of its success in influencing government policy. The Colbertist movement triumphed in 1791 and then, having fulfilled itself, disappeared. On the other hand, the free trade movement of the Physiocrats failed in the eighteenth century and lived on into the nineteenth to influence historians in their interpretation of the economic history of the *ancien régime*. It led them to write as though in matters of customs reform the government and administration of the country were dragged unwillingly along by the physiocratic movement until its efforts were partially rewarded by the reforms of the Revolution. The mercantilist forces, according to this view, succeeded in retaining the frontier customs, but the expectation was that these, too, would eventually be abolished. It is hoped that this book will show that, on the contrary, the reforms of the Constituent Assembly crowned the efforts of practical administrators who for a hundred years had been planning a reform to which the physiocratic system had little relevance. As for public opinion in the matter, Professor Beatrice Hyslop has rightly said, in contradiction to René Stourm, that popular demands in favour of internal free trade, like those in favour of the uniformity of weights and measures, 'were not due to the influence of eighteenth-century economic liberalism, but to a natural protest against the complex hindrances to commerce'.[1]

The relation of the Physiocrats and the customs reform movement may be clarified through a comparison of their aims, methods and achievements, but first something must be said about the Physiocrats themselves. Their movement may be said to have begun in 1757 when François Quesnay and Victor Riquetti, marquis de Mirabeau, came to an agreement on basic principles and began to attract disciples by writing and talking about economic questions.[2] During the decade that followed, these two leaders were joined by Pierre-Paul Mercier de la Rivière, Pierre-Samuel Dupont, known after 1789 as 'Dupont de Nemours', Guillaume-François le Trosne, Louis-

[1] Beatrice Hyslop, *French Nationalism*, p. 56.
[2] The Physiocrats are best studied in Georges Weulersse, *Le Mouvement physiocratique*.

Paul Abeille until 1768, abbé Nicolas Baudeau, abbé Pierre-Joseph Roubaud and Jean-Nicolas-Marcellin Guérineau de Saint-Péravy, all of whom took part in regular discussions and wrote books and articles expounding physiocratic ideas. These writers together formed the physiocratic sect proper, but there were many friends of the sect such as Condorcet, Condillac, Turgot and Bertin, to mention only the most important, who were influenced by it. Vincent de Gournay cannot be called a Physiocrat, although he was venerated by the sect as an enlightened administrator and an early advocate of liberty in economic affairs. The Physiocrats had a vision of a Natural Order of the universe of which the fulfilment would bring maximum prosperity and they hoped by preaching and writing to restore this Natural Order. Accordingly, when they posed the question, 'Are customs barriers a good thing or not?', in terms of their system they would necessarily answer in the negative.

The adherents of the customs reform movement were, on the other hand, for the most part administrators, faced with the problem of how in a competitive world they could best assist the endeavours of Frenchmen in the face of efforts by other governments to favour their own nationals. This was a practical problem the complexities of which were exhibited daily in the complaints of manufacturers: for example, of one Monsieur Varnier, who petitioned that he could not sell his vitriol in Paris as cheaply as the importers of foreign vitriol because of the *octrois* and the *douanes*.[1] The reformers' theme was not, 'Customs barriers are a bad thing and should be abolished', but 'How can they be changed to benefit French trade and industry?' From Anisson at the beginning of the century to Mahy de Cormeré at the end of it, these administrators believed that it was essential for the progress of the French economy that all *internal* duties should be abolished and a single duty set up on the frontiers. Moreover, they were all aware that this had been Colbert's plan,[2] and defended it as such against the attacks of the Physiocrats.

---

[1] A.N., F^{12} 830, memoir of 11 March 1779.
[2] E.g. Anisson, *Sur la suppression des bureaux intérieurs*, etc., A.N., F^{12} 827; de Betz, *Mémoire sur les finances*, etc., B.N., ms. fr. 7771, fol. 206; de Montaran, *Mémoire sur les tarifs*, Paris, 1762, p. 84; Cormeré, *Rech. fin.*, vol. i, pp. 217 ff.

The method of the Physiocrats was to develop their doctrine at great length and on a highly theoretical level. They might well have supported the single duty project as a step in the right direction, but there is no evidence that, in general, they did so. In fact, some of them were contemptuous of it, especially, of course, its plans for the single duty itself. Le Trosne, in his *De l'administration provinciale et de la réforme de l'impôt*, got the factual material for his chapter on the customs duties, as he tells us, from Moreau de Beaumont, so he could hardly fail to mention the single duty project which de Beaumont describes in some detail;[1] but Le Trosne reviews it with the utmost contempt in such terms as 'the interests of the landowner and those of the consumer are thus counted as nothing and sacrificed to the interests of the manufacturer'.[2] Believing that all wealth comes from the earth and that agriculture is the only truly productive activity, Physiocrats such as Le Trosne condemned any scheme for encouraging trade and industry. They believed that the best interests of agriculture required total international free trade, and the mere abolition of the internal duties did not justify the single duty project in their eyes. Even Turgot made it quite clear more than once that he also was contemptuous of the single duty project, or any 'arrangement of import and export duties which it has been claimed would change the customs clerks into protectors of trade and the financiers into citizens'.[3] He wrote to Terray in 1773:

The truth is that all branches of trade should be free, equally free, entirely free, and that the system of some modern politicians, who expect to favour national trade by forbidding the importation of foreign goods, is a pure illusion.[4]

And in describing the project in general terms to the king in a memoir of 1776, he wrote:

Monsieur Colbert had the wise intention of converting all these duties into a single duty to be imposed at the frontier on the goods entering or leaving the kingdom. The idea of suppressing them

---

[1] Moreau de Beaumont, *Mém. con.*, vol. iii, pp. 347 ff.

[2] Le Trosne, *De l'admin. prov.* (written in 1779), vol. i, p. 338.

[3] Turgot, *Œuvres*, vol. ii, p. 509; vol. iii, p. 618, Turgot to Terray, 24 Dec. 1773. Cf. vol. ii, p. 493.

[4] *Ibid.*, vol. v, pp. 358–68.

altogether in order to free commerce was too far removed from the accepted ideas of his time for him to be able to think of it.[1]

Turgot made no attempt to put the reform into effect—it was hardly to be expected that he would, in view of his attitude to it—and the only other person of physiocratic leanings who was familiar with the project, Dupont de Nemours, regarded it as at best a step in the right direction.

The reforming officials were well aware of the difference of approach. Rousselot de Surgy made fun of Dupont's extravagant generalities about the national benefits of abolishing all customs barriers.[2] Another, Jean-François de Tolozan, wrote:

If the advocates of unlimited freedom confine themselves to a demand for the suppression of those duties imposed on the trade from province to province, then our wishes conform in this respect to theirs; but if they ask for a complete and absolute suppression of the duties on the imports and exports of the kingdom, we observe that the means for replacing their financial product must first be found; in the second place the foreign powers must be induced to follow our example. . . .[3]

The relation of the physiocratic movement and the customs reform movement becomes evident in the difference between their approaches to commercial relations with England, especially the Treaty of Commerce of 1786. The Physiocrats advocated international free trade not only because they believed there was no point in protecting industry, it being only a non-productive manipulation of agricultural products, but because they thought the erection of trade barriers anywhere tended to stifle agricultural production, the only source of real wealth.[4] But according to physiocratic doctrine there was yet another reason for abolishing all French trade barriers, and this was that foreign competition, English included, was not to be feared, because industrial and commercial gains and losses were only illusory. England, they thought, was dominated by a government of merchants and manufacturers who did not

---

[1] Dupont, *Tableau comparatif*, p. 73.

[2] Rousselot de Surgy, *Enc. méth.*, vol. i, pp. 2 ff., note.

[3] Jean-François de Tolozan, *Mémoire sur le commerce*, p. 89.

[4] To the land as a source of wealth, the Physiocrats added the sea and the earth's mineral resources, as might be expected: see Roubaud, *Les Ephémérides du Citoyen*, January 1767, p. 67, and Quesnay, 'Hommes' (1757), *F.h.d.e.s.*, 1098, p. 59.

realize that trade and industry were the results and not the cause of wealth, and who were violating the Natural Order for the sake of a momentary and precarious national power.[1] In order to promote their industrial and commercial advantages the English were erecting trade barriers, passing laws such as the Navigation Acts, and thus stifling their agriculture. In addition, having started well with a solid agricultural development, they had begun to reach the end of their productive expansion, because of their small territory, and to support political ambitions beyond their natural capacity had contracted enormous public debts which would eventually overwhelm them. It was in the development of this doctrine that Le Trosne entitled one of his chapters: 'That the position of France is infinitely superior to that of England', and began, 'This thesis is not difficult to prove. The territory of France is more than double, and the population twice as great. . . . '.[2] From this, he and the other Physiocrats drew the conclusion that in the Natural Order of the universe France was destined to be richer and stronger than her rival and had only to develop her agriculture to realize her destiny. Thus Dupont de Nemours proposed in 1790 that France should warn England not to declare war, because she was loaded with debts, whereas France, 'has just provided herself with two or three million *livres* worth of capital in very good funds of earth'.[3] Similarly, Quesnay had said ' . . . the violation of natural law . . . will some day be fatal to England',[4] the elder Mirabeau could rejoice that English splendour, based on the moving sands of loans and indirect taxes, would crumble,[5] and Le Trosne announce that 'the prestige of England will fade away like a dream, and the reawakening will be terrible'.[6] This notion

[1] Quesnay, 'Dialogue sur les blés', in E. Daire, *Physiocrates, Quesnay*, etc. Paris, 1846, p. 154; Mirabeau, *Lettres sur le commerce des grains*, p. 92; Le Trosne, *L'Ordre social*, p. 194.

[2] Le Trosne, *De l'admin. prov.*, p. 282.

[3] Dupont, *Considérations sur la position*, p. 23. In 1790, the Minister of Public Contributions, Clavière, wrote, 'M. Dupont a contracté une singulière habitude: celle de se tromper chaque fois qu'il parle de l'Angleterre ou des Anglais' (*Réponse au mémoire*, p. 86 (B.N., Lb³⁹ 4176)).

[4] Quesnay, *Physiocratie*, p. 211.

[5] Mirabeau, *Lettres sur le commerce du grain*, pp. 92–4.

[6] Le Trosne, *Réflexions politiques*, p. 60.

runs, in association with pleas for complete free trade, right through physiocratic literature. It is echoed by J.-F. Sérane, deputy for the Hérault in the Constituent Assembly, who published a speech, said to have been delivered to the united committees of Marine and Commerce, in which he attacked the single duty project and then demanded a total abolition of all customs barriers saying 'France is a solid house, England a ruined one'.[1]

This attitude to England was no mere bravado but firmly rooted in physiocratic doctrine. Therefore there was no question in the physiocratic mind of a calculated mutual reduction of trade duties; any reduction at all was bound to be beneficial to France. In 1775, during war with England, Le Trosne wrote that if France should win, ' . . . the greatest advantage the King could get from the victory would be to force England to allow absolutely free trade with us, while offering to treat British trade in the same way'.[2] In his *Mémoire sur la vie et les ouvrages de Monsieur Turgot*, Dupont de Nemours writes,

He is said to have proposed to the King the suppression of all customs duties. Their abolition was a great political project which was to give us such a prodigious superiority over England that it would henceforth have been impossible for that power to struggle against us. . . .[3]

Since their doctrines led them to such a conclusion, it is obvious that the whole business of negotiations with England was irrelevant to the Physiocrats. It was doubtless worth while to induce the British government to lower duties as far as possible but tariff reductions could equally well be carried out without reference to the British government, as Turgot had thought, unilateral reductions being certain to benefit France.

There can be little doubt that physiocratic doctrines had a strong influence upon the French side in the negotiations of the Commercial Treaty of 1786, especially through the agency of Dupont de Nemours, who was the chief, if not the sole, economic advisor to Vergennes and Gérard de Rayneval.[4]

---

[1] *Opinion de Monsieur Sérane*, p. 25.   [2] Le Trosne, *De l'admin. prov.*, p. 52.
[3] Paris, 1782, 2e partie, pp. 195–6. Quoted in Georges Weulersse, *La Physiocratie*, p. 164, and in Rousselot de Surgy, *Enc. méth.*, vol i, p. 2, note.
[4] F. Dumas, *Etude sur le traité*, 1904.

Article 18 of the Treaty of Versailles (1783) binding England and France to make such a treaty of 'new arrangements for trade on the basis of reciprocity and mutual expediency',[1] was insisted upon by the French rather than by the English,[2] and the treaty, both in its own time and since, has generally been regarded as a triumph for physiocratic free trade principles.

The attitude of the reforming officials to commercial relations with England was very different. It was based on the belief that English goods enjoyed an advantage over French goods, not only because of the superiority, in many cases, of British machines and manufacturing processes, but also because there were no internal customs duties in England and the frontier duties were adjusted more or less in favour of British national trade and industry; that is, duties on exported manufactured goods were low, those on imported manufactures were high, and this arrangement was reversed for industrial raw materials. Anisson reckoned that most French exports, on the contrary, were priced at least 6 per cent or 7 per cent, and often 15 per cent higher than was necessary because of the internal duties,[3] and that within France foreign goods were often cheaper than French goods for the same reason. The disadvantage under which French trade and industry were working is implicit in the writings of most adherents of the internal free trade movement. Mahy de Cormeré wrote, 'So long as the internal duties remain, the national manufactures which are affected by them will not be able to stand up to the competition of English manufactures.'[4] Rousselot de Surgy, after quoting Dupont's view that the abolition of all customs as planned by Turgot would have given France a tremendous superiority over England, asked very pertinently how this result was to come about when even such goods as were smuggled from England to France did considerable damage to French industry.[5] The Deputies of Commerce quoted a letter from John Holker, General Inspector of Manufactures, asking on

[1] Amé, *Etude sur les tarifs*, p. 22.
[2] *Loc. cit.*
[3] Jean Anisson, *Sur la suppression des bureaux intérieurs*, etc., A.N., F[12] 827.
[4] A.N., F[30] 111, memoir beginning, 'L'Execution du traité . . .'.
[5] Rousselot de Surgy, *Enc. méth.*, vol. i, pp. 2 ff., note.

behalf of a certain manufacturer for a dispensation from paying internal duties,

'because', Holker writes, 'if our woollens cannot be sent freely through the interior of the kingdom, our merchants will not be able to engage in speculative trading nor even to send our lower priced cloths to Spain and Portugal'. He adds that English woollens are manufactured in provinces where labour is cheap, that they are subject to no duties nor taxes of any kind at all, and that they may move freely from one province to another. From this he concludes that there should be no hesitation in granting the same immunity and the same freedom for cloths which are manufactured in the Provinces Reputed Foreign, where labour is cheap, to trade in competition with the English; but without these concessions, he adds, *it is useless to think of it*.[1]

A senior (and for some years the sole) Intendant of Commerce, de Tolozan, wrote despondently to the Secretary of State for Foreign Affairs in 1789 that the English had long been ahead in the manufacture of hardware, steel and leather goods, in spite of the persistent efforts of the Bureau of Commerce to promote those industries in France. 'It is only with time', he concluded, 'that we can hope for success'.[2]

The adherents of the customs reform movement believed that the reform which they advocated was absolutely essential if French industry were ever to withstand foreign, and especially British, competition, and a desire for adequate customs protection appears as a major factor in foreign trade relations almost from the beginning of the century. Most English manufactures had been prohibited by the *arrêt* of 6 September 1701, and when a commercial treaty was signed on 11 April 1713 re-establishing a degree of mutual trade with England, one of the French delegates to the conference at Utrecht, Nicolas Mesnager, wrote to Paris begging that some means be found for keeping English sugar and woollen goods out of France or else the country would be flooded with them and ' . . . a great many people who sail to our colonies and many who manufacture

---

[1] A.N., F12 714, *avis* of 11 April 1766.

[2] A.N., F12 157, Tolozan to comte de Montmorin, 20 Nov. 1789. Comment on the superior quality of British goods was very common; e.g Jean Paganucci, *Manuel historique*, article 'Quincaillerie'.

these same goods would soon find themselves without employment.'[1] Anisson and Fenellon, the Deputies of Commerce sent to England on an official mission in the same year, wrote from London on 19 July 1713,

Before our departure we said several times that this treaty was disadvantageous for our commerce, but that we could console ourselves with the fact that it had brought us peace. This idea, which we had in Paris, has grown very much since we began to work here. . . .[2]

Anisson put forward the single duty project as the only way of preventing an economic disaster, but the French ministry curtly rejected the suggestion. Later, he and Fenellon were relieved to hear that the British Parliament had refused to ratify the treaty, for if it were ever carried out, they wrote, France would be inundated with British goods: 'Their goods are so well made that, as they are cheaper than ours, the concession of the Tariff of 1664 would cause the ruin of our manufactures of wool, hosiery, locks, hardware and hats.'[3]

Seventy years later, when the question of a commercial treaty was raised again, the officials warned the government once more that a treaty would almost inevitably be disadvantageous. On 29 December 1785 John Holker wrote a long letter to Gérard de Rayneval in which he explained that the effects of admitting English goods into France would be disastrous in view of the fact that French goods could never withstand their competition.[4] Edouard Boyetet, another reforming official, was keenly aware of the English industrial and commercial superiority, and early in the negotiations over the treaty he tried to persuade Calonne that there was great danger.[5] On 30 August 1786, by which time the treaty had for several months been accepted in principle by the government, Boyetet sent Calonne his *Supplément aux observations* in which he replied to a British argument that British goods could in any case be

[1] A.N., G⁷ 1699, letter of Mesnager dated 10 May 1713.

[2] A.N., G⁷ 1699, Anisson to Desmaretz, 19 July 1713.

[3] A.N., F¹² 1699, letter of Jan. 1715 initialed 'M.A.'; cf. A.N., G⁷ 1704, Anisson's *Mémoire sur la négociation à Londres pour le Traité de commerce*, 1713 et 1714.

[4] Edouard Boyetet, *Recueil de divers mémoires*. Holker's letter is fully quoted in part 2, pp. 85–105.

[5] *Ibid.*, second set of numbering, 23.

introduced into France as contraband, and that therefore it would be advantageous to France to admit them with moderate duties.

It would be most unfortunate if such an argument were to make the least impression on the administration for if it were at all well-founded, all projects for the encouragement of the industry of the kingdom would have to be abandoned. In particular, the government would have to give up that great and glorious project, so useful and even essential, for the suppression of all the duties on internal trade; because, if the guarding of the frontiers could not be relied upon, this project would then become just as harmful as it is now expected to be beneficial.[1]

If a treaty were inevitable, he concluded, then the single duty project should be carried out first to enable the French economy to sustain its effects. This was the attitude also of the Chamber of Commerce of Normandy which, while the treaty was being negotiated, sponsored a comparative study of the English and French economic situations. Two men, Rabasse and the younger Husard, were sent to study trade and industry in England, and on the basis of their report le Couteulx prepared the famous memoir which supported the views of Holker, Boyetet, Cormeré and all the other reforming officials that if a treaty were to be made, some serious reforms, and particularly the single duty project, would have to be put into effect first to prevent disaster.[2]

In the defence of the treaty which he wrote in reply to this memoir on 12 February 1788, Dupont de Nemours claimed that the government had received the memoir only on 30 September 1786, four days after the treaty had been signed.[3] It is possible that he was trying to protect the government and himself from charges of deliberately ignoring the information and advice which the memoir contained. In any case, the French government had been sufficiently warned of the need for radical reforms to aid French industry and trade in their struggle against the forthcoming British competition on internal markets,

---

[1] Edouard Boyetet, *op. cit.*, second set of numbering, p. 39.

[2] *Observations de la Chambre de Commerce de Normandie sur le Traité de Commerce avec l'Angleterre*, Rouen, 1788. That this memoir was drawn up by le Couteulx is mentioned in Condorcet, *Mémoires sur le règne de Louis XVI* (tomes vii and viii of *Œuvres choisies de M. le Marquis de la Rochefoucauld-Liancourt*), Paris, 1862, vii, 282.

[3] Dupont de Nemours, *Lettre à la Chambre*, p. 102.

and it seems clear that this was one reason why Calonne was so anxious to carry out the single duty project. Cormeré says,

It was decided that the establishment of the new tariff and the suppression of the internal duties should take place before the treaty of commerce with England was put into effect. Presumably the ministry would otherwise have avoided signing a treaty so pernicious for our national industry.[1]

Boyetet, Dupont and Gérard de Rayneval all agree that this was the case.[2] In fact, as Léon Cahen remarks, the government set up a special committee on 14 October 1786 under the presidency of Bouvard de Fourqueux to say what action was necessary to offset the evil effects of the treaty.[3] Almost immediately—and Cahen does not say this—the committee recommended the execution of the single duty project and of the subsidiary projects to abolish such taxes as the *marque des huiles*.[4] The report of this committee may have had something to do with the submission of the project so soon afterwards to the Assembly of Notables: at least, it shows that some government circles were urging the importance of the single duty project in preparing the French economy to resist the effects of the commercial treaty.

On 11 January 1787, well before the treaty had been put into effect, Michau de Montaran, a reforming official whose father had played a major role in the preparation of Bertin's project, wrote to de Colonia, *Intendant du département des fermes* in the *Contrôle général*, warning him to have the Farmers General put on their guard against the evil effects of the treaty.[5] English merchants were already travelling through France, he said, and selling considerable quantities of cotton and woollen goods. He also pointed out that the discovery of smuggled goods would be more difficult, it being no longer sufficient merely to identify

[1] A.N., F³⁰ 111, memoir beginning, 'L'Execution du traité . . . '.

[2] Dupont, *Lettre à la Chambre*, p. 43; Boyetet, 'La lettre du Parlement de Rouen . . . ' in A.N., F¹² 658ᴬ. The contents as well as the hand-writing identify these memoirs as Boyetet's; Gérard de Rayneval, quoted in His de Butenval, *Etablissement en France*, p. 180.

[3] Léon Cahen, 'Une nouvelle interprétation du traité franco-anglais de 1786–87', *Rev. hist.*, 1939, p. 272.

[4] Dupont, *Lettre à la Chambre*, p. 102.

[5] A.N., F¹² 131, Montaran to de Colonia, 11 January 1787.

them as English. During the spring and summer of 1787, there was still an expectation that the single duty project, recently reviewed by the Assembly of Notables, would be put into effect shortly, and Boyetet urged during those months that this reform should be promised in the introduction to a questionnaire which at his suggestion was to be sent out to ask the merchants for their ideas about the obstacles to trade.[1] Early in 1788, English goods having been regularly admitted under the terms of the treaty for about six months, Boyetet wrote, 'The harm is done, the greater part of the industry of the kingdom is crushed and destroyed; the way to stop the harm is known and its success is certain.' He went on to recommend industrial subsidies and the immediate implementation of the single duty project which, he said, had been held up for eight months by 'intrigue and the cabal devoted to those who have a private interest in stopping and delaying its execution'.[2] Cormeré and even Dupont were also chafing at the delay.[3]

The Farmers General and other enemies of the project, such as Douët de la Boullaye, maintained as an alternative solution that imported English goods should be made to pay the internal duties. This appears to have been the only practical suggestion which the Farmers General made in reply to the many industrial complaints blaming the internal duties for the inability of French goods to compete with British imports. The Farmers General did not hesitate to express their views, as for example in a controversy which arose early in 1789 over a request by the manufacturers of acids and mineral salts at the Moulin de Javel for exemption from internal duties on their products. The manufacturers pointed out that oil of vitriol, for instance, was protected at the frontier by an import duty of 15 per cent which would be adequate if costs could be reduced by exemption from the internal duties. The Farmers General replied that to exempt goods from paying customs duties on that principle would be to undermine all taxes on trade, and eventually to destroy them as a source of revenue, because the

---

[1] Boyetet, *Nouveau recueil de mémoires*, p. 39. The questionnaire was actually sent in August 1788 according to Menard, *Observations sur l'état actuel*, preface.

[2] A.N., F^{12} 658^A, 'La lettre du Parlement de Rouen . . . '.

[3] See *infra*, p. 125.

principle could be applied to every type of goods manufactured in France.[1] Thus the old argument between financial and economic interests continued.

Meanwhile, among the officials directly concerned with the economic welfare of the kingdom, Boyetet and Dupont in particular, a different argument developed. Although Dupont de Nemours shared the impatience of the reforming officials for the execution of the single duty project, it must not be forgotten that as a Physiocrat and, according to his own declaration, as one of the architects of the treaty, he regarded it as a necessary treaty and a great step forward, regardless of its effects. Even so close a friend of the Physiocrats as Condorcet blamed him for this attitude and for trying to attribute the harm assumed to have been done to French industry to the way in which the treaty had been carried out; that is, to the indifference of the Farmers General and the dishonesty of the English.[2] And Boyetet attacked Dupont because he had urged the signing of the treaty purely on doctrinal grounds and had failed to recognize the primary importance of the single duty project.[3] Boyetet was expressing the opinion common among the reforming officials.

It has been fashionable to accept Dupont's viewpoint in the dispute over the treaty and to regard Boyetet's statements with suspicion as uncharitable personal attacks.[4] As a consequence, Boyetet's argument, which was that of all the reforming officials, that the single duty project should have been executed before the treaty, has never received proper attention. The replies to Dupont, for example that of the Normandy Chamber of Commerce, appear to have been ignored while Dupont's views have been solemnly repeated down through the nineteenth century and after. Indeed, Henri Sée, in an article on the controversy of Dupont and the Chamber of Commerce over the treaty, mentions neither the replies of the Chamber, nor the internal duties, nor the internal free trade project.[5] In one

---

[1] A.N., F12 658A, 'Note pour la conférence demandée à Mr. le Mis. de la Luzerne'; and A.N., F12 724, *Avis des députés du commerce du 21 avril* 1789.

[2] Condorcet, *Mémoires sur le régne de Louis XVI*, tome vii, p. 282.

[3] A.N., F12 658A, 'Je vous envoie, Monsieur, . . .'.

[4] Even Léon Cahen suggests this, *Rev. hist.*, 1939, pp. 283–5.

[5] Henri Sée, 'The Normandy Chamber of Commerce and the Commercial Treaty of 1786', *Economic History Review*, 1930.

of the replies of the Chamber which Sée ignores, the *Réfutation des principes et assertions contenues dans une lettre qui a pour titre: Lettre à la Chambre de commerce de Normandie sur le mémoire qu'elle a publié relativement au traité de commerce avec l'Angleterre par M.D[u]P[ont]*,[1] the Chamber commented in the same vein as Boyetet upon Dupont's report of the government's intentions:

> The Chamber of Commerce is doing full justice to the good faith of M. d[u] P[ont]. It believes in fact that the minister who signed the treaty did not have the unwise intention of exposing French industry, without defences and without weapons, to the attack of the enemy whom he brought into his own home. But would it not have been justly prudent, and was it not essential even, to begin by giving our industry at least the force, the means and the weapons needed to hold its ground? It is a cruel and insulting excuse to say that this unexpected attack will give industry an energy and stimulation which it needed.[2]

Henri Sée, F. Dumas, Pierre Clément and René Stourm, among others, do not seem to allow for the fact that the French customs system was ill-prepared for the commercial treaty. They accept the view of Dupont de Nemours that the treaty would not have harmed French industry if the dishonesty of the English and the indifference of the Farmers General had not combined to turn it to French disadvantage, and if the English negotiators had not been so well-advised about the condition of industry in the two countries. Furthermore, most of them defend the treaty with what the Chamber of Commerce called the 'cruel and insulting excuse' that it gave a useful stimulation to French industry.[3] They take no account of the internal duties and the reform project. They pay no attention to the reforming officials, Tolozan, Boyetet, Cormeré and others, all of whom shared the conviction that the treaty was a monstrous mistake which could be rectified only by carrying out the single duty project.

To say that the reforming officials had something important to contribute to the debate on the commercial treaty is not to say that they correctly appreciated the effects of the treaty on

---

[1] A.N., AF IV 1318, 45 fols.

[2] *Ibid.*, fol. 14.

[3] Dumas, *Etude sur le traité*, p. 187–92; Clement, *Histoire du système*, p. 92; Stourm *Les Finances*, vol. ii, p. 38.

French industry and trade. The studies of C.-E. Labrousse[1] have shown that the economic crisis of 1787–91 which contemporaries attributed to the treaty was the climax of a recession which had begun as early as 1778. A widespread and prolonged failure of the wine harvest, a cotton famine after the War of American Independence, a shortage of forage for sheep in 1785 resulting in a drop in wool production, and poor grain harvests—each of these factors probably did more harm to French industry than did the influx of cheap English manufactures. After all, the treaty did not go into effect until summer 1787 (though certain goods had been admitted since the Treaty of Versailles four years previously) when industry was already showing signs of recession. What the Physiocrats and the reforming officials wrote tells us less about the effects of the treaty than about the contrasts in their ideas. While the reformers exaggerated the immediate effects of British imports on the French economy, the Physiocrats were too optimistic in their smug doctrine that England was in a state of imminent collapse. The reforming officials had little conception of the complex forces which lay behind the economic crisis and over-rated the effect of administrative action; the physiocratic movement, condemning all government controls, clung to an optimistic belief in the benevolence of natural economic forces. The one sought to make government control more efficient; the other sought to destroy it. The one made concrete plans for action; the other preached that Reason and Liberty must prevail. The one wished to strengthen France through a national customs union; the other through the operation of Natural Law. Both movements were important in different ways. In the matter of customs reform, however, the essential fact is that the law of 30 November 1790, by which the Constituent Assembly abolished the internal duties, was the victory not of the Physiocrats but of the reforming officials of the customs reform movement.

[1] C. E. Labrousse, *La Crise de l'économie française*, 664 pp.

CHAPTER IV

The Reforming Officials, the General Farm and the Crown

THE reforming officials believed that, in the words of Michau de Montaran, 'a good tariff should be clear, simple, unique and uniform'[1] so that the customs might perform their proper function, that of discouraging the import of foreign manufactures and the export of raw materials and encouraging the export of French manufactures and the import of raw materials. This meant adapting the customs in such a way that they would create a favourable balance of trade. And indeed Anisson, de Betz, de Montaran and others among them expected that one result of the single duty project would be, in the words of de Betz, that 'without exploiting the mines [of gold and silver] we shall share in their product'.[2] But they held no crude bullionist theory. Theirs was in the main a theory of what E. A. J. Johnson has termed 'the export of work' and 'foreign-paid incomes'.[3] They believed, in brief, that surplus earnings in foreign trade accrued in payment for the labour, not the materials, that had been used in the manufacture of exported products. Therefore, as de Betz put it, 'our object in setting the import and export duties must be to keep the profits of labour so far as possible for the subjects of the King in preference to foreigners, not only in the fabrication of manufactures, but also in the preparation of all the materials which are used in them'.[4] To achieve this purpose, the single tariff was to impose low duties on imports in proportion to the labour which could be usefully applied to them, and on exports

[1] Michau de Montaran, *Mémoire sur les tarifs*, p. 27.
[2] Lallemant de Betz, B.N., ms. fr. 7771, fol. 206; Anisson, A.N., F¹² 827.
[3] E. A. J. Johnson, *Predecessors of Adam Smith*, chapter xv.
[4] De Betz, ms. B.N., ms. fr. 7771, fol. 208.

in proportion to the degree of finish which they had been given in France. This idea was sometimes taken to extremes, as for example when the Chamber of Commerce of Rouen suggested encouraging the import of underfed livestock and the export of fat ones.[1] But there can be no doubt that it was a theory according to which the uniform tariff would serve the economic purpose of maintaining a high level both of prosperity and of employment at the expense of foreign customers. Combined with the twin purpose of restoring and preserving complete freedom of trade within France, it formed a policy of state encouragement for national trade, industry and (said Montaran) agriculture which was to depend entirely upon the transformation of the customs into an instrument of national economic policy.

In accordance with this view, the reformers distinguished between the duties on the foreign frontiers, which they thought economically useful, and those in the interior which they regarded as mere taxes. When this distinction was brought to the attention of the Farmers General, who ignored it in their administration of the customs, some of them argued that the internal customs also served an economic purpose. 'Commerce can be flourishing and beneficial to the kingdom', ran their argument, 'only if it is widespread and shared among all the provinces, which requires that it be subject to duties proportional to the advantages which they find in it. This proportion is kept today in several provinces only by the inequality of the local duties levied on them, and it is to be feared that the suppression of these duties, and the uniformity of the proposed single duty, will end the competition between all the provinces of the kingdom which has always been recognized by the Council. . . . '.[2] But the reformers were convinced that, in the words of de Betz, 'the collection of these duties, no less arbitrary than their administration, is based on ancient tariffs so full of omissions, contradictions and double counting (*double emplois*) that the majority of them have degenerated into customary

---

[1] Bib. Mazarine, ms. 2778 and 2779, *Projet de tarif pour servir à la perception des droits de traites à l'importation des marchandises de l'étranger dans le Royaume* . . . , vol. i, fols. 1–3.

[2] B.N., nouv. acq. fr. 22253, fol. 276–301, *Projet du travail nécessaire.* . . .

tariffs which often impose different duties in the bureaux of the same district'.[1] Not planning, they thought, but the accidents of the kingdom's growth had given rise to the internal duties.[2] Even supposing that some of them did nevertheless fulfil an economic function, as for example in allowing merchants in provinces like Brittany and Alsace to carry on foreign trade without fear of competition from merchants in the area of the *Cinq Grosses Fermes*, their effect was to favour provincial rather than national trade and was therefore unjustifiable to the reformers, who were hoping to create a national customs union. Yet believing as they did in the necessity for customs protection of the kingdom as a whole, they thought it essential to defer the abolition of the internal duties until the customs on the frontiers had been strengthened and rationalized. The various duties on the frontiers were not at all adapted to the kind of control which the reformers had in mind, for although properly placed, they were no less confused, arbitrary and contradictory than the internal duties. Even the Tariff of 1667 and the *nouveaux droits*, mainly because they included many high duties and many outright prohibitions, did not satisfy the reformers.

In the preparation of the projected single tariff, the official reformers distinguished themselves at every stage by their insistence on moderate protective duties rather than on prohibitive duties or actual prohibitions. They thought it impossible, even if desirable, to maintain 'a commerce always active on our part and always passive on the part of other countries',[3] international trade being necessarily in large measure to the mutual advantage of all countries. In their view, most foreign products ought to be admitted on payment of preferential rather than prohibitive duties. They argued that prohibition was necessary only because the costs arising out of the internal duties raised the prices of French products by as much as 12 per cent or 15 per cent so that they had difficulty in competing with cheaper foreign goods even inside France.[4] If the internal

---

[1] De Betz, B.N., ms. fr. 7771, fol. 207.
[2] Jean Anisson, A.N., F12 827, *Sur la suppression des bureaux intérieurs . . . (1720).*
[3] De Betz, B.N., ms. for 7771, fol. 208.
[4] Anisson, A.N., F12 827.

duties were removed, the French could then afford to charge lower prices for their goods and would consequently need less protection from foreign competitors. But a much more important reason was that, as Anisson wrote, 'high duties are almost always evaded and rarely paid'.[1] They inevitably encouraged smuggling;[2] high duties could not be enforced and therefore destroyed the effectiveness of customs control. As smuggled foreign manufactures could be sold very cheaply they constituted serious competition on the domestic market for the equivalent French products, competition far more damaging, according to the official reformers, than would be that of foreign goods which had paid a moderate preferential duty. It was the belief of the reformers that if duties were kept low, then the customs barriers could be made really effective against smugglers. Anisson and de Betz each in turn pleaded for moderate duties, but de Betz was instructed by the *Délibération* of 9 July 1728 to observe the spirit of the *nouveaux arrêts*, many of which imposed prohibitions, or duties of 50 per cent and more, on foreign manufactures.[3] When he submitted his tariff to the Crown in 1737, the Royal Council of Commerce raised the duties on a variety of important products.[4] Bertin's tariff would have imposed duties of not more than 20 per cent *ad valorem*, but the Chamber of Commerce of Rouen proposed that this maximum should be raised to 30 per cent. The officials who were active in the reform movement during the last years of the *ancien régime* successfully defended their point of view. When a tariff of high duties and prohibitions was being drawn up for the Constituent Assembly in 1790, they pointed out that it was useless to attempt to collect more than 15 per cent *ad valorem* because there were *assureurs* in every port who would smuggle goods into France for such a charge and even less.[5] As a result of this protest, the tariff was revised, before it was brought into

---

[1] *Ibid.*

[2] Michau de Montaran, *Mémoire sur les tarifs*, p. 25.

[3] De Betz, B.N., ms. fr. 7771, fol. 210.

[4] A.N., G1 79, *Etat des droits du projet du nouveau tarif sur lesquels le Conseil du Commerce a fait des changements avec un précis des motifs qui ont déterminé à fixer ou proposer lesdits droits et de ceux qui ont engagé le Conseil à les changer* (ms.), 22 fols. (1738).

[5] Mahy de Cormeré, *Situation exacte des finances*, pp. 14 ff.; and Marcel Marion, *Histoire financière*, vol. ii, p. 90.

force in 1791, so that the customs might serve as a more efficient protective barrier.

There were several reasons why the reformers wished to render the customs more effective as an instrument of economic policy. 'It will never be possible', wrcte Anisson, putting forward one such reason, 'to draw up an exact balance of the merchandise which enters and that which leaves the kingdom without the establishment of the customs bureaux on the frontiers, and in consequence those who govern will never be able to know what direction to give to the commerce of the King's subjects, which types of manufactures to encourage, which kinds of trade to neglect and which to protect'.[1] This argument for the single duty was put forward by the Deputies of Commerce at a time when the Crown appears to have had no regular statistics of imports and exports. True, annual reports of imports and exports had been sent to Paris frcm a few important customs bureaux ever since the time of Colbert, and in 1700 the Controller General had asked the Farmers General for quarterly reports which were turned over to Savary des Bruslons, author of a well-known dictionary of commerce of the time, for the preparation of studies and tables.[2] Yet there had been no attempt to make a comprehensive, accurate and regular calculation of the balance of trade.[3] When administrative machinery for doing so was set up a few years later it was partly owing to the efforts of the Deputies of Commerce. They clamoured for the calculation of these statistics for several years without result. Then, in May 1710, Nicolas Mesnager, sometime Deputy of Commerce for Rouen and one of the French representatives at the Utrecht treaty conference, demonstrated an urgent practical need for such figures, and arrangements were made with a Farmer General, Poiret de Grandval, 'to compile the general balance of imports and exports of the kingdom'.[4]

The organization for this work was as yet of a rudimentary

---

[1] Anisson, A.N., F12 827; B.N., ms. fr. 14294; A.N., F12 1910, 'Mémoire sur le nouveau Tarif' (29 March 1702), and note beginning, 'Dispositions pour parvenir'.

[2] A.N., F12 115, Amelot to Savary des Bruslon, 18 Jan. 1701.

[3] Léon Biollay, *L'Admin.*, pp. 485 ff.

[4] *Ibid.*, p. 488.

character. Three years later, however, Jean Anisson discovered while in England on an official mission that statistics of English trade had long been published in weekly reports and regular summaries; and furthermore, that these statistics as interpreted by Charles Davenant proved that, contrary to the belief of the French government, the balance of trade between France and England had been in favour of the latter 'by several millions' for the previous fifty years.[1] Whatever the truth or falsehood of this information, Anisson reported it to the Controller General in France. When Desmaretz replied that Davenant's book was 'a work of passion and animosity upon which one cannot, there-fore, place any reliance',[2] Anisson spent some time in checking the information in order to impress upon Desmaretz, in a later report, that it was true.[3] It can hardly have been a coincidence that during their exchange on this matter an *arrêt* was passed on 18 April 1713 setting up on a firmer foundation the organization for compiling statistics of imports and exports under the name of the *Bureau de la balance du commerce*.[4]

The proper constitution of this *Bureau* was a tacit admission by the ministry that they were ill-informed about the movements of French trade. But they were not yet ready to admit Anisson's charge that no accurate statistics would be possible until the single duty project had been put into effect, and they were content to leave the *Bureau de la balance du commerce* under the direction of the General Farm where it remained until 1781. In the meantime, Amelot and de Betz struggled each in his turn to compile more accurate statistics. De Betz wrote a detailed account of the diffi-culties he met. Even after 1781, when Necker reorganized the *Bureau* in an attempt to make it more useful, Mahy de Cormeré was obliged to work out his own statistics because the *Bureau* found its task so difficult that by 1788 it had produced complete figures only for the year 1782.[5] As the reformers were aware, the *Bureau* could not fulfil its task satisfactorily because of two

[1] A.N., G⁷ 1699, Anisson to the Controller General, 6 April 1713; Controller General to Anisson, 13 April 1713.

[2] *Loc. cit.*

[3] A.N., G⁷ 1699, Anisson to the Controller General, 17 June 1713.

[4] *Arrêt* of 18 April 1713 presented in resumé in *arrêt* of 29 Feb. 1716 listed under date in Amelot's correspondence, A.N., F¹² 116.

[5] For Cormeré, see *infra*, p. 124; Léon Biollay, *L'Admin.*, p. 490.

defects of the customs system: its complexity, which made analysis of the registers extremely difficult, and its weakness in controlling trade, which resulted in the smuggling of great quantities of goods that could not be taken into account.[1]

To some of the reformers, the effective protection of a unified national free trade area was essential if France were to benefit from commercial negotiations with other countries. Lallemant de Betz and Michau de Montaran seem, from what little they say on the subject, to have held this view.[2] Jean Anisson expressed it clearly and vehemently in a letter to the Controller General during the negotiations with England leading to the Treaty of Utrecht. The circumstances which provoked Anisson to write the letter are interesting. As the War of the Spanish Succession was drawing to an end, one of the conditions of peace upon which the English and Dutch representatives insisted was that exports from their countries should be admitted into France upon the payment of only the duties established in 1664 or earlier. A commercial treaty with England was to be negotiated on this basis, and to assist the French representatives Anisson was sent to London on a mission to study English trade. He had to form some idea of what the effect on Anglo-French trade would be if the Tariff of 1667, the *nouveaux droits*, the *arrêt* of 6 September 1701—in fact, the whole fabric of Colbertist protection—were to be suspended, leaving only the duties of the Tariff of 1664 to be collected at the bureaux around the provinces of the *Cinq Grosses Fermes*, and the old local duties in the Provinces Reputed Foreign. Anisson soon decided that if his government adopted this course the duties on goods sent from England would amount to less than the internal duties on goods travelling from the *Cinq Grosses Fermes*, and in consequence French manufactures of the *Cinq Grosses Fermes* would not be able to compete with English manufactures in the Provinces Reputed Foreign. The competition of English woollen cloth

---

[1] Ambroise-Marie Arnould (*sous-directeur* of the Bureau), *De la balance du commerce*, cf. the figures of Cormeré in A.N., ms. fr. 7772, fol. 499; *Extraits du mémoire sur la réforme des Traites par Monsieur de Cormeray* (sic), in Arch. Ass. Pub., papers of Auget de Montyon; and A.N., F30 111, *Précis* of 20 memoirs, by Cormeré; and Cormeré, *Rech. fin.*

[2] Michau de Montaran, *Mémoire sur les tarifs*, p. 14 and *passim.*; de Betz, B.N., ms. fr. 7771, fol. 208 and fol. 211.

and hosiery was most to be feared, and Anisson believed they would be smuggled into the territory of the *Cinq Grosses Fermes* and even there compete favourably with the French products.[1] This danger was also recognized by others, such as Ravat, *prévôt des marchands* in Lyon, and d'Angervilliers, Intendant of Dauphiné, who pointed out the threat to the woollen manufactures.[2] How could French industry be protected? Ravat, d'Angervilliers and the Deputies of Commerce recommended a ban on the export of raw wool and abolition of the internal duties on it. But Anisson, in one of his letters to Desmaretz, the Controller General, offered a more radical solution:

The customs must be reduced to a single duty and the Tariff of 1664 established at every port of entry so that there will no longer be any distinction between the provinces of the *Cinq Grosses Fermes* and the Provinces Reputed Foreign.[3]

On the one hand, he continued, the English could not complain, because once their goods had paid the entry duty, they would be free to go anywhere in France without paying internal duties. On the other hand, the whole kingdom would be equally protected against English goods and the Provinces Reputed Foreign would find French goods to be cheaper. In reply the Controller General merely sent Anisson a curt reminder that his function in London was to study trade and industry, not to make recommendations regarding the treaty.[4] Although the offending clause in the draft Treaty of Utrecht was eventually dropped without any commercial treaty having been signed, nearly seventy years later a clause in the Treaty of Versailles (1783) once more raised the question of a commercial treaty with England. And once more the reforming officials proposed that the single duty project should be put into effect before any such treaty were signed.[5] On both occasions the reformers were arguing for the adaptation of the customs to economic purposes.

[1] A.N., G7 1699, Anisson to the Controller General, 29 April 1713.
[2] A.N., G7 1702; register labelled, 'Matière de commerce, 4 vols', pp. 109 ff. It was here calculated that internal duties raised the price of raw wool by 6 or 7 per cent to manufacturers in many parts of the country.
[3] A.N., G7 1699, Anisson to the Controller General, 29 April 1713.
[4] A.N., G7 1699, Desmaretz to Anisson, 29 April 1713. [5] *Supra*, p. 79.

They had in mind the economic interests of the kingdom as a whole rather than those of individual merchants. 'There is, in truth, only one Merchant in the State,' wrote de Montaran, 'which is the State itself. All the businessmen (*négociants*) are only the factors and commissioners to whom it leaves the task of cultivating the various parts of its commerce. Their profits are also the profits of the State and enrich it; but they impoverish it if they harm agriculture, manufacturing and the population'.[1] The other reformers, too, were thinking of the general welfare.

Because of this, they believed that their intentions were fundamentally the same as those of the Crown. Most laws and regulations touching upon the customs were prefaced by a statement of the Crown's benevolent intentions for the trade, industry and agriculture of the kingdom and the reformers professed to see the basic ideas of their own reform programme expressed in all this legislation. 'To overcome the evils of the present system', wrote de Montaran, 'a good tariff is needed, and for this it is perhaps only necessary to perfect a work already begun by the collection of *arrêts* and regulations successively passed since the tariff of 1664.'[2] In 1737, Lallemant de Betz had already collected five or six thousand regulations, and after studying them had concluded that they betrayed 'a concern to increase the trade of the nation, to perfect and to multiply its manufactures, and to establish with our neighbours a mutually useful commerce'.[3] He believed that all these regulations, though they had disturbed the tax farms in their administration of the customs almost continuously except for a ten-year period from 1677 to 1687 when few such regulations had been passed, had proved inadequate and ineffective in assisting industry. Few merchants had profited by them because even those laws which had reduced duties had failed to improve the conditions of trade. In short, government regulations appeared to de Betz to have been inconsistent, contradictory and unprincipled.[4] Behind de Betz's analysis lay the view that the Crown, in spite of its

[1] Michau de Montaran, *Mémoire sur les tarifs*, p. 160.
[2] *Ibid.*, p. 88; cf. Michel Amelot, *Mémoire sur la suppression des droits intérieurs* (1720), in ms., A.N., F¹² 827.
[3] De Betz, B.N., ms. fr. 7771, fol. 211.
[4] *Loc. cit.*

sound intentions, had passed its regulations in response to the exigencies of diplomacy or to the petitions of special interests. As the merchants and manufacturers who petitioned for the reduction of duties or for special protective duties were invariably asking for privileges or 'freedoms', the regulations of the Crown had encouraged certain trades but not trade in general, certain manufacturers but not manufacturing. They had engendered a system of monopoly and privilege. Far from implementing a national economic policy, the customs had been dissipated in concessions and favours.

Privilege was a disease which tended to infect the reform projects also. The single tariff would be an effective control device only if it retained its general uniform character; being a sort of dyke of protection against the sea of Anglo-Dutch trade, the tariff could be weakened by exceptions, just as a dyke may be undermined by holes. Yet because the Crown could not resist the petitions of private, local, regional and even foreign interests, each tariff project had lost its virtue even before it had been abandoned. In 1720 Anisson himself, usually so confident, was sure that the Crown would not be able to overcome the opposition of Breton and Flemish interests. He therefore proposed a limitation of the project in its opening phase to the south-eastern region.[1] In the same year Amelot, who had at first planned to confiscate the *coûtume de Bayonne* and to grant its part-owner, the duc de Gramont, an equivalent revenue, in reply to a strong complaint from Gramont was forced to reassure him that no such change would be made.[2] It was plain, furthermore, that exceptions would probably have to be made in favour of the free fairs of Bordeaux, Beaucaire, Toulon, Troyes, Rouen and Dieppe and the free ports of Marseille, Dunkirk and perhaps Bayonne.

The history of the later projects, too, shows that the further a tariff project was developed, the more its uniform character came under attack. Thus Lallemant de Betz was forced to take into account a vast range of privileges which he reduced to nine

[1] Jean Anisson, *Proposition subsidiaire sur la suppression des bureaux intérieurs dans les provinces de Lyon, de Dauphiné, de Languedoc, d'Auvergne, et de Provence*, A.N., F¹² 827, 12 fols. (1720).
[2] A.N., F¹² 119, Amelot to Gramont, 23 Sept. 1720.

categories: those granted to foreign countries, to the East Indian
and African trades, to the West Indies and French American
colonies, to the Indies Company, to the ports of Marseille,
Bayonne and Dunkirk, to interests in the Provinces Reputed
Foreign, to fairs and manufactures, to cities, towns and communities, and to religious houses and institutions, hospitals, the
Hôtel Royale des Invalides, and the suppliers of munitions, food and
equipment for the armed forces.[1] Again, Bertin in his uniform
tariff proposed to make no exceptions beyond those in favour of
the free ports, to which it was planned to add Strasbourg as a free
city.[2] But once published, the project roused the opposition of
all those whose privileges it would have destroyed. 'A privilege
attacked', wrote Montaran at this time, 'finds defenders in all
those who have privileges to preserve.'[3] It was to avoid adding
to the numbers of privileged that the Deputies of Commerce in
the mid-1760's opposed a series of petitions for exemptions from
customs duties. If these were refused, they wrote, the private and
provincial interests concerned might be more willing 'to lend
their support to the execution of the general uniform tariff with
which the Council is occupied'.[4] Yet when it appeared to the
Deputies in the summer of 1767 that the general reform project
was not to be put into effect after all, they began to support local
and private interests once more, according to their usual practice. Indeed, it was difficult for them to avoid doing so because
decisions on customs matters were usually taken only after
consulting the representatives of the General Farm and the
Deputies of Commerce. Unless the Farmers General were to
have everything their own way, the Deputies had to speak up
in defence of petitions from merchants and manufacturers and
provincial economic interests. A concern for special interests
was at the very heart of the *ancien régime*. While hopes for a
single, uniform tariff barrier on the frontiers were disappointed
again and again, the government continued to issue regulations,
adding to the list of *nouveaux arrêts* and other laws which usually
favoured the dealers in certain types of merchandise or the

[1] A.N., G¹ 3-5, *Inventaire raisonné des opérations concernant le tarif du droit unique,*
No. 22.
[2] Michau de Montaran, *Mémoire sur les tarifs*, p. 107.
[3] *Ibid.*, p. 116.   [4] *Supra*, p. 58.

interests of a province but not national trade and industry as a whole. In spite of this, the reformers believed that the Crown wished to use the customs in the national interest and had not done so partly because it was obliged to bow to the opposition of special interests.

The Crown had another reason, however, of which the reformers were fully aware. In practice, the government valued the customs for their financial yield. It treated them primarily as a tax rather than an instrument of economic policy. And here, indeed, was the crux of the problem facing the reformers: the customs served a double function, a financial as well as an economic one, and whatever the reformers thought on the matter they had to take the financial function seriously because the Crown did so. In consequence, their writing reflects a determination to reconcile the two functions and in most cases an unwillingness to admit that if the duties were reduced to an economically useful barrier on the frontiers, customs revenue might suffer a decline. They were forced at every step to justify the single duty project in financial terms, even though they believed in it fundamentally for the economic benefit which they expected from it. Anisson was concealing an interest in the growth of trade and industry beneath an apparent concern for revenue when he wrote 'It is certain that the increase of commerce [resulting from the reform project] would create more jobs for workers and thus make them better able to pay the *taille*, the *gabelle*, the *aides*, and the other royal taxes which this sort of people pay badly when they are unemployed'.[1] The tariff of Lallemant de Betz was clearly designed to be an economic control, and yet he felt obliged to describe it as 'a single duty which is nothing but the price of the permission which the King gives to foreigners to trade in his kingdom and to his subjects to trade with his neighbours ...'.[2] De Montaran, after defining the customs duties as nothing more nor less than taxes on consumers' goods, went on to say, 'if it were only a question of securing a good financial yield the Tariff would be very short: a single duty of 5 per cent or even 6 per cent on all types of merchandise imported and exported would doubtless be the surest means of producing a considerable yield ...

---

[1] Anisson, A.N., F^{12} 827.   [2] De Betz, B.N., ms. fr. 7771, fol. 208.

But Agriculture, Trade and the Population demand their rights, which are as precious for Finance as for all the other parts of the body politic and the State'.[1] Like all the others, de Montaran believed that in the long run revenue would probably increase as a result of the reform.

Unlike most of the earlier reformers, however, he admitted that it would cause a considerable loss in the immediate future. Most of his predecessors had had little success in convincing the Crown and the General Farm that the reform project was financially feasible. Even de Betz, for all his detailed and optimistic calculations, appears to have convinced them only momentarily. It was difficult for them to see how the revenue from the internal duties could be sacrificed without reducing the total customs revenue, especially as de Betz's calculations[2] and those of a later reformer, Mahy de Cormeré, showed that internal duties produced normally from one-third to one-half of the customs revenue and even more in wartime.[3] Again, the government's experience appeared to have been that the use of the customs for the purpose of controlling foreign trade inevitably reduced their yield: as late as the period 1768–77, the *nouveaux droits* produced only 881,787 *livres* annually (not much more than the *douane de Lyon*) and the Tariff of 1671 only 562,210 *livres*, whereas the Tariff of 1664, which was mainly a revenue tax, yielded 3,296,483 *livres*.[4] To abolish duties such as the latter in favour of protective duties such as the former, as the reformers projected, seemed to many like a financially disastrous course. And not all the sceptics would accept the argument that if only the *nouveaux droits* were reduced from high prohibitive duties to moderate protective ones they would yield more revenue. High duties on foreign manufactures seemed necessary to make up for the revenue sacrificed in reducing duties on French manufactures.

The reformers' argument that high duties were evaded did not carry much weight with those interested only in revenue, because if, for example, a 45 per cent duty were collected on only one-third of the taxable goods passing across the frontiers, no less

---

[1] Michau de Montaran, *Mémoire sur les tarifs*, p. 13.
[2] Bib. P. et C., *Le projet du droit unique*, tome xiv.
[3] See tables, pp. 10–12.   [4] *Loc. cit.*

revenue was taken than if a 15 per cent duty had been collected on all of them. Moreover, it was characteristic of the government of the *ancien régime* to impose duties which could not be collected and prohibitions which could not be enforced. As the records of royal laws and regulations show, the Crown in some matters seemed to prefer to publish and re-publish unenforceable regulations at frequent intervals, meting out severe punishment, as a public warning, to the few offenders whom it did catch, rather than to restrict itself to more moderate regulations of a type which could be made effective. Thus, smugglers and *faux-saulniers* were heavily punished when arrested, but the chances of arrest were not great and the incentive to smuggling was strong. Furthermore, the confiscation and sale of smuggled goods was profitable both to the employees making the seizure, who were allowed to divide between them usually about half of the proceeds, and to the General Farm itself which kept the other half. Records of the average annual customs revenue for the years 1768–77 listed a yearly receipt of 232,576 *livres* for fines and the sale of confiscated goods out of an annual gross total of a little over 18½ million *livres*—about 1 per cent of gross revenue.[1] This amount was pure profit for the Farmers General because the price which they paid for their lease was always calculated on the known product of the duties themselves. For this among other reasons the case for moderate duties had little appeal to them. It also roused opposition in the government. In practice the Crown regarded the customs duties, like the *aides*, the *gabelle*, the *tabac*, the *droits de marque* and certain *octrois*, as indirect taxes: it added the surtax or *sols pour livre* to them as to all the others; it joined the *péages royaux* to them and certain of the *aides* as well; and it included them in the tax farms which were leased to the Farmers General.[2]

At almost every stage plans for reform had to make allowance for the lease, usually signed every six years, by which the Farmers General assumed control of the tax farms in a formal contract. By its terms, the Crown could make no change in the

---

[1] *Supra*, p. 10. These figures are from the same source.

[2] A.N., F¹² 1910, Farmers General to Chamillart, 3 January 1702; A.N., F¹² 1903, 'Etat des Droits que S. Templier prétend que perdra . . .'; A.N., F¹² 1910, 'La vérification a été fait par M. de la Vigne . . .'. See *supra*, pp. 2 ff.

customs, or any other part of the tax farms, unless it were willing to pay the Farmers General an indemnity equivalent to any loss caused by the change. There was never any money for an indemnity because as soon as the lease was signed the Crown almost always spent or committed the sum which the Farmers General had contracted to pay, and it was never at any time prepared to use other funds. When, for example, the government proposed in its *arrêt* of 24 December 1701 to lower the duties on certain French exports, a bill from the Farmers General for a mere 713,029 *livres* led to drastic amendments of the original proposals by *arrêts* of 4 April 1702 and 9 October 1703. This incident made it perfectly plain to the reformers that they must prepare their projects for inclusion in a new lease. Michel Amelot, director of reform plans at that time, was already aware of this necessity. In 1701, he had instructed Le Febvre and de Blair to complete their draft proposals by the end of March 1702 so that they might be reviewed in the Council of Commerce and finished a year later, ready for the six months of negotiations with the Farmers General that would end with the signing of a new lease in October 1703.[1] But this date came and a new lease was signed before the reform plans had been finished. During the next six years the reformers hoped that a change might be written into the lease to be signed in October 1709.[2] But all in vain. Later, the planners of the other projects had the same concern for the leases. It was no co-incidence that de Betz completed his project in 1737, just a year before the lease Forceville was to be signed, and that the project which Bertin sponsored was ready early in 1762, just six months prior to the signing of the lease Prévost, and given up for lost by some of its supporters in 1767 when it became apparent that it would not be implemented the following year in the lease Alaterre.[3] Amelot in 1720 had not been bound by the necessity of meeting such a deadline, the tax farms being part of Law's *système* and the Farmers General mere directors of the *Com-*

---

[1] A.N., F12 115, Amelot to Le Febvre, and to de Blair, 17 Nov. 1701; Amelot to de la Bourdonnaye, 3 June 1701; A.-M. de Boislisle, *Corresp.*, vol. ii, de Blair to Amelot, 26 Dec. 1701.

[2] A.N., F12 54, sessions of 11 March 1707 to 7 June 1709.

[3] A.N., F12 714, *avis* of the Deputies of Commerce of 28 August 1767 on a request of a wire manufacturer of Lorraine for exemption from the duties of the *Cinq Grosses Fermes*.

pagnie des Indes. But not until 1783, when the customs were placed under an administrative commission (*régie*), was the government again free to change the customs without reference to the lease of the tax farms.[1]

Until that time, there were hopes that provision might be made in a lease for a general reform, hopes that were disappointed again and again. In bargaining over the terms of each new lease both the Crown and the General Farm were prepared to sacrifice reform projects for a variety of reasons but fundamentally because they regarded the customs as a source of revenue which could not be sacrificed to any reform project, whatever its eventual benefits might be. The Farmers General knew they were making a powerful appeal to the Crown when in 1702 they wrote, 'this farm, with all its product, still leaves the ministry with pressing needs ... we are operating machinery which should produce, and we could make it produce, twice as much ... '.[2] This attitude to the customs continued to prevail, especially during the reign of Louis XV when the General Farm was being steadily built up: in 1730 the *tabac* was added to it, in 1732 the *domaine d'Occident et du Canada,* and in 1738, in effect (though legally not until 1762), the various tax farms of the duchies of Bar and Lorraine. Because of this growth and the prosperity of France in this period, the price of the lease was driven up from 80 million *livres* in 1726 to 152 millions in 1774.[3] Every lease in this period was the result of a struggle between the parties for maximum financial benefits. The leases of 1703, 1709, 1744 (de Betz's project was still being considered in the early 1740's) and 1762 were all signed under the shadow of war, which rendered any reform project quite unacceptable, first because the government needed every *sol* it could find, and secondly because the interruption of foreign trade, especially by sea, drastically reduced the yield of import and export duties and diverted a great deal of trade to inland routes, thus swelling the doubly precious revenue from the internal customs duties. Not all the reform projects failed because of war-time pressure on the financial system:

[1] By an *arrêt* of 9 Nov. 1783 (a copy in A.N., AD IX 489).
[2] A.N., F12 1910, 'La verification a été fait par M. de la Vigne ...'.
[3] G. T. Mathews, *Gen. Farm.*, pp. 78 and 285.

H

that of Amelot collapsed in 1720–1 apparently because it was associated with Law's abortive financial schemes. It is not clear why the plans of de Betz were rejected when the lease Forceville was signed in 1738. Throughout the history of these early projects, however, there is little to suggest that the Crown and the Farmers General did not continue to hold the view that the customs were primarily a revenue tax.

The Crown and the General Farm shared the same point of view with respect to the reform project as well as to the customs. In the plans and debates of the reform movement during the first three-quarters of the eighteenth century they appear almost as allies. Sometimes one and sometimes the other took the initiative in supporting the reform plans—or, at times, in opposing them—yet at every stage their attitudes were similar and they sometimes worked together. During the years following the creation of the Council of Commerce in 1700 the reform projects which the Deputies of Commerce were invited to discuss and criticize were prepared by a team of royal and Farm officials. And when Anisson and his group proposed their counterplan for a single uniform duty they found that they had to convince the Farmers General as well as the Crown of its value. Hardly had the government of the Regency adopted the principle of the single duty as a basis for reform than the Farmers General, at the instance of Lallemant de Betz, accepted it also. The harmony between them, still undisturbed when the reform was abandoned in the 1740's, survived during the preparations of the 1760's. Even though the Farmers General took little part in the project of those years they do not appear to have disapproved of it. It is significant that the opponents of the project believed the Farmers General to be the power behind the reform movement. 'We are assured', wrote one, as late as 1770, 'that the Farmers General, on the specious pretext of establishing a perfect uniformity in the levy of import and export duties on all the territories of His Majesty, have at last had their project approved and that the King's commissioners are themselves to propose it to the Estates.'[1] These

[1] Montaudouin de la Touche (?), *Mémoire concernant le droit unique, nouveau droit d'entreé et de sortie par mer que les Fermiers généraux proposent de faire établir dans tous les ports et havres de la Province de Bretagne* (ms. 1770).

beliefs were strengthened when two partisans of the project, de Montaran and Abeille, defended the Farmers General against various charges by these opponents.[1]

In view of the co-operation of the Farmers General and the Crown over the previous fifty years, the Provinces Reputed Foreign and the Foreign Provinces had every reason to suspect that the official project of the 1760's was sponsored by the Farmers General, despite official assurances to the contrary. It is no matter of surprise, therefore, that provincial opposition was founded partly on the suspicion that the project was a financial scheme disguised as a plan for national economic improvement. Such suspicions were naturally strengthened by the association of the customs with other indirect taxes: the royal *péages*, the *gabelle*, the *aides*, and the *tabac*. All these were unequal, being collected at different rates in different provinces and in some provinces not at all, so that the arguments for uniformity, simplicity and efficiency applied to them as well as to the customs. The *gabelle* and the *tabac*, in particular, were closely linked with the customs: many of the barriers needed to divide their various price zones one from another coincided with internal customs barriers, and the General Farm had taken advantage of this situation to combine the bureaux and brigades of guards. If this system of tax collection were to be reformed by abolishing internal barriers in order to levy an equal tax by a uniform collection system, then what could be more probable or more reasonable than the imposition of the *gabelle* at an equal rate throughout the entire kingdom? Nothing would have suited the Crown and the Farmers General better. As Antoine Lavoisier explained:

... if the government would undertake to establish a uniform system of collection throughout the kingdom and to suppress the privileges of individuals and provinces, administrative costs would be reduced, as a result, by more than four million *livres* through the abolition of all the brigades of guards which separate the privileged provinces from those where the salt monopoly is maintained, and through the abolition of more than a thousand customs bureaux, quite apart

---

[1] Michau de Montaran, *Mémoire sur les tarifs*, p. 128; Abeille, *Eclaircissements sur un mémoire attribué au commerce de Nantes et envoyé au mois d'8bre 1770 aux Etats de Bretagne* ..., A.N., F¹² 2427, 71 fols.

from the increase in financial yield which would necessarily follow from that uniformity.[1]

The authorities of the Provinces Reputed Foreign and the Foreign Provinces, always on the watch for any attack on their privileges, saw each single duty project as a plot to subject them to the hated *gabelle* and perhaps all the other indirect taxes of which they were free. Only eighteen months after Bertin had made public his single duty project, the Estates of Brittany, after hearing the report of their permanent commission (*commission intermédiaire*), and after studying some memoirs from the Farmers General and the replies of several Breton communities, recorded in their deliberations:

The Estates charge their *Deputés-en-cour* to be on their guard, and to oppose any attempt of the Farmers General in their administration of the *gabelle* in the provinces to obtain the enactment of any regulation, and notably the one proposed in their memoir which is to be placed on record together with the said replies to serve as an introduction; and the *Procureur général sindic* of Brittany will oppose registration by the Parlement of all edicts and declarations in favour of the Farmers General which would tend to molest the citizens of the province in the said consumption of the salt which they need.[2]

Even the Breton, Montaudouin de la Touche, who understood the economic purpose of the single duty project, rejected it partly because the customs were just one of a number of taxes administered by the Farmers General. 'Providing the tax farmers can make a prodigious fortune during one or two leases of their farm', he wrote, 'it will matter little to them what becomes of the trade of the kingdom after that.'[3] He was convinced that the new general tariff would be used in the interests of finance rather than trade because, he said, 'representations of the Chambers and Deputies of Commerce are almost never heard; the credit of the tax farmers, like an irresistible torrent, always prevails'.[4] To judge from the past, he was right.

---

[1] Antoine-Laurent Lavoisier, *Œuvres*, vol. vi, p. 160.

[2] B.N., ms. fr. 8292, *Précis des délibérations des Etats depuis 1567 jusqu'en 1762 rédigé par ordre alphabétique*, 4 vols., vol. iii, article 'gabelles'.

[3] 'Suite des Considérations sur les finances et le commerce de France', *Journal de Commerce*, Oct. 1761, p. 11.

[4] *Ibid.*, p. 12.

Already, however, a change was taking place. During the twenty-five years following the launching of Bertin's project the Crown gradually ceased to look upon the customs as a tax with economic uses and began to view them primarily as a potential instrument of economic policy. The ideas of the reforming officials came to prevail and the alliance of the Crown and the Farmers General in customs matters weakened and broke. The first unmistakable signs of this change may be seen in the growing enthusiasm for the project among certain royal officials who were in no way involved in the planning of it. Calonne, Intendant of Trois Evêchés and future Controller General, gave it support in an address to the Royal Society of Metz on 18 November 1772,[1] and he was only one of many who spoke favourably of it in these years.[2] Then in 1778 a minister was appointed who—the first since Bertin—gave it wholehearted backing. This was Jacques Necker who committed himself to the project in his *Compte rendu au Roi* (1781), widely published and widely read, in which he condemned the customs system as 'barbarous' and announced that he was preparing a reform programme to be ready whenever the War of American Independence, in which France was currently engaged, should come to an end. This commitment did not mean that he was prepared to sacrifice the revenue from the customs; he believed that the reform would not necessarily even reduce it. But his main argument for the reform was that national trade should be free of internal barriers and protected from foreign competition.[3] Soon after he came to office, he appointed an official, Guillaume-François Mahy de Cormeré, to form and direct a Bureau for the Reform of the Customs (*Bureau pour la refonte des traites*). Cormeré believed that to accomplish his task, which was to transform the customs from a tax into an economic control, it was essential to take the customs out of the hands of the Farmers General and place them under a royal administrative commission (*régie*).[4] In spite of opposition from the General Farm, the single duty project now developed continuously under

---

[1] *Mémoires concernant la navigation.*

[2] *Supra*, p. 61.

[3] Necker, *De L'Administration*, vol. ii, pp. 165–224.

[4] Bib. Ass. Pub., Papers of Auget de Montyon, *Extraits du mémoire sur la réforme des Traites par Monsieur de Cormeray* (sic); and Cormeré, *Rech. fin.*, vol. i, pp. 414 ff.

government auspices, actively supported by most Controllers General, especially Calonne (1783–7), and by a growing body of public opinion, until it was eventually put into effect by the Constituent Assembly in 1790–1. For more than a decade, then, before the project was implemented, the reforming officials were also official reformers, and their programme enjoyed the full support of many ministers.

CHAPTER V

The Reform Movement during the Last Years of the *Ancien Régime*

JACQUES NECKER is generally thought to have accomplished little during his first term of office as head of French finances, beyond the publication of his famous *Compte rendu*, but there can be no doubt that it was he who launched the single duty project into its final phase. In doing so he did not consider the customs as an isolated problem but took account of the integrated nature of the system of indirect taxes, realizing that the *gabelle*, *tabac* and *aides* would also have to be reformed. He planned a wide range of changes in the financial system but believed customs reform to be one of the most important. Soon after his appointment as Director General of Finances he applied to Trudaine de Montigny's office for the records and papers relating to the single duty project.[1] And shortly afterwards, as though to test the force of the opposition, he made efforts to draw Lorraine into an immediate customs union with the *Cinq Grosses Fermes*.[2] Another sign that customs reform was

---

[1] A manuscript note, signed 'L.-H. Duchesne, 26 août 1790', is to be found in, Louis-Henry Duchesne de Voiron, *Projet d'imposition juste et facile propre a suppléer* ..., Paris, 1789, 34 pp. (B.M., F.R. 519 (10) inserted between pages 12 and 13.) It reads: 'Pendant la 1ère administration de Monsieur Necker, il fit demander à Monsieur Dureau, 1er commis de Messrs Trudaine, le travail fait par les Ministres pour porter aux frontières les droits de traittes et supprimer ceux de l'intérieur du royaume. Mr. Dureau le refusa, et ne le remis ensuite qu'à la sollicitation de Mr. de Fourqueux qui promit qu'on le chargeroit de la suite de ce travail. M. Dureau étant mort sans qu'il a été question de cette opération de finances, le travail est resté en mains de Mr. Necker; il seroit très utile de l'avoir pour procéder à celuy que se propose de faire Messieurs les députés à l'Assemblée Nationale attendu qu'il avoit été achevé et tous (?) concerté par Mrs. Trudaine, Mrs. les Deputés du Commerce, d'apres les avis des chambres de commerce, Mrs. les Fermiers Généraux et principaux négotiants du Royaume.' Cf. Duchesne, *Projet d'administration, remis a Monsieur Turgot quand il fut nommé Controleur général, et* ..., 1787, p. 10.

[2] *Infra*, p. 137.

uppermost in his mind is that an official, in urging him to reform the *aides*, could think of no better argument than that 'the freeing of the trade in wine, once decided, would win for the project of the single customs tariff several provinces which are opposing it only in the interests of their wine trade'.[1] But the best proof of Necker's interest in the single duty project is the founding of the *Bureau pour la refonte des traites* with Mahy de Cormeré at its head.

Guillaume-François Mahy de Cormeré was the chief planner and a constant champion of the project from 1778 almost to the institution of the project by the Constituent Assembly in 1791. Born on 10 November 1739 into an old and respectable family of officials of Blois[2]—his father and grandfather had in turn held office as receiver-general of the Domaines and Forests of the county of Blois, and his grandfather had also held posts in a *Chambre des Comptes*—he first became interested in the customs reform project in 1772 and wrote to the Controller General, Terray, offering his services in the preparation of the project which Bertin had launched. Terray encouraged him, so he tells us, and he spent the next few years 'gathering all the titles and information on the nature of the various duties, their rates, cases in which they were collected, &c.'[3] He showed his work to Turgot who advised him to continue, but it was Necker who first encouraged him to plan serious reforms;[4] and in 1777 or 1778 appointed him to work on a number of projects relating to internal free trade, of which the principal one was the single duty project. To this project Necker later referred in the *Compte rendu* of January 1781 and again in greater detail in his *De l'Administration des finances de la France* (1784), where after emphasizing the necessity of suppressing the internal customs duties, he went on to tell of the plans which he sponsored for this purpose during his first ministry: 'After all the research needed for the reform of the *gabelles* had been finished, I decided

---

[1] Arch. Ass. Pub., papers of Auget de Montyon, 'Aides—mémoire remis à M. Necker', 2 fols.

[2] Baptismal register of the parish of Saint Solenne for the year 1739, in the municipal library of Blois. Extracts were kindly sent to me by the Departmental Archivist of Loir et Cher, in Blois.

[3] A.N., F30 111, memoir beginning, 'Le plan d'uniformité . . .'.

[4] *Loc. cit.*

that the same *chef de travail* should undertake the analysis of the customs registers'.[1] It is clear that Necker's reference here is to Cormeré, who himself writes, 'It was after the completion of the work on the salt tax that Monsieur Necker charged me with the work involved in the reform of the customs'.[2]

The earliest account of Cormeré's work which I have found is a manuscript memoir of 1783 or 1784, written by Cormeré himself and entitled, *Extrait ou aperçu du travail contenant le plan de réforme sur la partie des traites*.[3] A progress report, probably to the Controller General, it shows that Cormeré had already been at work for some considerable time. Early in 1784 news of the project reached the author of Bachaumont's *Mémoires secrets*,[4] and by August he knew enough about it to write,

The work of Monsieur de Cormeré will not appear this year as had been hoped. For ten years this tireless calculator, with thirty-five clerks under his orders, has been preparing his project which, it will be recalled, involves the suppression of the *traites* and the freeing of the sale of salt and tobacco. Monsieur de Calonne, who appears very keen to have this great project carried out during his ministry, is encouraging the author and continuing to pay him the salary of 60,000 *livres* granted by preceding Controllers General. . . .[5]

In 1787, Calonne put the project before the Assembly of Notables in a memoir which Bachaumont reported to be 'a résumé of the work of the baron de Cormerai [sic] who was busy with this matter for a number of years, and under several ministries had an *ad hoc* bureau with lavish allowances'.[6]

Cormeré was indeed generously paid. From 1780, if not before, he received 12,000 *livres* a year. This was a fairly good allowance at the time, for Doublet de Persan for instance, Director of the Bureau for the examination and verification of the *péages*, was paid only 8,000 *livres* a year, and Nicolas-François, comte de Mollien, whose memoirs are frequently quoted in studies of the *ancien régime*, was a *premier commis* with a salary of 6,000 a year until his marriage in 1784, when it was

---

[1] Necker, *De l'Admin.*, vol. ii, p. 176. Cf. Necker, *Compte rendu*, p. 90.
[2] Mahy de Cormeré, *Mémoire sur les finances et sur le crédit*, p. 7.
[3] B.N., ms. fr. 7772, fols. 487 to 501.
[4] Tome xxv, 9 Jan. 1784, p. 22.   [5] Tome xxvi, p. 177.
[6] Tome xxxiv, 17 March 1787, p. 296.

raised to 10,000 *livres*.[1] Moreover, although there seems to be some doubt as to whether Cormeré's allowance was paid in full in 1781 and 1782, it was raised from the quarter of October-December 1783 to 12,750 *livres* every quarter, or 51,000 *livres* a year for himself and his employees, until 1787 when this amount was slightly reduced. The sums which the Crown paid to him, presented in a table of annual totals,[2] are not only an indication of his importance but also a record of the growth and eventual decline of his *Bureau pour la refonte des traites*.

1780	12,000	*livres*				
1781	4,800	,,				
1782	4,800	,,				
1783	35,270	,,	3	*sols*	4	*deniers*
1784	68,184	,,	5	,,	10	,,
1785	61,510	,,	12	,,		
1786	57,712	,,	14	,,	3	,,
1787	55,987	,,	8	,,		
1788	47,395	,,				
1789	27,800	,,				
1790	21,200	,,				
1791	17,200	,,				

With these allowances Cormeré was able to employ a considerable number of assistants. Bachaumont's estimate of thirty-five may be too high, but evidence for the enrolment in the years 1788–9 suggests that in the period 1784–7 there were more than a score. In 1788, 4,800 *livres* were distributed as 'severance pay' among six employees discharged from the bureau.[3] On 1 January 1789 five more employees, including

---

[1] A.N., DX 1; and A.N., DX 2 (14e *liasse*): letter of 21 October 1786.

[2] The registers of *Ordonnances* of payment from which most of the figures are taken, A.N., F4 70 and F4 71, begin in 1780 and, according to sums listed in A.N., DX 1, DX 3, and F⁴ 1040, are incomplete for the years 1788, 1789 and 1791. The figures for 1783 and 1784 are confirmed and supplemented in *Etats de comptant de l'année et des restes de l'année 1783* . . . , Paris (Imprimerie nationale), 1790, p. 78 (B.M., F.R. 551). Payments during the years 1790 and 1791 have been compiled from information in A.N., A.B XIX 327, *Registre de documents relatifs à la gestion de M. Dufresne comme directeur du Trésor public* . . . , p. 371, and A.N., F4 1040, two autographed letters of Cormeré to Dufresne dated 15 June 1791. The fact that all these records supplement each other suggests that even taken all together they may be incomplete.

[3] A.N., DX 1 (Appointments et traitements, 1788). These were: Millon, awarded 1200 *livres*; Baconel, 1200 *livres*; d'Orvilliers, 600; Testu, 600; Raymond, 600; and Reignier, 600.

Cormeré's brother, Mahy de Chitenay, were discharged and also awarded gratuities.[1] And after the loss of these eleven men Cormeré still headed a bureau comprising five clerks and an office boy, for which he received an allotment of 23,000 *livres* for the year 1789.[2]

Given a staff and remuneration on such a scale, who can doubt that Cormeré and his bureau held a prominent position in the official movement for customs reform? Their role naturally declined as soon as the Constituent Assembly had assumed power and set up its various economic and financial committees. But it is significant of Cormeré's prominence even during the Revolution that in 1790 his enemies published a satirical *Dialogue entre M. A . . . Député à l'Assemblée nationale, M.B. . . . Fermier Général, et M. le Baron de C . . . sur les impositions indirectes*,[3] in which Cormeré is defeated in a struggle with a Farmer General for the support of a Deputy to the Assembly. The economic committees of the Assembly, especially the Committee on Taxation and the Committee on Commerce and Agriculture, consulted Cormeré and used his material in the preparation of their own project. On the suggestion of a member of the Committee on Finance, the Assembly published Cormeré's *Mémoire sur les finances et sur le crédit*,[4] and one important Deputy, Théodore Vernier, who disagreed with him on many points, still thought that his financial plans were the only ones worth reading of the masses that were pouring from the presses.[5] On 28 September 1791 the Constituent Assembly awarded him a gratuity of 12,000 *livres* for the assistance he had given its

[1] A.N., DX 1. Mahy de Chitenay was awarded 1,800 *livres*; Pardon, 1,200; Bligny, 600; Langlois, 600; and l'Arbre, 600.

[2] Divided in the following manner: Mahy de Cormeré (chief), 12,000 *livres*; Arnier (clerk) 3,000; Chenet (clerk), 1,200; Le Clerk (clerk), 1,000; Vittermes (clerk), 1,200; Dupont (clerk), 1,200; one office boy, 600; office rental and lodgings for Cormeré, 1,000; office expenses, 1,200. (A.N., DX 3, 15e chapitre, signed by Bertrand Dufresne on 27 August 1789.) Cf. A.N., DX 3, *Compte général des revenus et des dépenses fixes au premier mai, 1789*, Paris, 1789, p. 167.

[3] Published without place or date, this book has been dated 1790 by André Monglond, *La France révolutionnaire*, tome i. The contents of the book show beyond a doubt that 'Monsieur le Baron de C . . .' is intended to be Cormeré.

[4] Paris, 1789. Officially published at the suggestion of the Baron d'Harambure.

[5] Vernier (Deputy for Aval in Franche Comté), *Nouveau plan de finances*, p. 1; cf. the anonymous, *Considérations sur l'impôt des gabelles et sur celui du tabac*, 1789, p. 21.

committees, and suppressed his bureau.[1] Undoubtedly he had
already enjoyed his greatest reward a few months earlier when
the Assembly had adopted the single duty project and taken
steps to implement it. His official career ended, Cormeré
emigrated to San Domingo in January 1792.[2]

He first began to work seriously on the single duty project
when, in 1777 or 1778, Necker employed him to head an
official team for that purpose. Having set up the *Bureau pour
la refonte des traites*, Necker was naturally disposed to give it
every possible assistance though Cormeré had difficulty in
gaining access to the customs registers essential for the study of
the effects which the single duty would have upon the trade of
the various provinces, and Necker passed out of office before
he was able to wrest these registers from the hands of the
reluctant Farmers General.[3]

This failure to procure the customs registers held up Cormeré's work for some considerable time, and Joly de Fleury, on
succeeding Necker as Controller General, announced that he
would make no changes and proceeded to pay little attention to
the reformers. During Fleury's two years of office Cormeré got
no satisfaction. He appeared to Cormeré to be favourably disposed towards the project, but that Fleury's support was at best
half-hearted is shown by some notes which he made at the time
the single duty project was presented by Calonne to the
Assembly of Notables:

Barriers to the frontiers

This project is good in itself. Well informed people who have
reflected on it doubt whether it will be so advantageous as is believed.
It is something to be worked out and discussed in both its financial
and its commercial aspects. The power of Louis XIV and the genius
of Colbert failed over it. In our time all ministers have worked on
this project, but their efforts have always been unsuccessful. More-

---

[1] A.N., AB XIX 327, *Registre de documents relatifs à la gestion de Monsieur Dufresne comme directeur du Tresor public . . .*, ms. fol. 371; Gerbaux and Schmidt, ed. *Procès-verbaux des Comités*, 4 July 1791; *Assemblée constituante, procès-verbaux*, 28 Sept. 1791, p. 51; *Ancien moniteur, table chron.*, p. 191 (No. 275); and B.N., ms. fr. 6799, fol. 167, *Reprises actives du cy-devant Trésor royal.*

[2] La Rochefoucauld, *Lettre à un membre de l'Assemblée nationale législative*, note on p. 13.

[3] Cormeré, *Rech. fin.*, vol. i, p. 2.

over, the consent of the provinces is necessary because of the King's promise to let them continue to enjoy their present status. If they consent they will have to be indemnified. Indemnity presents the same problems. Can they have confidence in the one that will be offered to them.[1]

Characteristically, Joly de Fleury temporized by appointing Douët de la Boullaye, in 1782, to prepare a report on the project.[2] According to Cormeré, the report of de la Boullaye was favourable but before Joly de Fleury could take any action he passed out of office. The next Controller General was Lefèvre d'Ormesson who, although he held office only from March to November 1783, did at last get Cormeré his customs registers in July 1783.[3]

In the same month a movement was begun to bring the customs more firmly under the control of the government and the effect of this was to remove one of the obstacles to the single duty project. Vergennes was negotiating the Peace of Versailles with Britain and having difficulties on the commercial side. A Farmer General, Jacques-Mathieu Augéard, writes:

... he complained to me that the General Farm did not want to concede two free ports; he claimed that its refusal would cause the failure of the peace negotiations.[4]

Augéard told Vergennes that if the Farmers General were properly indemnified the customs could be struck off the current Farmers General's lease and treated as a *régie*, whereupon Vergennes would be able to make whatever customs arrangements were necessary for the peace treaty. The two then agreed that since three years, or half of the lease, had passed, the amount of the indemnity for the remaining three years could be set at exactly the sum which the Farmers General had already earned on the customs during the first half of the lease. Augéard says

---

[1] B.N., Collection Joly de Fleury, ms. 1040. Mollien reports that Fleury opposed the project: 'il appelait cela des innovations'. (*Mémoires d'un ministre du Trésor public*, vol. i, p. 202.)

[2] Gabriel-Isaac Douët de la Boullaye, *maître des requêtes* since 1762, was at this time in charge of affairs relating to the *péages*, to the *bureaux des finances* and to *les projets*, and it was doubtless in this latter capacity that he was asked to study Cormeré's project (*Almanach royal*).

[3] A.N., F³⁰ 111, 'Le plan d'uniformité ...'.

[4] J.-M. Augéard, *Mémoires secrets*, p. 117.

that his colleagues gave their consent to this arrangement and that he personally delivered it to Vergennes on 31 July, never doubting that Vergennes would discuss the matter with d'Ormesson. Soon afterwards Vergennes and d'Ormesson quarrelled and for this and perhaps other reasons d'Ormesson never heard of Vergennes's negotiations with the Farmers General over the customs. D'Ormesson, on his side, without consulting Vergennes, proceeded with plans of his own to convert the whole General Farm into a *régie*; on 24 October 1783 he went alone to see the King and induced him to sign an *arrêt* which ordered this reform for 1 January 1784.[1] If, as Augéard says, d'Ormesson had had sixty or seventy million *livres* with which to reimburse the Farmers General, this reform might have been possible, 'but as there was not a *sol* in the treasury, this operation became impracticable; moreover it provoked alarming reports in Paris, and raised all the financiers and moneyed people against the minister. . . . '.[2] On 31 October Augéard went as the representative of the Farmers General to see Vergennes and demanded that d'Ormesson be discharged. Calonne succeeded him on 2 November, and a week later the offending *arrêt* was cancelled by another which recognized Vergennes's agreement with the Farmers General. In this *arrêt* and in the next lease, the customs duties were, by formal arrangement with the Farmers General, removed from the hallowed protection of the lease and administered for the King. As far as the customs were concerned, the Farmers General were no longer farmers but simply paid administrators. This meant that the customs duties could be reformed without indemnity to the Farmers General—an important step forward, for previously any plans for customs reform had either to provide for such an indemnity or to be incorporated in a new lease.

The only reason for the change, according to Augéard, was that for diplomatic purposes the French Secretary of State for Foreign Affairs wished to create two free ports. This was,

---

[1] Moreau de Beaumont, *Mém. con.*, tome v, p. 491 (supplement by Vieuville). A copy of this *arrêt* and the *arrêt* of 9 November 1783 may be found in A.N., AD IX 489. The Farmers General were heavily recompensed for this loss by an *arrêt* of 3 February 1786. This *arrêt* is reproduced and discussed in *Convention Nationale. Rapport des commissaires réviseurs des trois compagnies de finance, avec représentans du peuple.* . . .

[2] Augéard, *Mem. sec.*, p. 119.

indeed, a major reason, and the ports of Lorient and Bayonne were duly freed from customs duties in 1784. But it is more than probable that the change was made partly to promote the single duty project; for all three of the ministers who took part in the events of July to November 1783, d'Ormesson, Vergennes and Calonne, were in favour of the project. D'Ormesson's views are made clear in Cormeré's testimony, in the fact that d'Ormesson procured the needed customs registers, and in the intentions expressed in his short-lived *arrêt* of 24 October 1783. Vergennes, for his part, was not so all-important a sponsor of the project as His de Butenval has asserted, but there can be no doubt that he gave it strong support.[1] It was Calonne, however, who played the leading role. As Intendant of Trois Evêchés from 1766 to 1778, he had made an extensive inquiry into the economic condition of his generality, which had led him to study the customs barriers and the single duty project of the time.[2] According to a paper which he read to the Royal Society of Metz on 18 November 1772, he had studied all the literature on this controversy which had appeared since 1760, and had given much thought to the problem. His remarks, although diplomatically phrased in general terms, leave no doubt about his views:

Alsace, Lorraine and Trois Evêchés . . . are cut off [by the customs barriers] and harrassed only on the French side. Is it an advantage for them as they think and have always thought? Is it not rather a disadvantage, as people have been trying for several years to persuade them?[3]

Again, in a letter to the Bishop of Blois, dated 15 June 1789, Calonne wrote:

The ministry has perished, but the plan has survived . . . There is every hope that the freeing of internal traffic by the removal of the barriers [and other projects] will hold the attention of the national

---

[1] Comte His de Butenval, *Etablissement en France*, p. 20. A. Goodwin ('Calonne, the Assembly of French Notables of 1787 and the Origins of the *Révolte nobiliaire*', E.H.R., 1946, pp. 202 ff.) contradicts the views of Butenval. Calonne did doubtless play the greater role in preparing the project, yet Dupont asserted that Vergennes was '. . . un des deux ministres qui avaient déterminé le Roi à cette opération et préparé celles qui devaient en résulter . . .' (*Lettre à la Chambre*, pp. 88–89).

[2] Calonne, *Mémoires concernant la navigation*.

[3] *Ibid.*, p. 49.

representatives . . . If that happens, if the good that I have had in view is done, I shall not regret my efforts.[1]

These views, expressed before and after Calonne's period as Controller General, might be regarded as hollow sentiments, but there is no mistaking the seriousness of his intentions in two memoirs which he sent to the King in 1786, and in the part he played in the actual preparation of the project. Moreover, it could hardly be accidental that Cormeré drew his highest financial allowances during exactly the period of Calonne's ministry, that is, from the last quarter of 1783 to the first quarter of 1787.[2]

With the support of d'Ormesson, Vergennes and Calonne, Cormeré set up his offices, hired his staff and began to work in earnest on the single duty project during the autumn of 1783; that is, shortly after he had won access to the customs registers and about the same time that the customs were set aside to be administered for the Crown. He apparently hoped at that time to complete the project in one year. A long progress report which he sent to the Controller General late in 1783 or early in 1784 shows that the plan for suppressing the internal customs duties, the study of the probable effects of the project on the provinces and on the national customs revenue, the new *ordonnance* to govern the operations of the reformed system, the calculated effects of the reform on colonial trade, and the introductory survey of the existing system, would all be ready by April 1784, and by September Cormeré expected to have compiled a new comprehensive list of goods with their uses and most recent prices and on the basis of it to have drawn up the general customs tariff.[3] In fact he did not finish the project until near the end of 1785. The main reason for this delay was that the scope of the project was enlarged in 1784 by a decision to suppress not only the internal duties but also the *marque des fers*,

---

[1] Quoted in Marcel Marion, *Histoire financière*, vol. i, p. 399.

[2] Cormeré drew not more than 12,000 *livres* a year until summer 1783 when he drew an additional sum of 9,437 *livres*, 10 *sols*. On 12 October 1783 he received another sum of 2,146 *livres*, 10 *sols*, and beginning with the quarter of October–December 1783 he was paid 12,750 *livres* every quarter besides casual expenses. (See *supra*, p. 108.)

[3] B.N., ms. fr. 7772, fols. 487 to 510. *Extrait ou aperçu du travail concernant le plan de réforme sur la partie des traites.*

the *marque des huiles et savons*, and those *aides* which were levied in customs bureaux. Cormeré's *Mémoire sur la réforme des traites* written in 1786 or 1787, shows that by then the project had become much more comprehensive and was based upon a wider range of statistical calculations.[1]

In October 1785, Cormeré asked for the establishment of a commission to examine the project and it was appointed in April 1786.[2] There were eight commissioners: a *Conseiller d'Etat*, Michel Bouvard de Fourqueux (presiding); two Intendants of Finance, Pierre-Joseph de Colonia and Gabriel-Isaac Douët de la Boullaye; an Intendant of Commerce, Jean-Jacques-Maurille Michau de Montaran (the son); two *Commissaires généraux du commerce*, Pierre-Samuel Dupont (de Nemours) and Edouard Boyetet; and two Farmers General, Jacques-Joseph Brac de la Perrière and Jacques-Alexis Paulze de Chasteignolles. Although not named in the *arrêt* which set up the commission, Cormeré was admitted and took a leading part in the work and the discussions.[3] The purpose of the commission was first of all to verify Cormeré's conclusions about the effects of the project on national revenue and on the provincial economies, and then to prepare a final draft of the new tariff and the new *ordonnance*. According to fragmentary reports from Boyetet, Dupont and Cormeré, which together furnish an account of the commission's activities, the task proved to be long and difficult.

Calonne called the commission together soon after it was formed and, as Boyetet says, impressed upon them how important the single duty project was for the national welfare, and how essential it was for the commission to examine Cormeré's work carefully and to prove its worth.[4] But it soon became clear that

[1] Arch. Ass. Pub., papers of Auget de Montyon, containing extracts from this memoir.

[2] A.N., F^{30} 111, 'Le plan d'uniformité . . .'; Cormeré, *Rech. fin.*, vol. i, p. 229; A.N., K 677, fol. 144; A. Goodwin, *op. cit.*, p. 218, note 2; and 'Mémoire sur la réformation des droits de traites', *Collection des mémoires présentés à l'Assemblée des Notables*, Versailles, 1787, p. 10.

[3] *Loc. cit.*; Dupont, *Lettre à la Chambre*, pp. 43, 102 and 177. Bouvard de Fourqueux (1719–89), brother-in-law of Auget de Montyon, and father-in-law of both Trudaine de Montigny and Maynon d'Invault, succeeded Calonne as Controller General for a brief period, from 9 April to 3 May 1787.

[4] A.N., F^4 1032^2, ms. memoir by Boyetet, *Compte rendu à Mrs. de Villedeuil et Lambert et à Mgr. de Sens sur l'objet des places de commissaires généraux du commerce*, 5 fols. Henceforth to be cited as A.N., F^4 1032^2, Boyetet ms.

I

two of the most important members of the commission, de la
Boullaye and de Colonia, were habitually absenting themselves,
which held up the work, and that they and others were making
efforts to discredit Cormeré's memoirs as well as to cast doubt
upon the value of the project in principle.[1] De la Boullaye was
jealous of Cormeré, for he thought the reform project ought to
have been entrusted to him. Moreover, according to the
testimony of Cormeré, Dupont and Boyetet, de la Boullaye was
an agent or ally of the Farmers General and as such made it his
business to obstruct the single duty project.[2]

Why did the Farmers General use their influence against the
project at this time? They had opposed the earlier projects
only in so far as customs revenue might have been reduced, but
this difficulty had been removed in 1783 when they had con-
sented to administer the customs not as a tax farm but as a
régie. There was no longer any question of the Farmers General
making a profit from the customs, and any reduction of revenue
would not cause them any loss. Why then did they oppose
Cormeré's project? The answer is that the internal customs
could hardly be regarded as an isolated problem, but had to be
viewed as part of the whole structure of internal bureaux and
brigades maintained for the *gabelle*, the *tabac* and the *aides*
as well. For one thing, the inspection of vehicles by the customs
was an essential part of the prevention of salt, tobacco and wine
smuggling. For another, the cost of the internal barriers was
spread over all these taxes and would have been relatively
higher if the internal duties had been abolished. The indirect
taxes had therefore to be reformed more or less together or not
at all. There was general agreement on the reform of the customs.
The main question was how the *gabelle* should be reformed:
should it be abolished altogether or should it be imposed
equally throughout the whole kingdom? One or other alternative would have to be decided upon if the internal barriers
were to be removed. The planners of the earlier projects, by

---

[1] *Loc. cit.*; and Cormeré, *Rech. fin.*, vol. i, p. 299.

[2] *Ibid.*, p. 7; by clear implication in A.N., F⁴ 1032² Boyetet ms.; and in Dupont,
Procès-verbal de l'Assemblée baillivale de Nemours, vol. i, p. 334. Cf. the bitter but
coherent and convincing attack on de la Boullaye by Charles-Georges Fenouillot de
Falbaire de Quingy, *Mémoire adressé au Roi et à l'Assemblée nationale sur quelques abus
et particulièrement contre une vexation de Monsieur Douët de la Boullaye*, p. 47.

avoiding this issue, had left open the possibility that the single duty project might lead to the extension of the *gabelle*;[1] but Cormeré declared that the *gabelle* would have to be abolished and he worked on that assumption.[2] In his hands, the internal free trade project might well lead to the destruction of the *gabelle* and this, he knew, had earned him the hatred of the Farmers General. 'The General Farm', he wrote, 'has always considered the customs as the strongest support of the *gabelle*, *son impôt chéri*; it has realized that if the customs bureaux were removed to the national frontiers and the coasts, the local barriers, so numerous throughout the kingdom, would have no other *raison d'être* than the *gabelle* which the people hate. . . . '.[3]

The Farmers General now feared and hated the single duty project, but some of them appear to have hoped that if they could gain control of it they might be able to obstruct it indefinitely or even to use it to introduce an extension of the *gabelle*.

We feel it necessary to observe [they wrote in a memoir], that if the plan for changing the customs duties were adopted, the tax farmers, through their special knowledge acquired in managing the King's tax farms, would alone be capable of carrying it out successfully. Furthermore, there is every reason to believe that acting under the authority of the Council they would be able, in less than a year, to prepare the new tariffs, and to set up the new bureaux so far as local conditions would allow.[4]

This argument can only have been a bid for control of the project. Furthermore, during the 1780's they were continually trying to influence the *Département des fermes* of the *Contrôle*

---

[1] Amelot broached it in his first draft, but soon dropped it. (See Appendix II.)

[2] A.N., F[30] 111, Précis of 20 memoirs, memoir 3, art. 7.

[3] Cormeré, *Rech. fin.*, vol. i, p. 225.

[4] B.N., ms. fr. 11098: *Commerce et finance—Extraits des procès-verbaux de tournée de Monsieur de Chalut de Vérin fait en 1754, 1755 et 1756. Mémoire et projet du titre commun pour les fermes du Roy*, 61 fols. plus the coloured map of the internal duties which was first published in Michau de Montaran, *Mémoire sur les tarifs*. Another copy (ms. fr. 11097) lacks fol. 61, which is an important addition in another hand called 'supplément au mémoire'. The fear which the Farmers General had of the project is taken for granted, not only by the central figures in this narrative, but also by the Deputies of Commerce in an *avis* of 1 August 1786 (B.N., nouv. acq. fr. 2721) and elsewhere.

général in its work bearing upon the indirect taxes. In 1782, for
instance, they forced Rousselot de Surgy to retire from the
Contrôle général because, according to Cormeré, he was taking
too great an interest in reforms, especially the single duty project.[1] In 1786, when their new lease (Mager) was signed and
they were distributing gratuities to officials according to the
usual practice on this occasion, they gave specially large sums
to de Colonia, then Intendant of Finances in charge of the
Département des Fermes.[2] The following years, de Colonia was
replaced in this post by Douët de la Boullaye, who was in
league with the Farmers General and who lost no time in
proving it by discharging one of his clerks for taking too
great an interest in tax reform.[3] De la Boullaye is noteworthy for
his continuous obstruction of the single duty project. In the
commission set up in 1785 to examine the project he acted as a
sort of 'fifth column' of the Farmers General. The two Farmers
General on the commission, however, Paulze and de la Perrière,
proved to be loyal and useful members and earned Cormeré's
respect for their independent refusal to collaborate with the
obstructive tactics of the Farmers General as a body.[4]

In 1786, after the commission had held a few meetings,
Boyetet concluded that there were secret interests at work to
defeat the project, and that the commission as a whole would
never finish its examination of Cormeré's work. He therefore
proposed to Dupont that the two of them should examine it
alone without telling anyone. Dupont agreed and after four or
five months of hard study they announced to de Fourqueux that
they were satisfied with Cormeré's conclusions, that the project
would not be disastrous either for national revenue or for the
provinces. In several meetings with de Fourqueux they convinced him with the aid of their notes, surveys and extracts that
the work was sound, and he in turn informed Calonne of this
conclusion in the name of the commission. Calonne then

---

[1] Cormeré, *Rech. fin.*, vol. i, p. 48; the *Almanach royal* roughly bears out this statement on de Surgy's period of service; and accounts of payment in A.N., F⁴ 70 and
71 record the payment of his salary of 6,000 *livres* for only 1780 and 1781.

[2] *Loc. cit.*

[3] *Loc. cit.* This was Claude Vial, discharged on 27 July 1787 (A.N., D VI 8).

[4] Cormeré, *Rech. fin.*, vol. i, p. 229. Cf. the praise in *Convention Nationale, Rapport
des Commissaires réviseurs des trois compagnies de finance*, pp. 24 ff.

assembled the commission in Versailles and, announcing that he was satisfied with Cormeré's work on the financial aspect of the project, instructed them to get on with the preparation of the tariff and *ordonnance*.[1] The commission accepted an invitation to hold its meetings in de Fourqueux's house, but de la Boullaye thought his attendance unnecessary, the rest of the work being foreign to his department, and de Colonia also withdrew. The rest of the commission decided that the tariff should be studied by Montaran, Boyetet, Cormeré and de la Perrière, and the *ordonnance* by Montaran, Boyetet, Cormeré, Dupont and Paulze.[2] Regarding the *ordonnance* as particularly important, de Fourqueux gave it first to Paulze, and then to Cormeré and Montaran. The presence of Montaran is a link with an earlier phase of the struggle, for he possessed his father's *procès-verbaux* of the discussions of the *ordonnance* for the Trudaines's project. After Cormeré and Montaran had worked together on the *ordonnance* for a month, each article being discussed in committee meetings at Montaran's house, the whole was turned over to de Fourqueux, who checked it thoroughly himself, reassembled the whole commission to adopt the document formally, and finally submitted it to Calonne with the tariff. Four or five months had passed in the preparation of these two documents.

When Calonne himself had examined and approved them, he called another general meeting of the commission, presumably for a final review of the whole project. However, de Colonia and de la Perrière unexpectedly re-opened the old question of revenue losses, saying that although they admitted the usefulness of the project they believed it would entail a sacrifice of perhaps ten million *livres*. Cormeré maintained that on the contrary no revenue need be lost, and after a long discussion it was decided that de Colonia on the one hand and Cormeré on the other would try to establish the truth of their respective assertions. In the end Cormeré vindicated his calculations and de Colonia reported to Calonne that he was at last satisfied

[1] A.N., F[30] 111, three short memoirs by Cormeré; also in the same carton is a *Nouvelle Ordonnance des Traites*, ms. 147 fols., which is certainly part of some stage in the development of Cormeré's project.

[2] The relatively minor role assigned to Dupont de Nemours in this distribution of duties is to be noted.

that no revenue would be lost.[1] It was at this stage that the project was submitted to the Assembly of Notables.

As early as 20 August 1786 Calonne had presented a summary of this and his other projects to the King in a memoir in which he spoke of France as 'a kingdom where the provinces are strangers to one another; where the many internal barriers separate and divide subjects of the same sovereign'. He was already talking of 'the suppression of the internal customs, the removal of the bureaux to the frontiers, the formation of a uniform tariff'.[2] A short time later, in a memoir of 30 November 1786, Calonne explained the single duty project to the King in much greater detail, giving an account of its history and of the steps which he himself was proposing to take. He took great pains to make it clear that the strong objections of provincial interests to the plan were based on an expectation of financial loss which was purely conjectural and which seemed to be disproved by the official studies which he had sponsored. He concluded:

... the only way to cut through all these difficulties, which are based on misunderstanding, is to pay no attention to them but to continue working toward the public good. A general regulation must first be passed and after that an inquiry conducted to determine what may justly be awarded to the small number of provinces which may be able to prove that they have suffered a real loss; for we must not assume that there will be such loss. This is the plan that I shall follow if Your Majesty approves of it.[3]

We can only guess what passed between the King and his ministers. But one month later an official note in the *Journal de Paris* of 31 December 1786 announced to the public that the notables of the kingdom were to assemble for the consideration of reforms.[4]

The preparation of the single duty project was by no means a secret before the notables assembled. Bachaumont in 1784 had

---

[1] Cormeré, *Rech. fin.*, vol. i, p. 279.
[2] Calonne, 'Précis d'un plan d'amélioration des finances présenté au Roi le 20 août 1786', pp. 42–62 of *Réponse de Monsieur de Calonne à l'écrit de Monsieur Necker*, London, 1788, appendices, p. 52 and 3ᵉ partie, no. 5.
[3] A.N., K 677, No. 144. Cf. A. Goodwin, *op. cit.*, pp. 202 ff.
[4] Cited in G. Susane, *La Tactique*, p. 90.

devoted two entries in his *Mémoires secrets* to Cormeré's work.[1] The *Gazette de Cologne* of Thursday, 27 July 1786 (No. 60) mentioned the project in a passage which was reproduced the following week in the *Courrier de l'Europe*.[2] The *Mercure de France*, in an article of 17 January 1787, said that although the reforms to be discussed in the Assembly of Notables were not known definitely, 'there is talk of the plan announced for the suppression of the customs, for the equalization of the *gabelle*, and for the suppression of the *aides*'.[3] Obviously, so far as the single duty project is concerned, Calonne is not open to the charge of being so unprepared for the Assembly of Notables that his plans were hastily made up in the week preceding the opening of the Assembly on 22 February 1787.[4]

When Bachaumont received, on 17 March, a copy of the memoir on the single duty project, which had been submitted to the Assembly five days previously, he commented that it was easy to see from the title alone that few of the Notables would be capable of discussing it or even of reading it to any purpose: it was taking a good deal of their time, but they seemed to be making no progress at all.[5] Few, indeed, of the notables appear to have taken an intelligent interest in the project, and many like Joly de Fleury were bored by it. When Joly de Fleury, reviewing the events of the second day of the Assembly, made notes on Calonne's speech announcing his plans for reform, he mentioned all except the proposals concerning the customs barriers which he said he did not remember.[6] These proposals were given remarkably little space in the *procès verbaux*;[7] almost the only extensive comments on them were attacks by the notables from the Foreign Provinces.

In their observations, most of the six bureaux into which the Assembly was divided for close study of the proposed reforms gave the single duty project respectful approval and then repeated

---

[1] *Supra*, p. 107.

[2] Cited in *Réflexions d'un solitaire*, p. 55.

[3] No. 3, p. 115, cited in S.-P. Hardy, *Mes loisirs*, vol. vi, entry for 1 January 1787.

[4] This has been a widely held view: see G. Susane, *La tactique*, p. 167.

[5] Bachaumont, *Mem. sec.*, tome xxxiv, p. 296.

[6] B.N., *Collection Joly de Fleury*, ms. 1038.

[7] A.N., C 2, *Procès-verbaux du deuxième bureau*. Practically all accounts of the reforms put before the Assembly give little attention to the project.

all the objections which had been raised during the general discussion in the Assembly. They advised the government to examine very carefully the representations of the hostile provinces. The most important observations were those of the second bureau, under the comte d'Artois, to which the project had been assigned for special attention. The sixteen points raised by this bureau are a strange mixture of special pleading and general advice; and they illustrate admirably the diffuse way in which the Assembly of Notables dealt with the project.

(1) Before any duties are suppressed, the government should make certain that the customs revenue will not suffer;

(2) the customs are so intimately associated with the *gabelle* that the project must take into account whatever decision is taken on that;

(3) the duties affecting Alsace, Lorraine and the Trois Evêchés should not be changed until after the provincial assemblies have discussed the project;

(4) if imported raw materials and exported manufactures pay a duty of $1\frac{1}{4}$ per cent, the total cost to industry, over the whole process of manufacturing, will be $\frac{1}{2}$ per cent, which is too high a tax;

(5) certain goods, such as raw furs, beaver skins and medical drugs, should receive more favourable treatment in the project;

(6) a duty of 10 per cent on foreign iron might reduce foreign competition to the point of creating a dangerous iron monopoly in France;

(7) foreign white cotton should not be prohibited but regarded to some extent as a raw material;

(8) an export duty of 12 per cent on raw materials might tend to reduce stocks of them by deterring merchants from bringing into the country what they could not take out again;

(9) there must be some assurance that the projected right of *transit* and *entrepôt* will not again be suspended as it was in 1688;

(10) it would be desirable to suppress the royal *péages* if no revenue would be lost thereby;

(11) the *premier président* of the *Parlement of Bordeaux* complains

that the plans include an excessive and unfair duty on goods entering Bordeaux;

(12) de Villedeuil, Intendant of Rouen, complains that one of the local duties of Rouen is owned by the Chamber of Commerce which has contracted debts on the product of it and could not survive the suppression of it unless granted an indemnity;

(13) the duties of the new single tariff must never be raised arbitrarily, nor without taking into account the views of the Chambers of Commerce;

(14) this is such a vast and important reform that it should first be introduced for a trial period during which it could be amended in the light of criticism from various parts of the kingdom;

(15) soaps and oils should not be regarded as exports, because many industries need them as raw materials;

(16) the *prévôt des marchands* in Paris wants the duties reduced on coal entering Paris.[1]

Calonne's memoir to the notables had proposed to put the project into effect from 1 October 1787, but a number of circumstances combined to put off the date indefinitely. One of the strongest supporters of the project, Vergennes, died just before the Notables assembled, and shortly afterwards, on 10 April, Calonne was dismissed. His successor, Bouvard de Fourqueux, was replaced on 3 May by Laurent de Villedeuil who in turn was replaced on 30 August by Claude-Guillaume Lambert. The loss of Vergennes and Calonne and the prolonged ministerial instability had a damaging effect, for each new minister needed time to get a grip on affairs. Fortunately for the reform movement it was favourably regarded by Loménie de Brienne, President of the Royal Council of Finance from the fall of Calonne until August 1788, but he too had to proceed cautiously at first.[2] In May 1787, Boyetet sent a memoir to him urging the immediate execution of the project to offset the effects of the Commercial Treaty with England on French industry;[3] the treaty, signed the previous September, was to

---

[1] *Loc. cit.*

[2] Loménie de Brienne, *Compte rendu*, p. 10.

[3] Edouard Boyetet, *Nouveau recueil de mémoires*, p. 68.

be put into effect very soon. However, in accordance with the observations of the Assembly of Notables, such as those of the second bureau enumerated above, de Brienne asked Cormeré to carry out a general revision of the project and to prepare an abridged version of it.[1] Cormeré revised his work in the light of the customs registers of 1784 and of other material which he obtained from the *Bureau de la balance du commerce*.[2] It would have been possible, as Cormeré said afterwards, to follow Boyetet's suggestion of putting the project into effect provisionally for one year, during which the government could have adjusted the new régime to meet criticisms from different parts of the kingdom. However, de Brienne or de Villedeuil, or both, thought it would be prudent to submit the project once more to the Farmers General and the Deputies of Commerce.[3]

Hence, early in August 1787 the project was turned over to the Farmers General who were supposed to pass it on after a month to the Deputies of Commerce.[4] At the beginning of September, de la Boullaye suggested to the ministry that it would save time if representatives of the Farmers General and the Deputies of Commerce were to form a single committee of which he would be president. With the consent of de Brienne, he assembled four Farmers General and a number of Deputies of Commerce as a committee from which he deliberately excluded Cormeré. The work of this committee was supposed to be completed within a month, but more than six months later Cormeré was impatiently soliciting from the Controller General the results of the committee's work so that he could answer any objections or challenge any damaging amendments to the project. He wrote:

It is possible that Monsieur de la Boullaye's committee not knowing the principles which guided the one presided over by Monsieur de Fourqueux, holds a different opinion on some matters. It is therefore essential that these points of difference be thoroughly examined. But they can be known only if the committee held by Monsieur de la Boullaye will make its report, a report following which the sieur

---

[1] A.N., F^{30} 111, 'Le ministre paraît . . .', and 'Le plan d'uniformité . . .'.

[2] Cormeré, *Rech. fin.*, vol. i, p. 413.

[3] A.N., F^{30} 111, 'Le plan d'uniformité . . .'.

[4] *Loc. cit.* and Cormeré, *Rech. fin.*, vol. i, p. 232; cf. Dupont, *Procès-verbal de l'Assemblée baillivale de Nemours*, p. 334.

de Cormeré will then give his reflexions on the articles which the two committees disagree over.[1]

This view of the matter was reasonable enough because de la Boullaye, having taken practically no part in the proceedings of de Fourqueux's commission, was ignorant of the work on which the project had been based. Cormeré requested that the report of the committee be given to him for one week, after which it could be turned over to Antoine-Nicolas Valdec de Lessart, *maître des requêtes*, who had distinguished himself in an admirable report to the Bureau of Commerce on the question of *entrepôt* and *transit*.[2] De Lessart, as an impartial expert, could report on the project to a committee to be composed primarily of d'Ormesson and de Villedeuil but to which would be admitted Boyetet as a representative of de Fourqueux's commission, de la Boullaye or a representative of his committee, and Cormeré himself as author of the project. Cormeré suggested that if proceedings were begun immediately, the final report could be given to the Royal Council in May 1788 and the necessary laws passed soon afterwards. He grew more and more impatient as he saw that de la Boullaye's committee met rarely and was holding up the project by raising minor difficulties. A second and then a third memoir to the Controller General expressed in passionate terms Cormeré's feelings on the subject.

The ministry has announced this operation as imminent; *each month, each week, each day* of delay causes incalculable harm to trade ... nothing therefore should stop the *execution of the customs project* on next 1 July, the *suppression of the gabelle* on 1 January 1789, and the destruction of all local barriers on the following first day of July.[3]

Boyetet took the same stand in at least one memoir which he sent to the government, and Dupont was also impatient at the delay.[4]

---

[1] A.N., F³⁰ 111, 'Le plan d'uniformité ...'.

[2] For this report in full see A.N., F¹² 107, fols. 112–37 (*Procès-verbal* of the Bureau of Commerce, session of 10 April 1788).

[3] A.N., F³⁰ 111, 'L'exécution du traité ...' and 'Le plan d'uniformité ...'.

[4] Boyetet, 'La lettre du Parlement de Rouen présentée ... ', in A.N., F¹² 658ᴬ; Dupont, *Lettre à la Chambre*, pp. 43, 102 and 177, and *Procès-verbaux de l'Assemblée baillivale de Nemours*, vol. i, p. 334.

At last, in the course of the spring of 1788, Cormeré was allowed to study the work of de la Boullaye's committee,[1] and de Lessart was appointed to study the whole project and to report especially on the points of difference between the conclusions of de la Boullaye's committee and de Fourqueux's commission.[2] These were well-worn differences, such as whether or not the project would entail a loss of revenue. The Farmers General objected once again that there would be a loss of ten million *livres* and de la Boullaye supported them, even though de Colonia had proved, the last time this question had been raised, that there would be no losses.[3] Another difference was over maximum tariff rates. Cormeré had always maintained, in conformity with Necker's views in 1780 and those of de Fourqueux's commission in 1786, that duties of more than 15 per cent should not be imposed because they encouraged smuggling, and that 12 or 15 per cent would be enough to protect industry from foreign competition once the internal duties had been abolished.[4] De la Boullaye insisted that a maximum of 30 per cent would be needed.

This discussion went on for a long time, and in the meantime the government, considering the project to be of the greatest importance, reserved it for the attention of the Royal Council on Finance and Commerce.[5] The Bureau of Commerce was to deal with it only when invited to do so by the Royal Council. Although the project does not appear to have been discussed at all in the Bureau of Commerce before this rule was made, some of the problems which it raised occupied the best part of two meetings in April 1788. On the 10th, de Lessart gave a thorough report on the questions of *entrepôt* and *transit* in the course of

[1] A.N., F^30 111 contains a double sheet of paper bearing a note: 'Monsieur de la Boullaye a l'honneur de remettre à Monsieur le Contrôleur Général 1° la nouvelle ordonnance des traites proposée par le Comité et qui a éprouvé de légers changements dans quelques articles d'après les observations que M. de Lessart lui a communiquées, 2° une notice des motifs qui ont dirigé le Comite dans la réflexion du projet du nouveau tarif . . . '.

[2] Cormeré, *Rech. fin.*, vol. i, pp. 8 and 232.

[3] Cf. Loménie de Brienne, *Compte rendu*, p. 10.

[4] Cormeré, *Rech. fin.*, vol. i, p. 258; A.N., F^30 111, 'Le ministère paraît . . . '.

[5] This council was created by an edict of 5 June 1787 which combined the separate councils on Finance and Commerce. The Bureau of Commerce, temporarily suspended by the same law, was revived and its composition and functions defined in a *Règlement* of 2 February 1788. (A copy in A.N., F^4 1032².)

which he defended the usefulness of these freedoms and firmly contradicted the views of de la Boullaye and his committee.[1] At the conclusion of the meeting it was resolved that the main part of the project, that is, the reduction of all customs barriers to a single one on the frontiers, should be carried out first, after which the questions of *entrepôt* and *transit* could be decided in the light of experience of the reformed system. Some less important issues were raised at the meeting of 17 April, such as whether declarations of merchandise should be verified by quantity, weight, measure or number, and whether customs clerks should continue to add 10 per cent to the declared value of goods. On most of these questions the meeting adopted the views of de la Boullaye's committee with very little discussion.

Work on the project continued through the spring, and a report to the Controller General dated 30 June 1788 shows that it was by no means approaching completion even then. Although the *ordonnance* and the tariff were ready, and the study of trade privileges nearly finished, de la Boullaye was still working on the question of provincial rights and privileges and Cormeré was preparing a report on trade with the Indies. The latter question, along with others relating to colonial and foreign trade and the free ports, were yet to be discussed with the Marine Department. The report estimated that the project would not be ready for another three months.[2]

It was not ready in three months, however, nor in six. Necker had resumed control of finances in August 1788, and on 24 March 1789 Cormeré wrote a long letter to him outlining the project, which he said had been substantially finished long before, and complaining bitterly that it was being held up only by the subversive efforts of de la Boullaye and the Farmers General.[3] Not long afterwards, Cormeré published this letter as the introduction to his *Recherches et considérations nouvelles sur les finances*, in which he summarized his work on the single duty project. He was determined to do all in his power to interest the forthcoming Estates General in this and other financial reforms on which he and his staff had worked so long in the face of

---

[1] A.N., F^{12} 107, *Procès-verbaux* of the Bureau of Commerce, 4 April 1788 and later.
[2] A.N., F^{30} 111, *Note sur le travail des traites*, probably written by de Lessart.
[3] Quoted in full in Cormeré, *Rech. fin.*, vol. i, pp. 1–57.

jealousy, opposition and administrative confusion. In his *Observations à Messieurs les électeurs de la ville et vicomté de Paris*, he urged that the deputies to the forthcoming Estates General should read his account of the project and act upon it. By that time, his voice was only one of many. Public opinion, expressed in print and in attacks on the trade barriers, so impressed the National Assembly that, as Marion says, 'Everyone was agreed on the necessity of suppressing the duties of the interior and at the same time maintaining those on the frontiers'.[1] Thus the *ancien régime* passed on to the Revolution the problem of the internal duties which it had discussed so long.

[1] Marcel Marion, *Histoire financière*, vol. ii, p. 236; and 'Le recouvrement des impots en 1790', *Rev. hist.*, tome cxxi, 1916, p. 35; A.N., H 1441, letter from Soissons dated 8 August 1789, reporting the destruction of customs barriers.

CHAPTER VI

The State of Public Opinion on the Eve of the Revolution

BY 1789, French public opinion, taken over the whole country, was overwhelmingly in favour of internal free trade and of a single protective customs barrier on the national frontiers. This is shown by the general *cahiers de doléances* of which, out of a total of 522 studied by Beatrice Hyslop, 291 requested the immediate execution of this reform, 13 were favourably disposed towards it but with qualifications, and only 24 were opposed.[1] To take first the provinces of the *Cinq Grosses Fermes*, all their *cahiers* which expressed opinions on the subject supported customs reform. Other evidence, too, tends to support this impression of unanimity. The *épiciers* of Anger, for instance, wrote to the Controller General early in 1787: 'Weighted down by a host of local duties, the commerce of Anjou dares to beg your protection. . . .'.[2] The *juges et consuls* of Paris, of Orléans, of Chalon-sur-Saône, and many other towns wrote of the necessity of removing the customs barriers to the frontiers.[3] A book by a writer from Picardy, of which two editions were published in 1789, reviewed in impressive detail the damaging effects of the various obstacles to trade on the economy of the province and devoted a long passage to the problems involved in removing all barriers to the frontiers.[4] The provincial assemblies of Rouen, Ile-de-France and Orléanais, and the Chamber of Commerce of Normandy, all demanded the rapid conclusion of the single duty project.[5]

[1] B. F. Hyslop, *French Nationalism*, pp. 56–58.
[2] A.N., F12 828, letter and memoir of the Bureau syndic, Anger, 6 March 1787.
[3] A.N., C 9.   [4] Durand, *Considérations politiques*, pp. 60–72.
[5] P.-S. Dupont, *Lettre à la Chambre*, pp. 35 and 177; A.N., F12 658A, letter of 20 February 1789; Pierre Renouvin, *Les Assemblées provinciales*, p. 233; cf. A.N., F12 658A, précis of the *procès-verbal* sent to the Controller General on 1 December 1787.

The overwhelming weight of favourable opinion stands out all the more in contrast to the few rare expressions of opposition. Thus the representatives of the *toiles peintes* industry defended the internal duties and opposed the reform project because they feared the competition of Alsatian *toiles peintes* hitherto excluded from the area of the *Cinq Grosses Fermes*.[1]

In the Provinces Reputed Foreign, except for Brittany, the project appears to have drawn considerable support. Earlier in the century, the powerful wine interests of Guyenne had opposed all plans for a French customs union, but in the 1780's neither the *procès-verbaux* of the provincial assemblies nor the *cahiers de doléances* of the region betrayed any marked opposition. This was partly because the wine interests of Bordeaux, having lost their special privileges by an edict which Turgot drew up in 1776, had been reconciled to the prospect of reform; and partly because the latter project was clearly not a money-making device of the Farmers General and provided for little or no export duty on wine. The permanent commission of the provincial assembly of Haute-Guyenne had discussed the freeing of trade by means of customs reform as early as 1784 and in that year proposed to submit a plan to the government.[2] Eventually a general petition from the wine-growers of Guyenne, Périgord and Quercy persuaded the government to suspend the export duties on wine in all the ports of the Generality of Guyenne from the beginning of 1787.[3] Again, in June 1788 the Intendants of Languedoc, Auch, Béarn and Montauban solicited the abolition of the internal duties partly on the grounds that there was widespread agitation among merchants and industrialists. Meanwhile, as Pierre Léon records in his book, *La Naissance de la grande industrie en Dauphiné*, many merchants of Dauphiné were also protesting against internal duties.[4]

Feelings in Lyon were mixed, for there were many people

---

[1] Comte R. de Sèze, *Mémoire et consultation*, p. 9: ' . . . pour conserver l'équilibre entre les manufactures de l'intérieur du royaume et les manufactures d'Alsace, il est absolument nécessaire d'imposer un droit sur les toiles peintes et blanches de cette province'.

[2] *Procès-verbal des séances de l'Assemblée provinciale de Haute-Guienne tenue à Villefranche* (1779 to 1786), Paris, 1787, vol. 2, p. 56. Dion, *Histoire de la vigne*, p. 393.

[3] Comte de la Roque (in the name of the Deputies of Périgord), *Droits de traité*, p. 5.

[4] A.N., F12 650, dossier, 'Offices rélatives au commerce, 1788'; and Pierre Léon, *La Naissance*, p. 152.

with a personal interest in maintaining the extensive customs administration of that city. Customs employees such as the *maîtres crocheteurs* and the *affâneurs commissionés* were intent upon keeping their jobs.[1] When it became apparent that reform was inevitable, powerful interests attempted to secure the establishment of a *bureau de vérification* in Lyon such as the government intended to set up in Paris.[2] However, in 1790 the Society of Friends of the Constitution in Lyon attacked these interests and gave active support to the single duty project, as did many local merchants and industrialists.[3] It was a Deputy from Lyon, a silk merchant named Louis-Pierre Goudard, who led the final attack on the internal duties in the Constituent Assembly. In the towns of Saint Etienne and Saint Chamond, not far from Lyon, manufacturers gilds as early as 1779 had demanded that their merchandise be allowed to circulate freely throughout the country,[4] and in the province of Auvergne feeling against the internal duties had been very strong, as the *procès-verbal* of the provincial assembly shows.[5] In Franché Comté opinion was divided. Here there was a widespread provincial loyalty which often favoured the maintenance of provincial 'privileges'. Since there were guards and bureaux on every frontier many people's jobs depended upon the maintenance of the *status quo*, and those whose interests lay in foreign trade, legitimate or otherwise, were against any reforms that would strengthen the barriers along the eastern frontier of the province. But only one *cahier de doléance*, that of the nobles of Besançon, was opposed to the single duty project.[6] In 1780, an Inspector of Manufactures, Antoine-François Brisson, reported of Franché Comté that 'the existence of internal bureaux seems intolerable to the manufacturers, to the merchants, and to all the inhabitants of the mountains'.[7] Miss Hyslop concludes that, judging from the

[1] *Observations des Maîtres crocheteurs et affâneurs commissionés.*

[2] A.N., F³⁰ 111, *Mémoire que l'on croit important que la Ferme générale connaîsse avant la clôture de son travail sur le reculement aux frontières des douanes du royaume*, 38 fols.

[3] *Avis aux négotiants de Lyon.*

[4] A.N., F¹² 831, *Mémoire* of July 1779, prepared in the bureau of de Cotte.

[5] *Procès-verbal des séances de l'Assemblée provinciale d'Auvergne . . .*, 2 vols., Clermont-Ferrand, vol. ii, p. 285.

[6] Hyslop, *French Nationalism*, p. 57.

[7] A.N., F¹² 650, *Cahiers faisant partie des mémoires d'une tournée en Franche-Comté faite par . . .* : 'Sur l'état de la Franche Comté rélativement aux traites', 14 fols.

K

general *cahiers de doléances*, the generalities of Moulins, Riom, Lyon, Grenoble, Aix, Montpellier, Toulouse, Auch, Bordeaux, Montauban, Limoges, La Rochelle, Besançon and Dijon all favoured the abolition of the internal customs duties.[1]

Brittany, long regarded as the arch-enemy of the project, was strangely inactive compared with the north-eastern provinces. At the Assembly of Notables, the Breton representatives had not submitted memoirs of protest but had simply announced that they could speak only as private individuals about the liberties and privileges of their province which must therefore be excepted from any reforms planned.[2] But by 1789, according to the *cahiers de doléances*, opinion was decidedly in favour of the single duty project. There were two important reasons for this change. First, the greatest cause of opposition had undoubtedly been the fear that if the province joined a national customs union it would have to submit to the *gabelle*. Brittany had been the chief opponent of any plans for imposing the *gabelle* equally throughout the kingdom.[3] When it became apparent, however, that the *gabelle* was likely to be abolished at least as soon as the internal barriers, Breton opposition to customs union with the rest of France largely disappeared. Another reason is that certain industrial and commercial interests which traditionally preferred the freedom to trade abroad to the freedom to trade with France, believed they had suffered badly from the competition of British goods after the Commercial Treaty of 1786, and like many industrial and commercial interests on the frontiers they now wanted a strong protective customs barrier.[4]

In the northern provinces opinion was mixed, but there too industrial decline attributed to the damaging effect of British competition caused strong support for the single duty project. For instance, on 25 March 1788, Tolozan, director of commer-

[1] Hyslop, *French Nationalism*, p. 57.

[2] *Procès-verbal et observations présentés au Roi par les bureaux de l'Assemblée des Notables*, Versailles, 1787, second part, p. 55.

[3] See for instance, *Dialogue entre Monsieur A . . . Député à l'Assemblée nationale, Monsieur B . . . Fermier général, et Monsieur le Baron de C . . . sur les impositions indirectes*, 790, p. 40.

[4] A.N., F12 650, 'Offices rélatives au commerce'.

cial affairs, wrote to the Deputies of the Estates of Walloon Flanders:

I have received, Messieurs, the memoir in which you explain that the trade in woollen cloth manufactured in your province will be entirely destroyed if we do not suppress the duties levied in the internal bureaux of the kingdom.[1]

Early in 1790, the Chamber of Commerce of Lille seconded the sugar refiners of French Flanders in their demands for the reduction of export duties on sugar and the removal of the internal customs.[2] The *cahiers de doléances* reveal that even those who were not in favour of the project limited themselves to a demand for compensation if it were carried out. In the generality of Lille, three cahiers gave enthusiastic approval and three wanted compensation; in the generality of Valencienne four approved outright and two wanted compensation.[3]

In the smaller free territories also opinion was divided. The *pays de Gex* was generally in favour of maintaining its independence.[4] Marseille, which was to keep certain privileges after the reform of 1790, was jealous of its status as a free port. On the other hand, Bayonne and the *pays de Labour* were undecided. In 1784, as a result of agreements made by Vergennes at the Treaty of Versailles the previous year, Bayonne was granted full privileges as a free port by *lettres patentes* of 21 September and 4 July, the duc de Gramont being paid an indemnity of 12,000 *livres* a month for the suppression of the *coûtume de Bayonne*.[5] Later, we find the Deputy of Commerce for that city, Boyetet des Bordes, protesting to the Constituent Assembly that it was essential for Bayonne and for France to maintain that freedom.[6] However, a report of 25 November 1790 to the Assembly declared that there was a strong faction in Bayonne in favour

[1] A.N., F^{12} 157.
[2] Gerbaux and Schmidt, *Procès-verbaux des Comités*, sessions of 20 Jan. and 10 Feb. 1790.
[3] Hyslop, *French Nationalism* p. 57; and *Réflexions sur la nécessité de l'existence des douanes dans les Pays-Bas autrichiens . . .*, p. 45.
[4] Felix Gerlier, *Voltaire, Turgot, et les franchises*, 84 pp.
[5] A.N., F^4 70, DX1 and DX3. The National Assembly abolished the indemnity by decree of 2 Dec. 1790 with effect from 1 Jan. 1791. In Feb. 1791 Gramont applied to the Committee on Finance for redress.
[6] Boyetet des Bordes, *Précis sur la franchise*. The author is not Edouard Boyetet, although they are confused in the general catalogue of the *Bibliothèque nationale*.

of including the city within the national protective barrier, and that even the Chamber of Commerce had been forced to admit that the freedom of the city had favoured trade in foreign rather than French goods.[1] The controversy over the free ports became very involved and was hardly settled even when the Convention abolished free ports on 27 February 1794.[2]

The argument over the single duty project was most vigorous in the provinces of Alsace, Trois-Evêchés and Lorraine. The wine interests, both growers and merchants, raised vociferous and powerful opposition because they were fearful that the removal of the barriers to the frontiers would not only destroy their foreign trade, but would place them on an equal footing with the wine interests of the rest of France. Between them and the industrial interests which, although less outspoken, were in favour of the project, there was a great variety of opinion.

'One could never imagine the Alsatians accepting with pleasure the union of their province with those of the *Cinq Grosses Fermes* . . . .', wrote Lazowski, an Inspector of Manufactures, after touring Alsace in 1785.[3] This was an understatement, for the difficulties were so great that Cormeré thought the province would have to be left out of the national customs union. However, in order not to arouse the jealousy of Lorraine and Trois-Evêchés there was no special mention of Alsace in the project as presented to the Assembly of Notables. It was thought politic to make the distinction later when the representations of all three provinces had been duly weighed. Thus Alsace felt just as much threatened as the other two, and at the Assembly of Notables several of her representatives, notably the baron de Spon, first president of the sovereign council of Colmar, the baron de Flachslanden, the maréchal de Broglie, and the maréchal de Contades, attacked the project.[4] But when the government proposed to make an exception of Alsace, it

---

[1] Lasnier de Vaussenay (vice-president of the Committee on Agriculture and Commerce), *Rapport à l'Assemblée nationale.*

[2] Paul Masson, *Les Ports francs*; and the pamphlets in the British Museum, F.R. 541, 542, 580, 581, &c.

[3] A.N., F12 565, *Précis du journal de tournée de Monsieur de Lazowski en 1785 dans les provinces d'Alsace, la Lorraine et les Trois Evêchés*, 57 fols.

[4] *Procès-verbal et observations présentés au Roi par les bureaux de l'Assemblée des Notables*, Versailles, 1787, pp. 38 ff.; A.N., C 2, *Procès-verbaux du deuxième bureau de l'Assemblée des Notables*, 15e séance, 19 March 1787.

succeeded only in infuriating some supporters of the project in Lorraine and Trois-Evêchés.[1]

Opposition to the project was not unanimous in Alsace: the manufacturers were in sympathy with it. Reports show the strength of their support as early as 1770.[2] On 20 March 1787 the baron de Dietrich sent to Calonne an impressive number of petitions by the owners of forges, glass-works, dye-works and textile and other industries, all in favour of customs protection for their province, or of the removal of the internal barriers, or both.[3] The Alsatian industrial interests claimed that there was much more support for the project than appeared on the surface,[4] but the permanent commission of the provincial assembly, 'impressed with the alarm it saw spreading everywhere in the province over the removal of the barriers', circulated a *Programme* in November 1788 urging all those interested to submit their ideas so that all points of view could be studied and a report submitted to the National Assembly.[5] The weight of sentiment in the province against the project is indicated by the fact that seven *cahiers de doléances* opposed it and none gave it support.

For geographical reasons the Trois Evêchés was damaged more than Alsace by the internal duties, and also benefited less from free foreign trade. The project therefore found more support there than in Alsace, but even so most opinion was hostile. An Inspector of Manufactures, Alard, maintained that industry in the Trois Evêchés was hampered more by the *foraine* and by the barriers of the *Cinq Grosses Fermes* than by almost anything else,[6] and certainly the industrial interests were in agreement with this view. However, as early as February 1789 the Estates of Metz prepared an attack on the project which they sent to the representatives of the province in the Assembly of Notables.[7] Basing their calculations upon statis-

---

[1] A.N., 29 AP 81, Roederer to Brienne (?), 26 April 1788.

[2] A.N., F12 827, correspondence of d'Aigrefeuille.

[3] A.N., H 1448, (papers from the Bureau of Calonne, no. 5).

[4] *Aperçu sur le reculement des barrières jusqu'au Rhin*, p. 22.

[5] *Précis des opérations de la Commission intermédiaire*, p. 21. The question was discussed under the head, 'Bien Public'! Cf. Renouvin, *Les Ass. Prov.*, p. 223. *Programme*, Strasbourg, 19 Nov. 1788, 3 pp.

[6] A.N., F12 650, *Rapport du procès-verbal de la tournée faite aux mois de Juin et Juillet, 1789 dans la généralité de Metz, par M. Alard, Inspecteur des manufactures.*

[7] *Précis pour les Trois-Etats.*

tics taken from a memoir by Mahy de Cormeré,[1] they tried to show that foreign trade was the mainstay of the province and that except for a few manufacturers all citizens had an interest in maintaining the *status quo*. In the Assembly of Notables, Hocquart, a *premier président du parlement de Metz*, attacked the project in a long memoir of 21 March 1787.[2] The day before, a similar dignitary from the parlement at Nancy, Cœur de Roi, had made an assault on the project on behalf of the Trois Evêchés as well as Lorraine,[3] and Lambert had read a reply to Cœur de Roi prepared in the *Contrôle général*. This memoir from the *Contrôle général* was published together with much scathing criticism by the *Corps consulaire* and the merchants of Metz.[4] Later in 1787, the provincial assembly of Trois Evêchés appointed a commission to examine the project, but the report it submitted on 3 December did little more than repeat the criticism of earlier writers.[5] This report was itself reviewed critically by Pierre-Louis Roederer (1754–1835), a *conseiller au Parlement de Metz*, who was one of the most active and outspoken champions of the project in the provinces of Lorraine and Trois Evêchés.[6] The *cahiers de doléances*, like the many letters of encouragement and other papers preserved in his collected works, show that Roederer was not without support: seven from the generality of Metz approved the project, and only eight opposed it.[7]

In Lorraine, the question of customs union with France was raised much earlier than in other provinces. When in 1773 the

[1] The calculations in the large folding table are Cormeré's work. This table, reprinted in three subsequent pamphlets, is identified in a footnote to it in *Procés-verbal des séances de l'Assemblée provinciale des Trois Evêchés et Clermontois*, Metz, 1787.

[2] *Procès-verbal et observations présentés au Roi par les bureaux de l'Assemblée des Notables*, Versailles, 1787, p. 23.

[3] A.N., C 2, *Procès-verbaux du deuxième bureau de l'Assemblée des Notables*, session of 20 March 1787, 25 fols. A copy of Coeur du Roi's paper in Bib. Mazarine, ms. 2406.

[4] *Mémoire et observations pour et contre*. The original in the *procès-verbaux* (A.N., C 2) is entitled *Mémoire sur l'intérêt de la Lorraine, des Trois Evêchés et de l'Alsace*, 18 fols. These each contain a copy of Cormeré's table.

[5] *Procès-verbal des séances de l'Assemblée provinciale des Trois-Evêchés et du Clermontois*, Metz, 1787, pp. 232–45.

[6] Roederer, *Réflexions sur le rapport*; Roederer, *Œuvres*; and A.N., 29 AP 81, 85 and 86 (*fonds Roederer*).

[7] Roederer, *Œuvres*, vol. vii, p. 441; Hyslop, *French Nationalism*, p. 56.

French Academy offered a prize for the best *éloge de Colbert*, Joseph-François Coster, the famous Lorraine adversary of the Trudaines's project, took the opportunity to discuss it and to condemn it once again,[1] whereas Necker in his entry (which won the prize) made no mention of it, contenting himself with a brief favourable review of Colbert's attempts to reform the customs system.[2] It is certain, despite his tactful silence, that Necker was as strongly in sympathy with the project as Coster was opposed to it, and in 1778 he proposed in a long letter to the chief magistrates of Lorraine that the province should enter into a customs union with France immediately.

It has long been said, he wrote, that the only way to restore your manufactures is to remove the barriers which lie between France and Lorraine and to transfer them to the limits of the province on the foreign side . . . It is not a question, at the moment, of the uniform tariff; but while waiting for conditions to allow us to return to it, should not Lorraine join the *Cinq Grosses Fermes*, accepting the customs duties as they are now?[3]

In this way, he continued, the *foraine* of the province with its expensive apparatus of more than 700 bureaux could be abolished, but none of the other provincial privileges would suffer. He begged the provincial authorities to send favourable observations on this plan, proposed in the interests of Lorraine, so that steps could be taken to carry it out.

This letter caused a stir in Lorraine similar to that caused by Bertin's letter in 1761. According to Rousselot de Surgy, the greater merchants whose interests lay in free trade across the foreign frontier again called upon Coster to submit a formal protest against the project.[4] The most important response came from the Parlement of Nancy, whose *Observations sur le projet de réunir la Province de Lorraine aux Cinq Grosses Fermes*, drawn up on 12 December 1778, although on the whole unfavourable to the project, is nevertheless a careful and sensible review of

---

[1] Coster, *Eloge de Colbert*, p. 56.

[2] Necker, *Eloge de Jean-Baptiste Colbert*, p. 17.

[3] Necker's letter is fully quoted in Rousselot de Surgy, *Enc. méth.* article, 'Lorraine'.

[4] *Loc. cit.* The memoir by Coster was probably the *Premières idées sur le Tarif* (1779) which the merchants of Lorraine sent to Blondel (Intendant of Commerce) in 1786. Cf. Prugnon, *Aperçu des motifs*, p. 106; and Robert Parisot, *Histoire de Lorraine*, vol. ii.

the main issues. The Parlement praised the single duty project of 1761 for its intention to free internal trade from 'that mass of regulations whose number and variety defy human understanding and whose obscurity frightens commerce as much as it favours the greed of its own supporters'.[1] Such a plan, it continued, might well require a sacrifice of provincial interests to those of the whole country, but since Necker's proposal involves Lorraine alone we must follow his example and consider only the welfare of our own province. After summing up the effects of the project upon the interests of the consumer, the landowner, the manufacturer, the merchant, the state in general and the province in particular, it concluded that on the whole the province would lose and that for France in general there would be no substantial advantage. However, it admitted that the matter was immensely complicated and ought to be studied at length before any final decisions were taken.

As in the 1760's, the manufacturers were strongly in favour of the plan, but according to Brisson, who toured Lorraine in 1780, they were wary of saying so, 'because they were afraid of vexing on the one hand the owners of the vines, many of whom are their relatives, protectors, &c., and on the other hand the merchants whose co-operation they need every day'.[2]

Many of the writings provoked by the project submitted to Assembly of Notables, such as Roederer's *Observations sur les intérêts des Trois Evêchés et de la Lorraine rélativement au reculement des barrières des traites*,[3] dealt with the Trois Evêchés and Lorraine together, whereas others, notably two attacks on the project, were concerned only with the fate of Lorraine.[4] There was more favourable opinion in Lorraine than in the Trois Evêchés so that the two called for separate treatment, especially after it had become apparent late in 1787 that the provincial assembly of Lorraine could not agree on whether to accept or to reject the project.[5] It was then that Roederer wrote his *Questions proposées*

[1] A manuscript copy of this document, dated 1780, in Arch. Ass. Pub., papers of Auget de Montyon.

[2] A.N., F12 650, *Cahiers faisant partie des mémoires d'une tournée en Lorraine, faite par Monsieur Brisson en 1780*, No. 6, 'Sur l'état fiscal de la Lorraine rélativement aux traites', 17 fols.

[3] 1787, 24 pp.   [4] (1) Prugnon, *Aperçu des motifs*; (2) *Réflexions d'un solitaire*.

[5] Pierre Renouvin, *Les Ass. Prov.*, p. 223.

par la Commission intermédiaire de Lorraine concernant le reculement des barrières et observations pour servir de réponse à ces questions, to attempt to sway the balance in the assembly.[1] The assembly decided against the project but of the *cahiers de doléances* only seven were against it whereas seventeen were in favour.

The last decade of the *ancien régime* brought a profusion of written and recorded comment on the question of internal duties. It is difficult to say just how far the increase of books and pamphlets on the subject indicates greater public interest or how far it merely reflects a more relaxed censorship and cheaper publishing facilities. Such written evidence as there is suggests that earlier in the century interest was stronger than the small amount of published opinion might lead one to suspect.[2] Even so, the debate on the single duty project during the 1780's certainly aroused more public interest than had the discussion of earlier projects. The *cahiers de doléances* show this, for they contain a chorus of demands for 'le reculement des barrières' and 'la suppression des douanes intérieures'.

The evidence warrants no precise statement of the amount or the rapidity of the growth of public opinion, but it does at least suggest certain conclusions about the nature of opinion. First of all, some merchants and most manufacturers were in favour of the single duty project; but what must be emphasized is that the official side of commercial and industrial interests, namely, the Deputies of Commerce and the Inspectors of Manufactures, were also in favour. Even more important, in their common struggle against the internal duties, the official side of these interests adopted a strikingly different approach from that of the private side. Merchants and manufacturers were on the whole absorbed in their own personal, municipal, provincial, or regional conditions of supply, production, transport and sale. They were used to petitioning for privileges, and the freedoms they solicited were really privileges to be bestowed as a mark of favour. It was not 'freedom' in general but specific 'freedoms' which they wanted, and their requests were intended, as often as not, to secure a monopoly or to put competitors at a disadvantage. Government favour was thus a weapon in the

[1] 1787, 222 pp. Cf. de Lannoy, *Comité des Finances*.
[2] *Supra*, p. 44.

private warfare of commercial competition. National considerations, even in the face of foreign competition, were usually secondary. Thus, the import-export businesses in the Foreign Provinces and free ports wanted to preserve the 'freedom' of their provinces and ports from the national customs union even if it meant the ruin of industry. Conversely, industrial interests were in favour of the single duty project only because they thought it would afford them protection against foreign competition and would open larger domestic markets. The characteristic attitude of the merchant and manufacturer is shown in petitions not for general reform but for personal exemption from specific internal duties.

Such petitions were received by the *Contrôle général* and passed on to the Deputies of Commerce whose reports on them show a much different attitude to the problem of the internal duties. In the 1780's, as in the 1760's, the assembled Deputies often refused to support these petitions on the grounds that no privileged merchant or manufacturer would have anything to gain from the single duty project and would even suffer from the project because by freeing internal trade altogether it would rob him of his privileges. When the glass manufacturers of Trois Evêchés submitted a request for a reduction of the duties of the *Cinq Grosses Fermes*, the Deputies refused to support it on the grounds that 'this exemption would sustain in those provinces a harmful resistance to their union with the kingdom in respect of customs'.[1] They refused a similar request from the manufacturers of Sedan 'because plans are being made to remove the customs to the frontiers and to institute a uniform tariff, and their results will undoubtedly bear upon these matters . . . '.[2] The Inspectors of Manufactures in their reports also supported the general reform project rather than the requests of individual firms. Thus the private side and the official side of the trading and manufacturing world approached the problem of the internal duties in two quite different and sometimes contradictory ways.

---

[1] A.N., F12 724, *Avis des Députés du commerce du 23 août 1788.*

[2] A.N., F12 724, (1) *avis sur la demande du Sieur Cora, 29 July 1788*; (2) *avis sur la demande des selliers de Strasbourg, 14 June 1789*; (3) *avis sur la demande que font les intéressés aux rafineries de sucre de Toulon et de la Ciotat, 15 May 1789.*

The study of public opinion suggests, furthermore, that the views of officials on the problem of the internal duties were, on the whole, a great deal better informed and more carefully considered than those of merchants and manufacturers. All the good books were written by officials. The reason is obvious: not only did officials take a larger and more impersonal view of the problem, but they had access to information quite out of the reach of the common citizen and were closer to the planning of the reform project, even when they were not actually involved in it. The reform called for an understanding of difficult and sometimes technical matters which did not interest most merchants and manufacturers. Who among them showed himself as well-informed on customs matters as Necker in his *Compte rendu au Roi* and *De L'Administration des finances de la France*, or Mahy de Cormeré in his *Recherches et considérations nouvelles sur les finances*?

Another official with an outstanding grasp of the customs system and its shortcomings was Vivent Magnien. He is a shadowy figure and what little the dictionaries of biography write about him is full of errors, but there can be no doubt of his importance in the history of the reform movement. Born in Chalon-sur-Saône in 1744 or 1745, he attended school in Nantes and then entered the service of the Farmers General in 1764.[1] In 1785, by which time he had become a *premier commis* in the middle ranks of the customs service at Lyon, he was called to Paris to assist in the projected reform of the customs and later ordered to work with Cormeré.[2] Engaged on 1 October 1789 by the Committee of Agriculture and Commerce for work on the single duty project, Magnien was several times praised for his labours and eventually rewarded with an appointment to the post of *régisseur* of the

[1] *Etat des Régisseurs des douanes.*

[2] Acting on Calonne's orders, de Colonia authorized the payment of a salary of 3,000 *livres* annually to Magnien by a letter dated 31 Jan. 1786 (A.N., DVI 8; DX 2, *Etat des pensions accordées par MM. les Fermiers generaux* . . .). Proof of actual payment is in A.N., G¹ 46, which registers quarterly payments of 750 *livres* on 1 April 1788, 2 July 1788, etc. Also Mahy de Cormeré, *Recherches et considérations sur l'impôt*, Paris, 1790, p. 136. And Gerbaux and Schmidt, *Procès-verbaux du Comité*, sessions of 3 March 1790, 2 May 1791, 11 Nov. 1791 and 21 Nivose An III. Note that these editors, in their comments, are wrong about Magnien's name, the title of his book and the publication date.

customs on 1 May 1791. When a decree of 14 October 1792 reduced the number of *régisseurs* from eight to three he retained his post and appears to have held it almost until his death in 1811. What probably brought Magnien to the notice of the government in 1785 (and what brings him to our attention now) was a learned reference work on the customs which was published in 1786, apparently with financial assistance from Calonne.[1] In the introducton he wrote a passage to which he later referred with justifiable pride and which established him in the front rank of the reformers:

How much longer are these disparities, which hinder the movement of trade, going to last? Are we not soon to see the customs carried to the extreme frontiers and uniformity imposed on import and export duties throughout the kingdom? The devotion of the government to the welfare of commerce and the choice of persons which it employs to attend to the work involved in its revival are a sure guarantee that this vast and important project will be put into effect as soon as it is possible to reconcile the facilities demanded by national trade with the necessity of assuring the maintenance of the single barrier that will separate us from foreign countries . . . [2]

Just as enthusiastic, though less directly concerned in planning the single duty project, was Jacques-Philibert Rousselot de Surgy, the principal author of the *Encyclopédie méthodique, partie Finances* (1784–87).[3] In several learned articles in this book— 'Droits', 'Tarif', 'Traites', 'Finances', 'Bureau', 'Lorraine', and others—he left no doubt as to his attitude to the customs system. 'The pernicious effects of the internal duties are so striking', he wrote, 'that all ministers zealous for the happiness of the nation have sought means to end them.'[4] He had the highest opinion of Necker, even going so far as to declare him the equal of Sully and Colbert because of his plans for customs and other financial and administrative reforms.[5] De Surgy offered an elaborate set

---

[1] A.N., DX 1 (8e liasse), *Pensions accordées dans le département des finances sous le ministère de Monsieur de Calonne*, containing the entry: 'Magnien (Vivent), auteur d'un recueil des droits de tarif des traites. Par décision du ministre la somme de 1,800 *livres*, le 19 Decembre 1785.'

[2] Vivent Magnien, *Recueil alphabétique*, vol. i, p. cxxviii, 'Observations finale'.

[3] Paris (Panckoucke), 1784–7, 3 vols.

[4] *Ibid.*, article, 'Droit'.

[5] *Ibid.*, article, 'Contrôleur général des finances'.

of his own plans, which resembled those of Cormeré, and he heartily approved of the project that was presented to the Assembly of Notables.[1] His knowledge of the customs was by no means merely academic because for several years he served as a *premier commis* in the *Contrôle général* where he was in charge of affairs relating to the *traites*.[2] Cormeré thought so highly of de Surgy that he recommended him in 1791 to the Committee on Public Contributions as their best choice for the post of director of a bureau to supervise government accounts.[3]

Yet another reforming official was Jean-François Tolozan, who from the middle of 1787 to 1789 was the sole Intendant of Commerce and virtually the director of internal commercial affairs. In a book published in 1789 he wrote:

It is to be hoped that this great work [the single duty project], which we regard as one of the most important for national prosperity, will soon be finished, and we announce that the tariff is quite ready. But how can it be put into effect if the Foreign Provinces or those 'reputed foreign' do not wish to give up their privileges?[4]

The Constituent Assembly was soon to answer Tolozan's question, defeating all opposition by using the force of public desire for a national customs union. If public interest in this reform, nourished by the writings of officials, became an invaluable weapon in the hands of the Constituent Assembly, the government's single duty project remained the heart and soul of the reform movement. To this project we must now return.

[1] *Ibid.*, article, 'Traites'.
[2] *Supra*, p. 118.
[3] Mahy de Cormeré, *Situation exacte des finances*, p. 27.
[4] Tolozan, *Mémoire sur le commerce*, p. 77.

CHAPTER VII

The Reform Movement during the Revolution

THE Revolution inherited the single duty project from the *ancien régime* in a very real sense. The plans that had been prepared were presented to the committees of the Constituent Assembly, which continued to make use of Cormeré and his staff, of the *Bureau de la balance du commerce*, of the Deputies of Commerce, of the Farmers General and of Vivent Magnien. Necker, Lambert and de Lessart continued to play important roles in economic administration, and the committees of the Assembly, which in this matter replaced the commissions and committees of the Royal Councils, included among their members Roederer and Dupont de Nemours. Much the same problems were discussed. National financial needs were just as pressing as before, the opposed provinces still had to be considered, the new single tariff had to be worked out, it had to be decided whether to preserve the free ports, and there were still many with a personal interest in maintaining the internal duties. So far as the single duty project is concerned, the only real difference between the royal government and the revolutionary government is that the later was able to override opposition and execute the project whereas the former could not.

As early as 9 September 1789, the Committee on Agriculture and Commerce of the Constituent Assembly resolved 'to procure the work of Monsieur de Cormeré and to prepare to confer with the First Minister of Finances on the suppression of the internal barriers'.[1] In the meeting of 7 November, the president passed

---

[1] Gerbaux and Schmidt, *Procès-verbaux*, vol. i, 21 Sept. 1789. The work the Committee refers to is Cormeré, *Rech. fin.*

on to the Committee the draft of an *ordonnance* and a tariff, part of the single duty project which he had received from Lambert, and one of the Committee members asked that Cormeré should be invited to attend the meetings in which the project would be discussed.[1] The Committee did not disapprove and reserved the right to invite Cormeré, who was in fact admitted to the meeting of 23 November. On that occasion he presented the Committee with two copies of his *Recherches et considérations nouvelles sur les Finances*, a map of France showing the *péages* and internal duties, and a draft of a tariff together with various papers relating to it. A month later one of the members suggested that since the project was so important the Committee should solicit all possible aid. Accordingly, the Committee authorized its president to ask de Lessart for his memoir on the project, and a later report to the Assembly indicates that he duly sent it in.[2] Meanwhile, the Committee on Finance had resolved to hear a report on Cormeré's financial plans.[3]

The Committee on Commerce and Agriculture charged three of its members to make a special study of the project: Pierre-Louis Goudard (1740–99), a silk merchant from Lyon and Deputy of the Third Estate for that city, Pierre Roussillou (1746–1817), a merchant and Deputy of the Third Estate for Toulouse, and Fontenay (d. 1808), a manufacturer and Deputy of the Third Estate for Rouen.[4] To assist in technical matter they called in Vivent Magnien, and they later praised him very highly for his services.[5] The Committee undoubtedly called on the *Bureau de la balance du commerce* also, for in a letter written to accompany four boxes of paper sent from the Bureau to the Committee, Lambert mentioned to the president of the Committee that the Bureau was engaged in 'special research to determine the influence which the adoption of a uniform tariff and suppression of the internal barriers of the kingdom might

---

[1] *Ibid.*, session of 7 Nov. 1789.

[2] *Ibid.*, session of 21 Dec. 1789; Goudard, Roussillou and Fontenay, *Rapport fait à l'Assemblée nationale*, p. 13.

[3] Camille Bloch, ed. *Procès-verbaux*, session of 11 Nov. 1789.

[4] Robert, Bourloton and Gougny, *Dictionnaire des parlementaires*. Léon Dutil, 'Un homme de '89. Pierre Roussillou', *Mémoires de l'Académie des sciences, inscriptions et belles-lettres de Toulouse*, 1939 and 1940.

[5] Gerbaux and Schmidt, *Procès-verbaux*, session of 3 March 1790.

have upon public revenues'.[1] The Committee also acknowledged the help of the *Députés extraordinaires du commerce et des manufactures*,[2] who were sent to Paris in 1788 and 1789 as representatives of various cities, the regular Deputies of Commerce having lost their strictly representative character and become government officials. However, it is important to notice that the two *Députés extraordinaires* who worked on the single duty project had been regular Deputies of Commerce for many years and had almost certainly been members of de la Boullaye's committee in 1787 and 1788. François Tournachon had been Deputy of Commerce for Lyon since 1779, and de Rastigny, Deputy of Commerce for Marseille since 1772.[3] Four Farmers General continued to work on the project at this stage, three of whom, Paulze, Brac de la Perrière and Saint-Christau, had also been associated with it for many years.[4] With the assistance of all these experienced officials, Goudard, Roussillou and Fontenay prepared a version of the project which they presented to the Constituent Assembly on 27 August 1790, and they then acknowledged some of their debt to the *ancien régime*, particularly to the work of the Trudaines and to that of de Lessart.[5]

But both before and after the submission of this report, the single duty project of the Revolution was influenced by the reforming officials far more than these three Deputies cared to admit. The report did not, for example, acknowledge a *Motion sur un nouveau régime de finances* proposed on 2 October 1789 by the Baron d'Allarde, Deputy for Saint Pierre-le-Moutier. D'Allarde demanded

that the new customs régime be incontinently and without delay brought into force, this being the surest and only way of reducing the effects of the Treaty of Commerce with England, and that to facilitate these diverse operations and the imminent publication of

---

[1] A.N., F^{12} 652. Lambert to the Marquis de Bonnay (no date); cf. Gerbaux and Schmidt, *op. cit.*, session of 11 Nov. 1789.

[2] *Plan des travaux des Comités du Commerce et de l'Agriculture présenté à l'Assemblée nationale*, 8 May 1790.

[3] J. Letaconnoux, 'Le comité des députés extraordinaires des manufactures et du commerce de France et l'œuvre économique de l'Assemblée Constituante, 1789–1791', *Annales révolutionnaires*, 1913, tome vi, pp. 149–208, pp. 164 and 174; and Pierre Bonnassieux, *Cons. de Com.*, and Léon Biollay, *L'Admin.*, p. 541.

[4] Gerbaux and Schmidt, *Procès-verbaux*, session of 3 Nov. 1790.

[5] Goudard, Fontenay and Roussillou, *Rapport fait à l'Assemblée nationale*.

the new tariff on French foreign trade, Monsieur de Cormeré be summoned to the Committee which I wish to see formed, and that he submit the work he has been charged with for fifteen years as well as . . . such information as will facilitate the operation of this Committee.[1]

Cormeré had prepared much of the material on which d'Allarde based his motion,[2] and indeed the ideas on the single duty project were his also. On 19 November 1789 Cormeré sent a letter and a memoir to the president of the Constituent Assembly summarizing his financial proposals and asking permission to explain them to the Assembly.[3] Not only did he recommend the single duty project as urgently necessary, but he pointed out, as d'Allarde had done, that questions of taxation concerned most of the existing committees in general and none in particular, and that therefore a *Comité des impositions* (later called the *Comité des contributions publiques*) should be set up. On 21 November, when Cormeré's request came up in the Assembly it was decided to pass it on to the Committee on Finance, and on 19 December Cormeré was permitted to address the Assembly. Towards the end of December 1789, the Assembly duly set up the special Committee on Taxation recommended by Cormeré and d'Allarde. The election of its eleven members was announced on 21 January 1790 as follows: Monneron, Du Pont de Nemours, de la Rochefoucauld (its first president), Laborde de Méréville, Fermon, d'Allarde, Talleyrand, Roederer, Jarry, Douchy and Duport.[4] According to Cormeré this committee passed the first nine months of its life 'reflecting on the fundamentals of taxation', and he wrote his *Recherches et considérations nouvelles sur l'impôt*[5] especially for it.

From January 1790, then, there were three committees concerned with preparing the single duty project, guiding it through the Assembly and meeting the difficulties that stood in

[1] Pierre-Gilbert Le Roi d'Allarde, *Motion*, p. 39.
[2] Cormeré, *Situation exacte*, 1792, p. 5; d'Allarde, *Motifs et précis*, containing twelve extensive appendices which are probably the work of Cormeré. There are frequent references to his works.
[3] A.N., C 98 (136), Mahy de Cormeré, mss. (1) autographed letter, (2) memoir of 19 fols. beginning, 'Monseigneurs, La nation ne sera point déçue des espérances que lui . . .'.
[4] *Procès-verbaux de l'Assemblée constituante*, 21 January 1790.
[5] Cormeré, *Situation exacte*, p. 2.

the way of its execution. In spite of some common members, they approached the project differently because of their different functions. The Committee on Finance was mainly interested in finding ways of replacing the revenue that would be lost and was therefore less enthusiastic about the project than the other two. The Committee on Agriculture and Commerce shouldered the heaviest burden and, as we have seen, appointed a sub-committee under Goudard to complete the project and put it into effect. These two committees represented in some degree the interests named in their titles and were therefore less detached than the Committee on Taxation which took a broader view and concerned itself largely with matters of policy. All three consulted each other quite often and although they disagreed in some things, all three accepted the necessity of internal free trade and a customs barrier on the frontier.

The Committee on Finance concerned itself mainly with the old problem of the immediate loss of revenue that the internal free trade project might entail. Because the government needed money just as badly as before, the customs continued to be regarded as a source of revenue as well as a tool of economic policy, but there was now a difference: reform was inevitable and the government would have to make up any loss of revenue as best it could. The Committee on Finance expected the worst. The loss from the abolition of the internal customs alone was expected to be between five and six million *livres* annually,[1] and this was added to the revenue from the other indirect taxes to be reformed or abolished at the same time, notably the *gabelle, tabac* and *droits de marque*, to make a total sacrifice of 50,458,834 *livres*.[2] In fact, revenue dwindled away in 1790, the internal barriers being swept away by popular attacks and then suppressed by statute. Whatever revenue was collected was largely paid out, before it reached the treasury, in meeting claims on the government such as the *rentes* and the redemption of official credit notes.[3] As a result, during the first six months of

---

[1] Pierre de Delay, Deputy for Dauphiné, put it at seven millions (*Quatrième opinion de Pierre de Delay, sur l'organisation de l'impôt*, p. 13).

[2] 'Lettre de Clavière aux administrators du Département du Calvados', 5 June 1792, p. 124 of *Lettres et pièces intéressantes pour servir à l'histoire du ministère de Roland, Servan, et Clavière.*

[3] Frédéric Braesch, *Les Exercices budgétaires 1790 et 1791*, p. 14.

the year the Farmers General put not a single *sol* into the Royal Treasury. It was decided for the following year to collect the missing fifty millions by means of land and other taxes. Each of the eighty-three new Departments was to contribute the amount which had formerly been taken from it in customs duties and the other defunct indirect taxes.[1] There was a certain rough justice in this expedient, but once drawn up in a simple schedule the allotted sums looked arbitrary—they certainly varied—and some Departments resisted.

After the reform, the remaining customs produced very little revenue. In a joint report of 23 April 1791 the three committees reckoned that the *ancien régime* had collected in customs and associated duties on foreign and colonial trade a revenue of 28,200,000 *livres* at a cost of 14,000,000 *livres*; they hoped that in 1791 the reformed customs service and the taxes on colonial trade (*domaine d'Occident*) would procure 18,800,000 *livres* at a cost of 8,543,572 *livres*, thus making a real loss of only 3,965,000 *livres*.[2] A sceptical member of the Assembly, Pierre de Delay, proved to be much nearer the mark in predicting returns of only twelve millions, for in fact the year produced no more than fourteen millions.[3] Most of this sum was collected in taxes on colonial trade; there appears to have been no customs revenue at all until September and from then until the end of the year only 3,010,000 *livres* were received.[4] This was a very small contribution to the total regular receipts for that year of 249,374,506

[1] *Loc. cit.*; A chart showing the amounts for each Department and each of the former provinces was published by the Committee on Taxation on 1 May 1791 (B.M., F.R. 522).

[2] *Rapport sur l'organization générale de l'administration des Douanes nationales, et sur la dépense qu'elle exige . . .* ; cf. a table compiled by the Committee on Taxation and published 22 June 1791 (B.M., F.R. 524).

[3] *Quatrième opinion de Monsieur Pierre de Delay sur . . .* , 7 Jan. 1791, 45 pp.; Etienne Clavière, *Mémoire lu par le Citoyen Clavière*, p. 28. Official figures of customs yield were later given as follows: Dec. 1790: 679,083 *livres* collected at the Farmer General's expense; in 1791 : 22,129,449 *livres* of which 8,543,572 *livres* were deducted for the expenses of collection; in 1792: 20,839,858 *livres* of which again 8,543,572 *livres* were taken as costs of collection; and for the first eight months of 1793: 10,980,930 *livres* of which 5,619,648 *livres* went in costs. Late contributions were collected in 1792 for 1791 and in 1793 for 1792, but the amount of these was small and did not alter the downward trend of customs revenue (*Etats présentés à la Commission des douanes par les régisseurs, imprimés par ordre de la Convention Nationale le 2 Frimaire, an II*).

[4] Frédéric Braesch, *Les Exercices budgetaires de 1790 et 1791*, p. 14.

livres, and smaller still in the total budget, including *assignats*, of
895,890,006 *livres*. Wartime interruptions of foreign and colonial
trade, and smuggling, especially through the free ports, were
blamed for the deficit. Clavière, the Minister for Public
Contributions, expected even less in 1792, but he thought that
the original estimate and more could be collected in peace
time 'if instead of considering these duties as a premium granted
to industry, we follow the English example and make them an
integral part of the revenues of the Republic'.[1] In spite of this
hopeful view, the reformed customs system hardly justified
itself as a source of revenue. In 1793, a committee of the
National Convention pointed out that the customs were indeed
so unsatisfactory as a revenue tax that they might well be
abolished were it not for the fact that their main function was to
protect internal trade against foreign competition.[2] Under the
ancien régime the customs were worth a good deal because of the
internal duties and because the costs of administration were
shared with the *gabelle, tabac, droits de marque* and other related
taxes. After 1789, they became inefficient as a tax, especially in
wartime, and could be justified only as a protection for French
trade and industry. The government understood this. 'The intention of the National Assembly', wrote de Lessart, Minister
of the Interior, on 16 March 1791, 'was not so much to preserve
a tax as to furnish our manufacturers with the means of with-
standing foreign competition.'[3] In a way, events had proved the
Farmers General right in contending ever since 1760 that the
single duty project would cause a loss of revenue. It is well to
remember, however, that not only the customs but all the indirect taxes yielded less in these years, both in absolute figures
and in relation to other sources of revenue: after contributing
slightly less than half of the total revenue in 1788, in 1790 indirect taxes amounted to one-sixth or one-fifth of it and in 1791
only one-twelfth or one-eleventh.[4]

---

[1] Etienne Clavière, *Mémoire lu par le Citoyen Clavière*, p. 28.

[2] *Convention Nationale. Rapport général sur les contributions de 1793, et projets de
décrets qui doivent en précéder la fixation, présentes au nom du comité des finances, section des
contributions directes et indirectes*, Paris, 1793, 50 pp., p. 35, signed by Vernier, Fermon,
Ramel, Rouzet, Servière and Isoré.

[3] *Ancien Moniteur, réimpression*, vol. vii, p. 658.

[4] Braesch, *Les Exercices budgetaires de 1790 et 1791*, p. 44.

The single duty as a tax held little interest for the second of the three Committees, that on Agriculture and Commerce. ² ·
Roederer, a prominent member of it, adopts the common attitude when he criticizes Montaran's book of 1762 for treating the single duty as a tax.[1] Though not unaware of the financial problem, this Committee was chiefly interested in the welfare of commerce and industry and set itself the task of carrying out the project with all possible speed. As before, the Farmers General obstructed the project by withholding information and declining to co-operate, even though a few of their more far-sighted colleagues were on the planning team. The Committee's inquiries about customs revenue, costs and numbers of employees remained unanswered until its vice-president, Lasnier de Vaussenay, appealed in exasperation to the Controller General. Thereafter the information came in less than a fort-night, on 5 April 1790.[2] Protests against the project from regional and other special interests were firmly treated as individual cases to be studied carefully but not allowed to interfere with the project as a whole. Goudard and his sub-committee had already made a draft of their main proposals when the Committee announced its 'profond et pénible travail' on the customs to the Constituent Assembly on 8 May.[3]

The most striking characteristic of these draft proposals is their simplicity, suggesting, as indeed the text implies, that action is imminent and that details will have to be worked out afterwards. In all previous projects, the main ideas had been gradually lost, gradually smothered under a growing pile of evidence and argument on minor issues, which in many cases could only have been decided empirically after the principal reform had been carried. Here we have, in the first three of thirteen articles, a plain proposal to abolish the internal customs bureaux and the duties collected in them. A fairly compre-hensive list of the internal and other local duties, which has been quoted with wonder and ridicule ever since, follows. A

---

[1] A.N., AP 29 68, Roederer papers, ms. 'Théorie des Tarifs de droits de traites'·
[2] Gerbaux and Schmidt, *Procès-verbaux*, sessions of 12 Dec. 1789, 2 and 6 Feb. 1790, 24 March 1790, and 5 April 1790.
[3] *Plan des travaux du Comité de l'Agriculture et du Commerce présenté à l'Assemblée nationale le 8 Mai 1790*, Paris, 8 pp. The main proposals are stated in Gerbaux and Schmidt, *Procès-verbaux*, sessions of 24 April and 5 May 1790.

fortify borders first

number of other articles are intended to strengthen the national customs and maintain the existing local tariffs until a new organization and a single tariff can be instituted. Comments are invited on the new tariff to be published in draft with the law embodying these proposals. The proposals are to take effect on 1 November 1790—a deadline that was to be almost met, for with some minor changes they became law on 5 November and took effect on 1 December.

During the intervening months the Committee dealt with day-to-day problems of customs administration in the spirit of these proposals; that is, they distinguished in a practical way between the internal and the external duties. Customs barriers everywhere were being flouted and even attacked, yet the Committee took steps to reinforce only those on the national frontiers. On 17 May, they proposed to strengthen the most exposed borders with reinforcements of personnel from the *gabelle* service, which had been abolished by a law to take effect on 15 August. Shortly afterwards, a refusal of the inhabitants of Vendres to obey customs regulations prompted urgent letters from the Committee to the Controller General and the Minister of War and Marine to have troops and ships patrol the coast of Roussillon. But in October the Director of the tax farms in that region was still complaining that employees were deserting because of threats from the populace. A rising tide of foreign contraband was beginning to break through in so many places throughout the country that such patchwork operations were plainly inadequate.[1]

The abolition of the *gabelle* weakened the customs barriers even further and the resulting increase in smuggling spurred the Constituent Assembly and its committees to act more quickly than they might otherwise have done. The reform project was intended, as it always had been, to strengthen the customs barriers on the frontiers as well as to abolish those in the interior

---

[1] A.N., D VI 8, Letters of Fremond (Director at Narbonne) dated 24 October 1790; Gerbaux and Schmidt, *Procès-verbaux*, sessions of 28 May and 30 July 1790; Pierre Vidal, *Histoire de la Révolution*, pp. 62 and 175 ff. On 27 June, the customs and other tax officials at Ingrande were terrorized by smugglers who, with support from the local population, broke into the bureaux and took away confiscated goods in the boats of the customs service (*Extraits de la lettre écrite par le Receveur de la Régie générale à Ingrande . . . du 3 Juillet*, 1790, B.M., R 628).

and it was now urgent that this be done. But the customs were not an isolated problem. Practically minded reformers like Cormeré and Goudard had long recognized that the indirect taxes, especially the *gabelle, tabac* and *douanes*, which shared so many expensive brigades of guards, ought to be dealt with together.[1] This task fell to the Committee on Taxation. Three of its members, La Rochefoucauld, Roederer and Jarry, had visited the Committee on Agriculture and Commerce on 14 May 1790 to ask that the report on the customs reform be withheld from the National Assembly pending a committee decision on the *tabac*. The report was in fact held up until after La Rochefoucauld and Roederer had appeared before the Committee on 16 August with the decision that tobacco was to be freely grown and sold throughout France. The barriers of the *tabac* were to be pushed back to the frontiers (with the possible exceptions of Alsace and the northern Provinces Reputed Foreign) and only foreign tobacco was to be reserved for sale by the State. Already on the previous day, 15 August, however, the law abolishing the *gabelle* had come into force, so that all those employees paid out of the *gabelle* receipts, including many customs officials, left their posts. Smuggling began to grow at an alarming rate.[2] The project was driven along by a mounting feeling of urgency in the Assembly and its committees, the Committee on Taxation even putting aside all its other work in its haste.[3]

When, on 3 October 1790, the National Assembly decreed that its committees should meet as soon as possible to plan the new administration for indirect taxes, it did so explicitly 'to speed the removal of the barriers to the frontiers of the kingdom'.[4] The committees believed that the existing organization of the Farmers General should not be trusted to carry out the single duty project, and that in view of all the reforms taking place the company's various branches would have to be con-

---

[1] Goudard's view is expressed in his report to the Assembly of 27 August 1790, p. 4; Cormeré's view is as stated *supra*, p. 117.

[2] Gerbaux and Schmidt, *Procès-verbaux*, sessions of 1 and 6 Sept., 11 Nov. and 13 Dec. 1790.

[3] (1) *Premier rapport fait au nom du Comité de l'Imposition, le 18 août 1790, ordre du travail*, 11 pp. (2) *Etat actuel des travaux du Comité de l'Imposition présenté à l'Assemblée nationale*, 1790, p. 7.

[4] Gerbaux and Schmidt, *Procès-verbaux*, session of 8 October 1790.

solidated. It was proposed, therefore, to form a new *régie* of 30 members of whom seven (raised to eight on 1 May 1791) would be concerned with the customs.[1] Already administrative control of the customs had partly been taken out of the hands of the Farmers General, for the Controller General of Finance was making new appointments to the posts of Director and Controller General of Customs.[2] Having ensured that within a reasonable length of time there would be machinery to put the single duty project into force, the Committee on Agriculture and Commerce could proceed to urge the enactment of Goudard's main proposals. These were put before the Assembly on 30 October and, in spite of continuing protests from the Foreign Provinces, were ratified on 5 November. While the destruction of 'nos foutues barrières' was being celebrated in such pamphlets as *Grande joie du Père Duchesne sur le reculement des barrières*, the Committee and the seven new *régisseurs* for the customs began right away to implement the new law. A printed circular letter to the departmental assemblies asked for their co-operation and told them to warn municipalities not to be alarmed at the number of customs employees who would be passing through on their way to the frontiers.[3] Goudard prepared a decree of 24 November which declared that from 1 January 1791 all leases of bureaux and other property for the internal customs service would be cancelled, with indemnities for the owners.[4] And many lesser problems were discussed, such as whether the royal *péage* of Trévoux should be abolished with the *traites* even though it was administered with the *aides*.[5]

How were the Farmers General to take this usurpation of their ancient functions and privileges? In spite of revolution in the capital and disorder in the provinces, the Farmers General continued to occupy the *hôtel des fermes*. They were prepared, as they had been in 1783, to accept a reorganization of the customs if the government were determined that there should be one,

---

[1] *Projet de réforme des différentes compagnies de finance chargées du recouvrement des impôts indirects, dans lequel on indique le danger qu'il y aurait de confier l'exécution du reculement des barrières à la compagnie de la Ferme générale, dans son organization actuelle*, 1790, B.M., F.R. 568.

[2] Gerbaux and Schmidt, *Procès-verbaux*, session of 29 October 1790.

[3] *Ibid.*, sessions of 10 and 11 Nov. 1790.

[4] *Ibid.*, sessions of 24 Nov. 1790.   [5] *Ibid.*, session of 17 Dec. 1790.

and after the new law had been passed they wrote to ask how the new customs service could be integrated into the General Farm.[1] They were less prepared for the sharp reply in which the Committee on Agriculture and Commerce explained that all the arrangements for the reform of the customs were to be under the direction of the seven new *régisseurs* who would appoint all employees in Paris and the provinces, would have office space in the *hôtel des fermes*, and would deal with all the correspondence and the accounts of the customs from 1 December 1790, leaving the Farmers General nothing more to do than finish any business begun before 1 December and collect money due before that date. To the Farmers General it did not appear so simple. In a detailed reply they protested that the seven *régisseurs* were already active and appeared to believe that they could exercise their new authority without even consulting the Farmers General. The new *régisseurs* even proposed to have all employees take a new oath as though they were no longer to be under the direction of the General Farm. As a result there was growing 'insubordination and confusion, which was very damaging to the service'. Legally, explained the Farmers General, the decree of 30 October 1790 had left untouched the terms of the lease Mager drawn up in 1786, and the administrators chosen to execute that decree must therefore be considered not as a new financial administration but as part of the existing one. Besides, if the collection of the customs and other taxes was not to be interrupted, if the new organization for the *tabac* was to be set up, and if remaining stocks of salt were to be sold, then, the Farmers said, the seven *régisseurs* would have to consult them about changes in the offices and personnel both in Paris and in the provinces and to put off their plan to abolish the internal brigades and bureaux. The Farmers General concluded with the warning that the reform planned would not only be expensive, thus preventing them from depositing much money in the Royal Treasury during the month of December, but once accomplished it would reduce customs revenue to fourteen million *livres* while maintaining administrative costs

Tales of woe of F. G.

---

[1] A.N., AB XIX 327, *Registre de documents relatifs à la gestion de Monsieur Dufresne comme directeur du Trésor public 1789 à 1791 et à ses rapports avec le Comité des Finances*, ms., 12e conference, art. 8 dated 8 Dec. 1790.

as high as nine millions. These prophecies of woe had little effect: the financial needs of the government were as great as ever, but the time had passed when the threat of a reduction of revenue could stop customs reform. The reformers were bent on transforming the customs from a hindrance to an aid in the national economy, and cost was no object.

By suppressing the internal duties, the law of 5 November 1790 created the national customs union which had been the goal of the internal free trade movement at least since the time of Colbert. But this law, though it realized the main aim of the movement, left undecided the question of whether Avignon, Alsace, the free ports and other controversial territories should be included within the national barriers or allowed a privileged status. By order of the National Assembly (12 February 1791) the fate of Avignon was settled by the Committee on Agriculture and Commerce in conference with the Committee on Diplomacy. These committees decided that the territory should be united with France and after a struggle with the authorities of the territory this was done according to a decree of 14 September 1791.[1] Alsace was at first included in the national customs union with eighty-seven bureaux, in the new Direction of Strasbourg, being placed on its outer frontier. But a decree of 7 July 1791 restored the time-honoured Alsatian privileges of *entrepôt* and *transit* for foreign goods. As for the free ports of Marseille, Dunkirk, Bayonne and Lorient, a bitter controversy had been raging for some years and had even broken out into open rioting between those who defended them as essential *entrepôts* and those who claimed that they facilitated smuggling—that is to say, between their big international trading interests and the jealous interests of unprivileged rival ports. The free ports were preserved for the time being and only abolished by the National Convention on 27 February 1794.[2] A number of other small territories, like the county of Montbéliard and the principality of Salm, were taken into the national customs union by agreements with their rulers, and a number of others, such as Gex and some islands off the coasts, were left out of it.[3]

---

[1] Mirot, *op. cit.*, p. 270.   [2] Sète was jealous of Marseille, Cherbourg of Dunkirk, etc.
[3] Gerbaux, and Schmidt, *Procès-verbaux*, sessions of 29 Nov. 1790, 16 May 1791.

But no effect & got bent on transformation

question of free ports, Alsace, Avignon & other controversial territories

The law of 5 November 1790 also left a great deal to be decided about the reorganization of the customs service. With much help from Vivent Magnien, Goudard prepared a comprehensive report and a decree of 23 April 1791 which guided the reorganization carried out over the ensuing months.[1] These planners reckoned that if France had 895 leagues of coastline and 623 leagues of land frontier, then in order to place a bureau about every two leagues they would have to establish 714 bureaux manned by 1,668 employees. The guards on the coast were to be stationed in a single line, a post of eight men every league, and there were to be two six-man posts per league on the landward frontiers, in order to have a double line. In all there were to be 1,775 posts comprising 13,284 guards commanded by 163 Captains-general. The administrative division was to be called a Direction, as before, and there were to be twenty Directors, sixty-three Travelling Inspectors and twelve Resident Inspectors, making a total senior staff of ninety-five. To complete the picture, a *régie* of eight (later reduced to three) was to direct operations from headquarters in Paris with a staff of thirty-eight officers and clerks. Vivent Magnien, who was appointed as the eighth *régisseur* on 1 May 1791, quickly gained and kept control over this organization and he succeeded in administering the customs with an even smaller number of employees than had been planned.[2]

Eighty years earlier, Jean Anisson had tried to answer the charge that the single duty project would put large numbers of men out of work. That charge was now proving to be well-founded. According to Goudard's calculations, about 10,000 men were made redundant, though this figure doubtless included employees of the *gabelle* and *tabac* as well as the internal customs. By decrees of 20 March and 31 July 1791, men discharged after more than ten years' service received pensions of 50 *livres* a month until re-employed, while some financial assistance was given to those who had been employed for less than ten but more than one year.[3] Probably some of the incum-

[1] *Rapport sur l'organisation générale de l'administration des Douanes nationales et sur la dépense qu'elle exige . . .* , 31 pp.

[2] *Etats présentes à la Commision des douanes par les régisseurs . . .* , 2 Frimaire, an II. Guards totalled 12,195 men and bureau employees 1,380.

[3] *Rapport et projet de décret sur les moyens de faire l'emploi le plus utile des sacrifices que*

bents of remaining posts, especially senior ones, were discharged so that the leaders of the new régime might place their friends and relatives in office, but the law of 20 March 1791 ordered that all new appointments to posts in the financial administration were to be made from among former employees of the suppressed services. Tarbé, the Minister of Public Contributions, seemed very anxious to enforce this law and requested monthly reports from the *régisseurs* on new appointments.[1] A few surviving Directors' reports suggest that comparatively few men from the suppressed services failed to find other official employment. It is true that of some 200 employees in the Paris headquarters, 50 were on the pension list in July 1791; but whereas most Directions numbered their employees in hundreds, their lists of unemployed at this time were numbered in dozens: the list of 41 reported at Charleville on 10 January 1791 had been reduced by 19 March to 28. In January, Saint Quentin reported 28 still unemployed and Chalon-sur-Saône 16. In March, Orleans listed 25, Langres 15, Tours 34 and Moulin 38. A report on the composition of the headquarters staff of the customs in August 1793 shows that most of the men in the middle and lower ranks had been employed by the Farmers General during the *ancien régime*. This was probably true of the entire reformed customs service, though there is no evidence to prove it.[2]

Customs employees appear to have been content, on the whole, with conditions in the reformed service, though in Autumn 1792 the Minister of Public Contributions was obliged to defend the clerks and guards against charges of corruption and of aiding *émigrés* by saying that they were grossly underpaid and had to live as best they could.[3] If loyal to the régime, they were certainly interested in getting the best possible con-

---

[1] A.N., G¹ 63, Tarbé to the *Régisseurs Généraux*, 22 June 1791.

[2] A.N., G¹ 63, 70; and *Etat des régisseurs des douanes de la République et des employés au bureau de leur administration au premier août, 1793.*

[3] Etienne Claviere, *Mémoire lu par le Citoyen Clavière, Ministre des Contributions publiques, à la Convention Nationale 1–5 Octobre, 1792*, Paris, 1792.

---

l'Assemblée nationale a fait par son décret du 31 Juillet dernier en faveur de la plupart des employés supprimés présenté au nom du comité d'agriculture et de commerce .. . . For pensions see A.N., G¹ 63, printed circular of 26 August and 13 and 14 September 1791. Service was counted up to the legal suppression of the General Farm on 1 April 1790.

ditions of service under it. As early as December 1790, the employees of Nantes, with a great deal of local support, drew up a document demanding a fair system of promotion to senior posts, which, they said, was denied them by a *Délibération* of 1778, and insisting on improved working conditions and the right of free speech.[1] With a backward look at the General Farm, 'cet antique colosse', they reminded the National Assembly that they were now 'public functionaries, working at the administration of the customs just as priests work at the administration of the faith, just as lawyers work at the administration of justice'. They wanted to be consulted about the forthcoming reorganization of the customs service.

Reorganization raised many problems which could not all be solved at once. One of the most pressing matters which remained after the abolition of the internal duties was the compiling of the new single tariff to replace all the local duties still being levied in the frontier bureaux. Goudard, with his team of experts, had been working on a tariff for many months, but unlike the other parts of the project it caused a heated debate when put before the National Assembly on 30 November 1790. Even before the tariff had been published, Cormeré had stirred up opposition to it, for he had seen at meetings of the *Députés extraordinaires des manufactures et commerce* that the tariff was being planned according to false principles. The planners were taking greater interest in the prohibition of foreign manufactures than in the more moderate aim of tariff protection for domestic industry.[2] Whereas he and the Committee on Taxation believed that when the internal duties were suppressed an import duty of 12 per cent or 15 per cent would be quite adequate to protect French industry from foreign competition, Goudard's sub-committee, doubtless under the influence of the *Députés extraordinaires*, took the view that many goods should be subject to duties of up to 20 per cent and many others prohibited outright. Experience has always proved, wrote Goudard, that prohibition makes smuggling more difficult.[3] Cormeré dis-

[1] *Département de la Loire Inférieure, District de Nantes, Douanes nationales*, 12 December 1790, 21 pp. (B.M., R. 496.)
[2] Cormeré, *Situation exacte*, 1792, p. 14.
[3] Goudard, Fontenay and Roussillou, *Rapport fait à l'Assemblée nationale . . .* (27 August 1790), p. 29.

agreed, for he knew that the customs barriers had never kept out contraband goods when the duties had been high enough to make smuggling profitable, and that the weakening effect of the Revolution on customs administration had resulted in a reduction of the rates charged by the *assureurs* for smuggling from 15 per cent or 20 per cent to 5 per cent or 6 per cent.[1] He attacked the tariff proposed by the Committee on Agriculture and Commerce:

I was alarmed and felt it incumbent on me to publish some important observations on the tariff: I believe they were not without effect, for the Assembly asked its combined committees on Agriculture and Commerce and Public Contributions to revise this tariff. The meeting of these two committees had the success which I had hoped for; the tariff was revised on the principles adopted in 1787.[2]

As Cormeré suggests, the combined committees did indeed publish a much more moderate tariff, which the Assembly accepted in a series of acts early in 1791; of these, a law of 2 March and a decree of 25 March put the new tariff into effect from 1 August 1791.

Credit for bringing about this revision has usually been given to Louis Boislandry, a Deputy from Paris who led the debate on it in the Assembly,[3] but he depended upon Cormeré's assistance. Boislandry admits himself that for some of the material in his *Opinion sur le projet du tarif du comité d'agriculture et de commerce*, he obtained 'reliable information from the *Bureau général des Traites*',[4] which was Cormeré's bureau. Cormeré may have exaggerated his own influence on this affair, but it is certain that he had much to do with the adoption by the Assembly of a tariff more or less in conformity with the principles which he had always defended. This tariff resembled, much more closely than Goudard's, the one that had been put before the Assembly of Notables in 1787. The more moderate party had for the time prevailed over the extreme partisans of prohibition. It is not too much to say that the reforming officials of the *ancien régime* had thus once again vindicated their principles.

---

[1] Cormeré, *Situation exacte*, pp. 14 ff.; and Marion, *Hist. fin.*, vol. ii, p. 90.

[2] Cormeré, *Situation exacte*, p. 14.

[3] Marion, *Hist. fin.*, vol. ii, p. 236.

[4] Louis Boislandry, *Opinion sur le projet de tarif du comité d'agriculture et de commerce*, Paris, 1790 (30 November), p. 10.

Summary and Conclusion

T HE heart of the movement for a French customs union in the eighteenth century was the single duty project. This was a plan, which Colbert had tried to implement early in the reign of Louis XIV, for replacing the internal customs barriers by a single uniform duty on the national frontiers. It was revived again and again during the eighteenth century. From 1702 to 1710 certain Deputies of Commerce, led by Jean Anisson de Hauteroche, proposed and defended this reform in the newly formed Council of Commerce. Under the duc d'Orléans, the Council of Commerce, presided over by Michel Amelot de Gournay, took up the idea and in August 1720 Amelot launched a project which, however, lasted scarcely more than a few months. The *projet du droit unique* was next taken up in 1726 by Michel-Joseph-Hyacinth Lallemant de Betz, a Farmer General, who with the collective approval and guidance of his colleagues worked out plans which were submitted to the Council of Commerce in 1737 and only abandoned in the 1740's with the advent of the War of Austrian Succession. From 1740 to 1770 Henri Bertin and the Trudaines, father and son, sponsored a single duty project which, although it had no immediate success, formed the basis of the work of Guillaume-François Mahy de Cormeré who, under Necker and Calonne, prepared the project which was passed on to the Constituent Assembly and finally put into effect in 1791.

One result of making a detailed study of this movement is the discovery that most of the key figures in it were men whom historians have hitherto ignored or regarded as unimportant. Of the more famous Physiocrats, only one, Dupont de Nemours, took any practical interest in it and his role was far less important than that of his contemporary, Mahy de Cormeré. Thus, in relation to the internal free trade movement various reassessments are needed. Necker and Calonne must both be regarded as playing a much more important role than Turgot, Anisson than Vauban, Amelot than Boisguillebert, Lallemant de Betz than Lavoisier, and the elder Michau de Montaran than Vincent de Gournay. At the same time there were some well-known men who, though neither very active nor very influential in the movement, must be regarded as sympathizers: Nicolas Mesnager, one of the negotiators of the Treaty of Utrecht, Jean Melon, Claude Dupin, Véron de Fortbonnais, Vincent de Gournay, John Holker, Moreau de Beaumont, Vergennes and Jean Tolozan, among many others.

The principal characteristic of the men who led the movement for internal customs reform is that they held official or semi-official posts. They were Controllers General, Councillors, Intendants of Finance, Intendants of Commerce, Inspectors of Manufactures, Deputies of Commerce, Farmers General, or holders of lesser positions in the bureaux of the government and the General Farm. Although the official world was not unanimous in its support, and although the movement found support in professional, literary, commercial and industrial circles also, it is not too much to say that the customs reform movement was inspired, planned and led from the *bureaux*. Government officials wrote practically all the best-informed and most influential books and memoirs on the subject of customs and customs reform; they made detailed, concrete, practical plans which they were continually bringing to the attention of the government; and finally they put their plans into effect in 1790 and the following years. This was, for most of them, only one of several reform projects, but many thought it to be vital, and for some it became a veritable passion. If the internal free trade project was only part of a larger programme of administrative change, it illustrates admirably the reforming efforts of the *ancien régime*.

The reformers wanted to organize the customs in such a way as to favour national trade and industry. A single uniform tariff imposed on the frontiers would, according to their plan, encourage the importation of raw materials by charging them with very low duties, while high export duties would be used to try to keep them within the country. At the same time, import duties on manufactured goods would be set high in order to reserve the domestic market for French industry, which would also be encouraged by very low export duties to send its products abroad. The most striking feature of this plan, however, was that it provided for the complete abolition of the local and provincial customs that were such a serious hindrance to internal trade. By reducing the customs to one uniform and efficient tariff barrier on the frontiers of the country, the reformers intended to favour French trade, industry and, indirectly, agriculture. Industry, which they regarded as of primary importance, was in their view a process of mobilizing national resources of men and materials for the production of finished goods that would increase national wealth by attracting money from abroad. Their goal of maximum industrial production for export was a national one which called for the co-operation of all French provinces in a common market and a customs union. A national economic policy was to be made possible through a reform of the customs.

Thus, the essential desire of the reforming officials was to transform the customs from a tax to an instrument of economic control. This was not a new idea; indeed, all the eighteenth-century reformers acknowledged that they had learned it from Colbert. But although the dual function of the customs had been widely recognized at least since Colbert's time, in practice the fiscal function had prevailed. Leased to the Farmers General, along with the *aides, tabac, gabelle* and other indirect taxes, the customs (*traites* or *douanes*) had been treated for the most part as a source of revenue. Colbert, in trying to reform the customs and use them as an effective control over the balance of trade, had encountered resistance in the provinces and financial problems. Yet his tariff reforms of 1664 and 1667, incomplete and inadequate though they were, inspired future generations of reforming officials to work towards internal free trade and a single uniform tariff on the national frontiers.

The customs as they existed in the eighteenth century were ineffective as a control on trade for a variety of reasons. The Farmers General were not so much out to make their barriers effective against prohibited or undesirable goods as to collect the greatest possible amount of money. The rapacious methods of their employees encouraged fraud, while the semi-

M

private commercial character of the General Farm, lacking
even the force of royal prestige, did nothing to deter it; and the
need to deploy forces on so many internal as well as external
frontiers made the barriers weak in the face of determined
smuggling. Moreover, foreign goods that were prohibited, or
charged 30 per cent to 50 per cent *ad valorem* at the frontiers,
could be smuggled in at modest cost through the agency of
assureurs who did a very profitable business. And as long as the
internal duties continued to raise the costs of French merchants
and manufacturers by 12 per cent or 15 per cent or more, then
the Uniform Duties on foreign imports had to be kept very
high; for imported foreign goods, once they had paid the
Uniform Duties, were exempted from paying all internal
duties providing they arrived at their destination with a certain
period, usually three months. What many of the reformers
wanted to do, therefore, was to remove the impositions on
internal trade so that the duties on foreign manufactures could
be reduced to 15 per cent or less, which would make smuggling
unprofitable for the *assureurs* and still afford protection for
French industry against undue foreign competition. To the
reformers it seemed essential to have low duties that were en-
forceable rather than high duties that were not. The reform
was to make the tariff barriers simple but effective and the
duties low but certain. The most important part of this project
was to abolish all those in the interior.

This was bound to be difficult because the fiscal function of
the customs was vital, especially to the Farmers General.
Being semi-private monopolists, they had no reason to distinguish between their various tax concessions and simply
exploited them as cheaply and efficiently as they could. In
doing so they naturally made no distinction in practice between
the internal and the frontier customs. Yet in theory they recognized the control function of the customs and although they
maintained in the early part of the century that the internal
duties were just as useful as those on the frontiers, in that they
maintained a necessary 'balance' in the trade of the different
provinces, by 1726 the Farmers General were convinced that
the internal duties were harmful to French trade and industry
and might well be abolished. Indeed, so interested did they be-

come in this reform that they undertook to plan it themselves. The problem for them resolved itself into one of devising a single uniform tariff of duties which, if collected on the national frontiers alone, would produce no less revenue than the system as it stood. And so willing were they to see the reform put into practice that for twenty years they supported the efforts of one of their number, Lallemant de Betz, to produce a reform project which they could accept. But the outbreak of war in 1743 reminded them that when foreign trade fell off, the maintenance of the customs revenue depended more and more on the internal duties, which were imposed almost exclusively on domestic trade. Moreover, Lallemant de Betz's conclusion that the reform need cause no loss of revenue was not really very convincing, or not permanently so, and indeed, after 1760 the Farmers General steadily predicted that the reform would result in a loss of over ten million *livres*. Although it was not in their interests to carry out the reform project themselves, they still recognized its value and were prepared, if properly indemnified, to give up the farm of the customs in order that the government itself might carry out the project. After all, the customs were by no means the most lucrative of the tax farms and the government could, in any case, remove them from the Farmers General's lease at any time by simply giving up a revenue of a few thousand *livres* a year and paying the necessary indemnity.

If the change were made at the time when a new lease was drawn up, no indemnity would be called for. Yet only twice in the century does the government appear to have felt it could run the risk of the revenue losses which the project might entail: the first time was in 1720 when it was still believed that all financial problems might be solved by an endless issue of paper notes, and the second in 1783, when for diplomatic reasons the government wanted to create new free ports. Therefore, the reformers were forced, right up to 1790, to plan the reform in such a way as to avoid sacrificing revenue. This was what much of the planning and calculating was for. And so deeply embedded was the view that the customs ought to justify themselves as a tax that it was not until the National Convention of 1792 that there was anything like a frank acceptance by the government of the fact that the customs, even if unproductive of revenue, might still be justified as an economic control. In short, although the government recognized that the customs would hardly serve as a satisfactory economic control until the customs reform project had been carried out, it continued in practice to regard them as a tax and to defend the internal duties out of sheer financial necessity. The reform was accepted in principle at least as early as 1720. The real problem was to put it into effect.

There was one major administrative difficulty. Not only were the customs collected without any distinction between internal duties and those on the frontiers, but they were also administered to a great extent by the same machinery that was used to collect the other indirect taxes. Many of the internal customs barriers were used to support, and at the same time had come to depend upon, the internal barriers of the *gabelle*, the *tabac* and the *aides*. While inspecting vehicles, the customs officers kept watch for illicit cargoes of salt, tobacco and wine. Many of the ubiquitous brigades of guards were deployed in such a way as to serve more than one tax farm, and they were paid out of the receipts of the *gabelle*, *tabac* or customs, according to convenience. The integration of these three tax farms, and to some extent of the *aides* and *droits de marque* also, seems to have been increased during the later part of the century when such able Farmers General as Antoine Lavoisier endeavoured to make the tax farms more efficient. As a result, it became more and more apparent that all the internal barriers ought properly to be abolished at the same time. Some of the Farmers General, indeed, were in favour of a general reform which would simplify and unify all the indirect taxes; but this would have entailed a single, uniform *gabelle* and *tabac* over the whole country, which the privileged and exempt provinces were ready to resist. These provinces in fact never ceased to regard the single duty project as a Farmers General's plot to subject them to the *tabac* and especially the *gabelle*, until they were at last convinced that these taxes were to be abolished. For the only alternative to extending the *tabac* and *gabelle* uniformly throughout the kingdom was to suppress them altogether. As long as they remained unequal, they required barriers to prevent smuggling from one zone to another. Until the 1780's, the reforming officials had usually avoided the problem of disengaging the internal customs barriers from those of the *gabelle* and *tabac*. The Farmers General could therefore reasonably assume that these taxes would be extended with the abolition of the internal barriers, and this prospect undoubtedly helped to make them look favourably on the single duty project during the greater part of the century. But during the 1780's, when the reformers became convinced that the *gabelle*, at least, would have to go, the Farmers General became opposed to the projected reform and threw every possible obstacle in its path. Thus, by planning to suppress the *gabelle*, the reformers excited the enmity of the Farmers General at the same time that they allayed resistance in some of the privileged provinces. Resistance in certain provinces that were free from the *tabac* was not overcome until as late as 1790 when the Constituent Assembly, on a report of its Committee on Taxation, decided to abolish the tobacco monopoly also. And it was not until then that the customs were at last freed from their paralysing association with the other major indirect taxes.

It was perfectly clear to most of the later reformers that the customs could never become an effective instrument of economic control so long as they remained in the hands of the Farmers General. This company not only collected money but also paid it out in the form of *rentes*, pensions, their own salaries and the salaries of their own and other personnel, and the expenses of their own and other official activities. They had their own independent *caisse* or budget which had to balance receipts and expenditures and show a profit. From this point of view they were a private firm. Many of the reformers believed that the customs would have to be transformed into a *régie* which, like any government department or crown commission, would do little more than collect revenue and send it to the Treasury. All payments, including the salaries of customs and other officials, would be made by the Treasury out of one central revenue fund. The administrators of the customs would thus have no interest in the amount of money they collected. The Constituent Assembly adopted this consolidation of revenue in principle, but so firmly rooted was the idea of an independent *caisse*, with the profit motive acting as a stimulus to the tax collectors, that the customs were at first organized in the old way as a *régie intéressé* with the whole paraphernalia of financial incentives, such as commissions (*remises*), or percentage shares of amounts collected, for the *régisseurs*. Again, it was the officials who turned out to be the real reformers, for the *régisseurs* themselves were the first to object to the customs being given 'the name and the character of a *régie intéressé*'.[1] Customs duties, they said, cannot be treated as indirect taxes without destroying public confidence in the administration and weakening it to the detriment of industry, commerce and agriculture. Accordingly, they begged the Assembly to accept their relinquishment of the commission (*remise*) which had been granted to them. Moreover, not only the *régisseurs* but even many of their subordinates expressed a similar desire to be regarded as civil servants performing a public service rather than employees engaged in a private business. It seemed essential to the customs officials themselves, as well as to most of the reformers, that the customs should be reorganized as a *régie*, or to use a modern expression, 'nationalized'.

From another point of view, the customs reform movement was a struggle for the formation of a national customs union to include all French territory. Several provinces and cities resisted this, partly because their internal tariff barriers seemed to protect them from the hated *gabelle* and *tabac*, which might be forced upon them if they agreed to the destruction of the barriers. Being, in practice, just one of several indirect taxes, the customs were viewed as an imposition from which it was a privilege to be exempt. A deeper cause of resistance was the fear in the Provinces Reputed Foreign and the Foreign Provinces of being taxed more heavily by the Crown as a result of any general reform to make taxes more equitable; for as things stood they were taxed less and subsidized more than most other provinces.[2] They were therefore inclined to reject any proposals to unify a tax. The resistance came mainly from the Estates and Parlements, which suggests that the struggle was really between

---

[1] *Pétition des citoyens chargés de l'administration des douanes nationales à l'Assemblée nationale.* Paris (Impr. Nat.), 3 pp. (B.N., Lf¹³⁰ 4).

[2] Frédéric Braesch, *Finances et monnaies*, fasc. II, part 3, pp. 205 ff.

the provincial authorities and those in Paris. But to some extent resistance in the provinces came from a preference for dealing with foreign countries and a real desire to protect provincial markets from the competition of goods from the rest of the country. The wine interests in Guyenne and Alsace, for instance, could sell their own products more profitably abroad and had no desire to see their home markets invaded by wine of perhaps better quality from other French provinces. Many commercial interests feared the formation of a national customs union, and supported the widespread idea that the internal barriers were maintaining a necessary 'balance' in the trade of the various provinces. On the other hand, most manufacturers were in favour of the national customs union. This opposition of merchants and manufacturers in the struggle over the internal barriers became so strong in Lorraine and Trois Evêchés that it seemed to Roederer to be fundamental.[1] A study of public opinion, however, shows that both merchants and manufacturers were primarily concerned with their own private interests. Theirs was a minor struggle, the main one being between various private and provincial interests on the one hand, and on the other, reforming officials working for a French customs union.

The single duty project was intended by the reformers to turn the tangle of provincial and local customs into a national system to be controlled from Paris and accountable only to the central government. They realized that in the execution of the project petitions from private firms and provincial authorities might have to be ignored in the general interest, which was coming to mean something more than the sum of provincial and private interests. A basic change in attitude towards such interests is shown in the increasing impatience of the reformers with the endless and crippling compromises which paralysed every attempt at reform. As the plans for reform were made and re-made, discussed and revised, it became apparent that the resistance of private and provincial interests was not a thing which would give way to persuasion or which could be fitted into some plan. It was something which would give way only to

---

[1] A.N., 29 AP 81, Roederer ms., *Balance du commerce des Trois Evêchés et de la Lorraine.*

force and, in the national interest, this use of force seemed
justified. This is clear in the urgent petitions in which Cormeré,
Calonne and others pressed the King to use his authority to
carry out the reform project. And the project itself was intended
to strengthen state control. The administrative system was to
be taken out of the hands of the General Farm and established
as a public service. As an efficient system of economic control
the customs would serve the national economy rather than the
financiers and the Royal Treasury. The internal customs duties,
mere taxes, would have to go in the national interest and any
revenue that was lost would have to be made up in some other
way. In short, the reform movement was a struggle to unify the
French economy, to equalize tax burdens, to create an effective
national system of administration, and to increase state control
of economic affairs.

The struggle has usually been interpreted as part of a liberal
or *laissez-faire* campaign to establish complete free trade and to
remove government interference in natural economic processes.
It has been thought of as part of the struggle against the despotic
system of inspection and controls set up by Colbert. At the
same time that men were struggling for freedom of speech and
freedom from arbitrary arrest—political tyranny, in short—
they were also endeavouring to free themselves from economic
tyranny. According to this view, the physiocratic sect were the
inspiration of the reform movement, and first the reformers and
then the revolutionaries were their disciples in economic
matters. The period from about 1760 onwards has been regarded as the time of a surge of liberal sentiment in favour of
abolishing all customs as an unnatural and unnecessary interference of the government in matters in which it ought not to
meddle. The Physiocrats, and public opinion formed by their
teaching, were thought to have influenced a certain number of
officials so that in government circles, as in the country generally,
progressive free traders were struggling against reactionary
mercantilists. This liberal interpretation has it that the Anglo-
French Commerical Treaty of 1786, a victory for the Physiocrats, might have led to complete international free trade if the
English, the Farmers General and mercantilists in the administration had not conspired to make the treaty a failure. It is

believed that the tariff that was established in 1790 was a compromise between the forces of free trade and the forces of mercantilism, but that it was nevertheless a step forward, forced on the *ancien régime* by the liberal upsurge of the Revolution.

This interpretation seems irreconcilable with the evidence. It is true that the Physiocrats did hold more or less liberal views, but they were not the views of the reforming officials and were quite irrelevant to the reform movement which finally triumphed in 1790. Historians have not seen the movement in this light because they were, in a sense, themselves converted to the Physiocrats' beliefs about the evils of all customs barriers and saw the reform movement as a step in the direction of their total abolition. As a result, they misunderstood the nature of the customs reform project: it was not intended to abolish all customs barriers but only those in the interior; it was not a concession to pressure from public opinion—the reforming officials did not follow opinion, they led it—but a plan of reorganization proposed by certain officials for various reasons of which the desire for economic liberty was only one. The reformers advocated internal free trade not because they wanted to favour dissatisfied industrial and commercial interests, but because they believed the internal duties to be harmful to trade and industry in general, inefficient and expensive as a method of tax collection and unjustified as barriers which separated French provinces from one another. The reform carried out in 1790 was never regarded as a step towards the total abolition of the customs, except by the physiocratic sect. It was not an early step towards the breakdown of Colbert's system, but a late step towards the completion of it. It was not intended as an extension of the terms of the Anglo-French Commercial Treaty but rather as a remedy for the economic ills attributed to the treaty. It was not a move to reduce government control but rather to increase it. And finally, the reform project was the work of the *ancien régime*, not of the Revolution. But when this has been said it must be added that if the Revolution did not conceive the project it had the more difficult task, which had frustrated reforming officials for nearly a century, of overriding the resistance of immeasurable vested interests and carrying it into practice.

APPENDIX I

Copies of some of the forms to be filled out at the customs bureaux by merchants or drivers carrying goods.

Déclaration, from a document in A.N., G^1 13

Acquit à caution, from a document in A.N., G^1 13

Acquit de paiement, from a document in A.N., H^4 2967[1]

Brevet de contrôle, from a document in A.N., F^{12} 726[A]

Modèle de Déclaration

Le . . . jour d . . . mil sept cent . . . à . . . heures après
. . . . midi, . . . M . . . . demeurant à . . . Paroisse d
. . . . Province d . . . . . a déclaré faire

Reçu . . . .   charger sur . . . . la quantité de . . . .

Na. Il faut
specifier la
qualité, le
poids, le nombre
des Marchandises,   (Et rien autre chose) pour être conduit par . . . .
les balots,   à . . . . Paroisse d . . . . près . .
caisses, & etc., ... Province d . . . . Election d . . . . . .
les droits que   . . . . . en . . . . .passant à . . . . en . . . . .
devraient les   jours & non ailleurs, dont il n'a été payé aucuns
marchandises si   Droits d . . . . qui montent à . . . . .attendu
elles sortaient.   la destination, pour sûreté desquels et du quadruple
                     d'iceux, meme de confiscation s'il y a lieu, led . . . .
                     et le sieur . . . . qui s'est présentement constitué
Na. désigner   Caution dud . . . . ont promis de rapporter dans . . .
la Ville ou   . . . . Certificat au dos de l'Acquit à Caution
Bourg le plus   tiré au bas de cette page, signé des Commis du Bureau
voisin.   des Traites d . . . . .ou des Curé, Juge,
                     Echevin, Syndic, ou Notaire d . . . . à deffaut de
                     Commis des Traittes, de la descente & déchargement
                     desd. Marchandises cy-dessus déclarées audit lieu d . . .
                     . . . . . . sans fraude & de certifier la vérité des sig-
                     natures du certificat de décharge, le tout aux peines
                     portées par les articles VIII & XII du titre 6 de
                     l'Ordonnance de 1687 & de l'Arrest du Conseil du 13
                     Mars 1722 & Lettres patentes sur icelui, ausquels
                     lesdits . . . . se soûmettent solidairement comme
                     pour deniers Royaux, reconnaissant la Jurisdiction
                     de Messieurs les Juges des Traittes, pour raison de ce,
                     & de faire certifier la sortie dans le jour par un Garde,
                     & ont signé.

                            . . . .
                            . . . .

                            [*verso*]

Le   Jour d   mil sept cent le sieur   a rapporté
l'acquit-à-Caution de l'autre part déchargé à   par le

Acquit-à-Caution

No . . . .
Bureau d . . . . .   Commis & Gardes des Fermes du Roy, laissez passer
pour . . . . demeurant à . . . .
Paroisse d . . . . Province d . . . . la
quantité de . . . .
. . . .
. . . .

(Et rien autre chose) qu'il a fait charger sur . . . .
. . . . pour être conduit par . . . . à . . . .
Paroisse d . . . . près . . . . d . . . .
Province d . . . . Election d . . . . .en . . . . . .
. . . . passant par . . . . & non ailleurs,
suivant la déclaration demeurée au haut de ce feuillet
No . . . . . . .dont il n'a été payé aucuns droits attendu la
destination, pour sûreté desquels & du quatruple, même
de confiscation, s'il y a lieu, ledit . . . . & le sieur
. . . . demeurant . . . . à . . . . sa caution ont promis de rapporter dans . . . . certificat au
dos du présent, de la descente & déchargement desd.
Marchandises audit lieu d . . . . signé des
Commis du Bureau des Traites de . . . . ou des
Curé, Juge, Echevin, Syndic d . . . . à deffaut
de Commis des Traites ausquels lesd. Marchandises
seront représentées sans fraude, même de certifier
la vérité des signatures dud. certificat de décharge aux
peines portées par les Articles VIII & XII du titre 6
de l'Ordonnance de 1687 & de l'Arrest du Conseil du
13 Mars 1722 & Lettres Patentes sur icelui ausquels ils se
sont soumis; ainsi qu'à la Jurisdiction des Fermes, pour
raison de ce, le présent nul après . . . . jours & si la
sortie n'est certifiée dans ce jour par un Garde. Fait au
Bureau des Fermes, à . . . . ce . . . . jour d . . . .
mil sept cent . . . . à . . . . heures à . . . . . .
midy.

. . . .
. . . .

[*verso*]

Na. Ceux   Nous soussignés
qui donneront   Certifions qu'il a esté déchargé en la maison de . . . .
le Certificat   à . . . . Paroisse d . . . . . . Election d . . . .
mettront leur   Province d . . . . la quantité d . . . . . .
qualité

        contenues en l'acquit de l'autre part, cejourd'hui
mil sept cent . . . . . .

DIRECTION DE DIJON

Bail de . . . .

Bureau   d . . . .

[SEAL]

No . . . .
de la Déclaration   Acquit de Paiement
No . . . .
de la Recette

Commis & Gardes des Fermes du Roi laissez passer le
Sr . . . . demeurant à . . . . venant de . . . .
Province de . . . . pour le compte de . . . .
Marchand à . . . . les Marchandises ci-apres détail-
lées:

Sçavoir

Na. Les commis   . . . .
auront attention   . . . .
de distinguer les   . . . .
balles, caisses, ...
tonneaux, & futailles . . ..
où chaque espèce de . . . .
Marchandise est   . . . .
renfermée & de   -———
remplir exactement
tous les blancs   ———

. . . .

desquelles Marchandises il a payé les droits d . . .
montant à la somme de . . . . . dont il fera la conduite en
déclarant qu'il passera par . . . . s'étant soumis de
représenter lesdites Marchandises à tous les Bureaux de la
Route, de même que le présent pour y être visé, à peine
de confiscation des Marchandises, & l'amende, suivant
les articles 16, 17, & 18, titre 2 de l'Ordonnance de 1687.
Fait au Bureau des Fermes du Roi à . . . . le . . .
jour du mois d . . . . mil sept cent quatre-vingt . . . .

. . . .
. . . .

DIRECTION DE LAVAL
Bureau d . . . . [SEAL]
Controlle
de passage

Brevet de Controlle
No . . .   Du . . . jour   de . . . . 174 . . à . . heure   a . . midi   au
Bureau des Fermes du Roy, à . . . . . le Sr . . . . du
lieu de . . . . venant de . . . . . allant à . . . . a
déclaré avoir charge à . . . . la quantité de

Cy-contre sera   . . . .
ecrit la quantité
& poids des marchandises . . . .
& les Droits tirés en
chiffre de la Même   . . . .
manière qu'ils sont
portés dans l'acquit que . . . .
l'on gardera   ————

                                                      ————
                                                      ————
                                                      . . . .

dont les Droits montent en total à la somme de . . . .
. . . . suivant   l'Acquit   dudi: Bureau   d . . . . en
papier timbré, signé . . . . resté en nos mains dont
copie ci-dessus. Fait à Laval par moy . . . .
. . . . . . ce . . . . . . jour   d . . . .
mil   sept   cens   quarante . . . .

. . . .

APPENDIX II

Droit unique avec la suppression des bureaux intérieures.

(Notes written by Michel Amelot, marquis de Gournay, on August 13 and 20, 1720, and now in the Archives Nationales, ms. F12 827)

[*Dated 13 August 1720*]

Deux questions ou difficultés générales qui tombent sur les diverses provinces étrangères comme sur la Bretagne.

1ère

Les droits qui se payent sur le sel comme marchandise, savoir si on les supprimera.

2ième

Savoir si les vins ou autres marchandises sortant de Bordeaux par exemple et allant en Bretagne doivent payer les droits ou en estre exemptes.

Na les droits sur le sel pourraient estre levés nons dans l'intérieur du royaume mais dans les lieux mesmes où sont les marais salans.

Embarras d'establir des Bureaux le long des Pirénées frontières d'Espagne, dans un pays qui a toujours esté entièrement libre.

Privilège des foires de Bordeaux, savoir s'il exemptera du droit unique ou d'une partie proportionnée au bénéfice que produisait cy devant tems de Foires suivant ce qui est proposé par le Député de Bordeaux.

Bretagne

Chaine de Bureaux sur la frontière où ils se lèvent des droits. Voir M. des Cazaux et l'engager à faire un mémoire pour répondre aux objections que les Bretons pourraient faire.

Mettre M. le M^{rl} d'Estrées au fait et proposer à S.A.R. de faire mettre un article sur cette matière dans l'instruction des M^{rs} les Commissaires du Roy qui doivent assister aux Etats.

Bureaux qui sont établis entre le Poitou, le Berry et le Bourbonnois et qui séparent d'avec la marche l'Auvergne le Limousin, etc. . . . . . .

Guyenne

Droit de Comptablie en Guyenne comme droit intérieur sur ce qui entre par terre dans la sénéchaussée de Bordeaux et qui en sort.

Patente de Languedoc, traitte d'Arzac dont les droits se perçoivent sur ce qui sort de cette province pour Guyenne.

Escrire à M^{rs} les Intendants de Bordeaux, de Pau et de Roussillon pour les consulter sur l'établissement de ces bureaux dont on pourrait reculer la ligne sans les pousser jusqu'à l'extrémité des frontières, en cas d'impossibilité de les y mettre.

On aura le bail fait de ce droit par M. le duc de Gramont auquel il s'agira de donner une indemnité.

Coûtume de Bayonne et pays de Labour. Le droit a été acheté par le Roy de la ville de Bayonne et S.M. en a aliéné la moitié en faveur de M. de Gramont, ce qui fait une grande difficulté.

2ième difficulté
Exemption des bourgeois de Bayonne pour ce qui entre et sort, chercher un expédient ou pouvoir donner la franchise à la ville et faire payer le droit unique aux entrées de la ville par terre.

Ce lieu n'étant pas fermé on ne peut prendre de mesmes expédients qu'à Bayonne. On pourrait reculer les bureaux en deça sans les pousser sur la fontière.

St. Jean de Luz a une pareille exemption que Bayonne. Le pays de Labour ne paye point de droits pour les denrées et autres choses de leur usage.

Droits nouveaux sur le tabac qui ne se lèvent que dans les pays anciens des C.G.F. aussi difficultés à Bayonne etc. . . . .

Roussillon
Il n'y aurait pas de difficulté à supprimer les droits intérieurs et à etablir le droit unique sur la frontière du Costé de Catalogne.

Languedoc
Nulle difficulté à supprimer les droits pour le passage dans le Dauphiné et dans la provence et établir le droit unique sur toute la coste sur la Méditerranée.

Na du costé du comtat d'Avignon laisser les bureaux d'y faire payer le droit unique.

[*Dated 20 August 1720*]

Provence
Nulle difficulté non plus qu'en Languedoc à supprimer les Bureaux intérieurs en établissant le droit unique sur les costes de la mer et sur les frontières du costé des estats de Mr le duc de Savoye.

Na Principauté d'Orange comme pour le Comtat d'Avignon

Dauphiné
Idem en établissant le droit unique
sur les frontières de Dauphiné où
il y a déjà des bureaux.

Lyon
Les 4 foires emportant l'exemption
entendre Mr Anisson & etc. . . .   de tous les droits de sortie, ce sera
une question de voir si on con-
Na la principauté de Dombes   servera cette exemption en tout ou
en partie, attendu la suppression
de tous les autres droits.

Franche Comté
Difficulté du tabac   On ne prévoit pas de difficulté
particulière en cette province si ce
Convient (?) plusieurs autres   n'est par rapport aux Suisses qui ont
provinces.   commerce avec cette province.

Alsace
Examiner ce qui convient avec cette
province et s'il n'est pas plus à
propos de la laisser comme elle est
aujourd'huy, ainsy que la Lorraine
Ajouter Sedan et sa principauté   et les Trois Eveschés, sans rien
changer aux Bureaux de Cham-
pagne, attendu l'extresme embarras
de multiplier les bureaux sur
touttes les frontières qui sont meslées
et enclavées avec les terres de
Lorraine et le Clermontois
Il faudra escrire à M^rs les
Intendants de ces provinces.

Flandre, Haynault et Artois
Deux grandes difficultes d'y établir
En escrire à M^rs les Intendants   les Bureaux du droit unique qui
sont présentement en Picardie.
Le bénéfice du transit accordé à
Lille & . . . .
les droits du tabac qui n'y ont jamais
eu lieu, et les plantations qu'il
faudrait y faire arracher.

N

APPENDIX III

Inventaire raisonné des opérations concernant le tarif du droit unique

(Copy of a manuscript memoir compiled in the 1740's and describing the records of the single duty project sponsored by the Farmers General and prepared under the direction of Michel-Joseph-Hyacinth Lallemant de Betz beginning in 1726. This manuscript is now in the Archives nationales G1 3–5.)

Comme il a été fait un inventaire de tous les titres, papiers, mémoriaux, et livres déposés dans le bureau des tarifs pour en faciliter la recherche, il suffira d'en joindre une copie à celui-ci, dans lequel on ne fera qu'exposer les diverses opérations concernant le Tarif du Droit Unique, et les motifs de ces opérations.

Opérations préliminaires qui ont servi d'instruction

1. Mémoires sur le tarif de 1664 au nombre de 191. Mémoires sur chacune des marchandises contenues au tarif de 1664 et sur les droits imposés par ce tarif, dans lesquelles sont rapportés au long les règlements postérieurs qui y ont apporté des changements pour travailler utilement sur le projet du Droit Unique; il était nécessaire de connaître à fond le tarif des Cinq Grosses Fermes, qui est comme l'esquisse de ce projet.

2. Cartes des droits des cuirs, drogueries, etc. au nombre de cinq. Cartes générales des droits dus à l'entrée et à la sortie sur les cuirs, peaux, et pelleteries, vins, étoffes, toiles, drogueries, et épiceries.

3. Extraits des règlements. Extraits des édits, arrêts, et autres règlements concernant la ferme des traites, et même des tarifs et des procès-verbaux de tournée de Messieurs les fermiers généraux. Ces extraits rangés par nature de droits et de privilèges ont été faits pour faciliter l'examen et la citation des règlements dans les mémoires sur les marchandises.

4. Compilation des marchandises: 1 volume. Compilation des marchandises dans laquelle sont rassemblées toute les dénominations comprises dans les tarifs et dans les règlements.

5. Compilation des tarifs à l'entrée: 1 volume. Compilation des tarifs contenant sous des titres génériques les noms de toutes les marchandises et servant à faire connaître tant celles qui sont tarifées sous différents noms, et à des droits différents, dans un même tarif, que celles qui y sont omises.

6. Mémoires sur les tarifs obscurs.

Mémoires particuliers sur les droits dont les tarifs sont obscurs, comme la Douane de Lyon, la Douane de Valence, la Foraine, les Drogueries, etc. Il résulte de ces mémoires que dans une infinité de cas, les droits de ces tarifs sont perçus à des taux arbitraires et introduits par un usage abusif et par conséquent que lesdits tarifs ont besoin de réformation.

7. Cartes par routes.

Cartes par routes et par départements imaginées pour prévenir les doubles emplois, dans lesquels le dépouillement dont il sera parlé ci-après semblait devoir entrainer. On a trouvé tant de difficultés à vaincre dans l'exécution de ces cartes qu'on a été contraint d'abandonner l'opération dont il ne reste qu'un essai.

Opérations formant le corps de l'ouvrage

8. Préface.

Mémoire servant d'introduction au travail du projet du Droit Unique.

(This memoir is to be found in B.N. ms. fr. 7771, fol. 206 ff.)

9. Dépouillement.

Le dépouillement des registres de recette du bail de Manis n'a pu être conduit à la fin pour laquelle il a été fait qu'après plusieurs opérations qui en font partie et dont on trouvera un détail exact dans la préface de l'ouvrage. Il renferme:

(1) les premier feuilles ou relevés des marchandises déclarées, et les droits perçus sur icelles. Ces feuilles contiennent le départ et la destination;

(2) les cartes qui ont servi de contrôle;

(3) les deuxièmes relevés qui contiennent la division des marchandises;

(4) les troisièmes relevés dans lesquels on a rassemblé tout ce qui a été déclaré d'une même marchandise où néanmoins les quantités sont divisées par espèces et par commerces;

(5) enfin, les quatrièmes relevés qui rassemblent sous des titres génériques, et par commerces séparés, tout ce qui a été déclaré d'une même marchandise pendant une année commune, en sorte qu'on voit d'un coup d'oeil combien chaque espèce de cette marchandise a produit de droits à l'entrée, à la sortie, et dans les autres commerces, le total des quantités de chaque commerce, et le total de tous les produits.

10. Principes des réductions: 2 volumes.

Tarif de rapport des différents poids et mesures usités dans le Royaume, au moyen du quel on est parvenu à réduire toutes les quantités des marchandises déclarées au quintal poids de marc, et à des mesures uniformes de contenance et d'étendue. Comme on y rend compte des principes sur lesquels les réductions ont été opérées on l'a intitulé *Principes des réductions*.

(To be found in the library of the Ecole nationale des ponts et Chaussees, ms. 1046, tome vii.)

11. Délibérations de la Compagnie.

Principes sur lesquels le Droit a été arbitré contenus dans la Délibération de la Compagnie du 9 juillet, 1728. Cette pièce est insérée dans la préface. (To be found in B.N., ms. fr. 7771, fol. 209).

12. Prix courants d'Hollande et de Rouen.

Etats contenants les prix courants des marchandises en Hollande et à Rouen. Les marchandises y sont rangées par ordre alphabétique et sous des titres génériques. Ces prix ont été rassemblés pour en tirer la valeur qui devait servir à l'arbitrage du droit unique, mais comme les feuilles ne contenaient qu'un très petit nombre de marchandises il a fallu avoir recours aux Chambres de Commerce.

13. Prix certifiés: 1 volume.

Autres états contenant par ordre alphabétique et sous des titres génériques toutes les marchandises dont les noms se sont trouvés dans le dépouillement, et dans la compilation des marchandises, et la valeur d'un quintal poids de marc de celles qui se vendent au poids, d'un muids, d'un cent en nombre, d'une pièce de tant d'aunes, et etc. conformément aux mesures usitées pour chaque espèce. Cette opération a occasioné un grand nombre d'ordres et de lettres missives qu'on a transcrit dans des registres tenus à cet effet. On a rassemblé dans des états généraux tous les états particuliers envoyés aux Chambres de Commerce et qu'elles ont renvoyés remplis et certifiés. En outre on y a rassemblé les prix donnés sur une même marchandise par toutes les Chambres, on en a fait un total dont on a tiré le pied commun. C'est ce pied commun qui a servi à l'arbitrage du Droit Unique.

(To be found in, Ponts et Chaussees, ms. 1046, tome vi.)

14. Mémoires sur les marchandises: 5 volumes.

Mémoires dans lesquels on a traité non-seulement de la nature, de l'origine, des propriétés, des apprêts, de chaque marchandise en particulier, mais encore de l'objet dont elle est dans le commerce soit extérieur soit intérieur. On y rapporte au long tous les règlements qu'elle a occasionné, tant pour les droits que pour les manufactures, on y touche l'origine et l'étendue des droits; on y rapporte les quantités entrées, sorties, et commercées dans l'intérieur pendant une année commune du Bail de Manis, le montant des droits que ces quantités ont acquittés, et la valeur d'un quintal poids de marc ou autre quantité, suivant l'espèce, tirée des prix certifiés par les Chambres de commerce. Sur les réflexions qui naissent du tout, on arbitre le Droit Unique à proposer; et même on expose les règlements qu'il conviendrait de faire pour l'avantage du commerce.

(To be found in, Ponts et Chaussees, ms. 1046, tomes ii, iii and iv.)

15. Table des règlements: 1 volume.

Table chronologique des ordonnances, édits, arrêts, ordres, et décisions cités dans les mémoires sur les marchandises.

(To be found in, Ponts et Chaussees, ms. 1046, tome v.)

16. Balances: 11 volumes.

Etats de comparaison par chaque espèce de marchandise contenant les quantités déclarées année commune et les droits perçus distingés par commerces d'entrée, de sortie, de port en port, intérieur des Cinq Grosses Fermes, intérieur des provinces réputées étrangères, comparées avec le produit de Droit Unique proposé pris sur les même quantités. Ces balances indiquent la porte qui doit resulter de la suppression des droits locaux et de l'intérieur et de la réduction des droits d'entrée et de sortie; elles ont servi à former la balance générale.

(To be found in, Ponts et Chaussees, ms. 1046, tomes viii to xiii.)

17. Index: 1 volume.

Table alphabétique des marchandises contenues dans le tarif du Droit Unique, et renvoyées à leurs titres génériques.

(To be found in, Ponts et Chaussees, ms. 1046, tome i.)

18. Nouveau tarif: 1 volume.

Projet du tarif du Droit Unique contenant les noms des marchandises rangés alphabétiquement sous leurs titres génériques; et à côté de chaque nom la quotité du droit proposé. On y a joint dans une colonne séparée les changements que le Conseil de Commerce y a faits.

(To be found in, Ponts et Chaussees, ms. 1046, tome xv.)

19. Cahier contenant les changements que le Conseil a jugé à propos de faire dans plusieurs articles du tarif proposé, et les motifs de ces changements qu'on appelle décisions. A côté sont les motifs qui ont déterminé à proposer les droits changés.

(To be found in, A.N., G¹ 79.)

20. Balance en conséquence des décisions du Conseil.

Etat de comparaison des droits contenus dans le tarif proposé pris sur les quantités déclarées année commune, avec le produit des droits arrêtés par le Conseil pris sur les mêmes quantités. Cet état sert à faire connaître la perte ou le profit résultant des articles réformés dans le nouveau tarif.

Privilèges

Les besoins de l'Etat ont engagé en différents temps de faire des traités d'alliance et de commerce avec plusieurs nations et villes étrangères et de leur accorder des privilèges qui consistent en exemptions et modérations des droits imposés sur les marchandises qu'ils apportent dans le Royaume, sur celles qu'ils en tirent, et sur celles qu'ils font passer par les lieux de leur possession enclavés dans les terres de France, et vice versa, ce qu'on appelle transit.

21. Mémoires sur les privilèges.

On a traité ces privilèges séparément dans des mémoires particuliers dans lesquels on a rapporté les époques et les titres de leur création, les différentes confirmations accordées de règne en règne, et les extensions et restrictions qui y ont été faites. On fait voir quels sont les avantages ou les détriments qu'ils causent au commerce; l'objet de ces privilèges par les quantités des marchandises qui en ont joui pendant une année commune du bail de Manis, soit à l'entrée, soit à la sortie, dans le cas du transit, et dans le commerce intérieur. Sur le tout on conclut à les confirmer, à les restreindre, ou à les supprimer, selon que le bien du commerce l'exige.

22. Tableau des privilèges.

Tous les privilèges sont exposés en détail dans neuf tableaux ou cartes qui sont le précis des mémoires et contiennent la consistance des privilèges et les titres sur lesquels ils sont fondés. Ces tableaux sont, savoir:

(1) privilèges accordés aux pays étrangers et droits auxquels ils sont sujets en particulier;

(2) privilèges accordés au commerce des Indes Orientales, et des cotes d'Afrique tant sur l'océan que sur la Méditerranée;

(3) privilèges accordés au commerce des Isles et colonies françaises de l'Amérique;

(4) privilèges accordés à la Compagnie des Indes, et droits auxquels elle est assujetie;

(5) privilèges accordés à la ville de Marseille, la ville de Bayonne, et la ville de Dunkerque;

(6) droits que payent les marchandises qui entrent et sortent par les Provinces réputées étrangères;

(7) privilèges accordés aux foires et aux manufactures du Royaume;

(8) privilèges accordés aux villes, bourgs, et communautés du Royaume;

(9) privilèges accordés aux communautés et maisons religieuses, à l'Hôtel Royal des Invalides, aux hôpitaux du Royaume, et aux munitionnaires et fournisseurs des vivres, bois, et autres Choses nécessaires à la Marine et aux armées du Roi.

23. Dépouillement, cartes, relevés, et balances.

Les marchandises qui ont joui des privilèges pendant le Bail de Manis ayant été dépouillées séparément, on en a fait des relevés semblables à ceux dont il est parlé plus haut. Et après la conclusion des mémoires on a dressé des balances particulières et une balance générale à l'instar et pour les mêmes fins que les balances du Droit Unique.

24. Droits non-répartis.

On a joint aux mémoires sur les privilèges des mémoires particuliers sur les droits qui n'ont point été répartis dans le dépouillement. Ces droits sont les droits d'acquit et autres de cette espèce, comme Patache, Quillage, Brieux, et autres semblables. On s'est attaché à en développer l'origine, et à fixer les cas dans lesquels ils sont dûs. Et l'on a inséré à la fin de chaque mémoire le produit total de chacun desdits droits pendant une année commune du bail de Manis. Na le Conseil n'a point vu les opérations sur les privilèges.

Opérations postérieures à l'examen du projet du Droit Unique

25. Mémoire sur les règlements concernant le commerce d'Hollande. Mémoire pour connaître de quelle considération les règlements concernant le commerce des Hollandais doivent être dans le projet du nouveau tarif. Les états de comparaison des droits des anciens tarifs de Hollande avec

ceux du Placard de 1725 démontrent que les Hollandais ont enfreint la Convention de 1699 et apporté une lésion considérable au commerce que la France fait avec eux.

26. Comparaison des droits du tarif de 1699 sur les marchandises d'Hollande entrantes dans le Royaume avec les Droits du tarif du Droit Unique sur les mêmes espèces de marchandises l'en ont des autres pays étrangers. Pour montrer que les droits auxquels les marchandises comprises au tarif de 1699 sont imposées par le nouveau tarif sont des droits exclusifs qui ne peuvent opérer une augmentation de produit.

28. Privilèges de Marseille.

Mémoire particulier en conséquence des décisions du Conseil dans la séance du 13 avril 1737 sur les privilèges de Marseille. On y établit qu'il suffit d'exempter les citadins de cette ville de la 10ᵉ partie des droits du nouveau tarif sur les drogueries et des trois quarts des droits dudit tarif à la sortie sur quelques espèces de marchandises y dénommées.

29. Etablissement du Droit Unique.

Mémoire dans lequel on examine différentes manières d'établir le Droit Unique, et l'on conclut à préférer l'établissement par provinces.

30. Etablissement du droit dans les Provinces réputées étrangères.

Mémoire à prouver l'utilité de l'établissement du nouveau tarif dans les Provinces réputées étrangères.

31. Réflexions sur les moyens de faire agréer le nouveau tarif par les Provinces réputées étrangères.

32. Etats concernant la Bretagne et la Franche Comté.

Etats dont le premier contient les quantités des marchandises entrées par mer en Bretagne pendant une année commune du Bail de Manis, et le montant des droits du nouveau tarif tirés sur ces quantités. Le deuxième contient tous quantités des marchandises qui ont fait pendant la même année l'objet du commerce de la Franche Comté avec l'étranger et avec les autres provinces du Royaume, et le produit du Droit Unique pris sur ces quantités. Il résulte de la comparaison de ces deux commerces que la Franche Comté serait extrêmement favorisée par l'établissement du nouveau tarif et la suppression des droits qu'elle paye dans son commerce avec l'intérieur.

33. Etablissement du Droit Unique dans les provinces de Dauphiné, Provence, & etc.

Projet d'un tarif de droits pour être perçus aux entrées et sorties du Royaume et substitués aux droits qui se perçoivent actuellement dans les provinces du Dauphiné, Provence, Languedoc, Roussillon, Gascogne, et Guienne. Cet état est fait pour faciliter le rapport au Conseil du tarif ci-dessus.

35. Balance du produit du Droit Unique tiré sur les quantités des marchandises déclarées année commune, pendant le Bail de Manis, à l'entrée et à la sortie des provinces de Dauphiné, Provence, Languedoc, et Roussillon, comparé avec le produit des droits perçus pendant ledit bail dans ces mêmes provinces, tant sur les marchandises qu'elles tirent de l'étranger et celles qu'elles y envoient, que sur celles qu'elles se communiquent réciproquement. Cette balance montre la perte résultante de l'établissement du tarif ci-dessus.

36. Suppression de frais de régie.

Etat des bureaux et frais de régie dont la suppression sera causée par l'établissement du Droit Unique dans les provinces de Dauphiné, Provence, Languedoc, et etc. comparés avec ceux qu'il convient de créer pour la perception du nouveau droit. Suivant cet état l'arrangement proposé ne doit opérer ni profit ni perte.

37. Etablissement du Droit Unique sur les frontières d'Espagne et Béarn. Balance du produit du Droit Unique tiré sur les quantités des marchandises déclarées pendant une année commune du Bail de Manis, à l'entrée et à la sortie, dans les bureaux situés sur les frontières d'Espagne et de Béarn, depuis le comté de Foix jusqu'aux Landes de Bordeaux, comparée avec les droits perçus dans les mêmes bureaux pendant le même bail. Il résulte de cette comparaison que l'établissement du Droit Unique au lieu des droits qui se perçoivent sur ces frontières opérerait un profit considérable.

38. Est-il préférable d'établir à toutes les entrées et sorties les droits tels qu'ils se perçoivent à Rouen au lieu du Droit Unique?

Balance des droits qui se perçoivent à l'entrée et à la sortie du Royaume dans les bureaux du département de Rouen comparés avec les droits adoptés dans le nouveau tarif. Elle fait connaître la proportion qu'il y a entre l'un et l'autre de ces droits, et conduit à juger lequel conviendrait le mieux d'établir à toutes les entrées et sorties des droits communs de tous, et qui se perçoivent dans la partie du Royaume où le commerce est le plus considérable, où des droits inconnus par l'étranger et par le français, quoi qu'arbitrés sur des principes de commerce, certain, et exactement pesés par le Conseil.

39. Autre moyens de supprimer les droits de l'intérieur.

Etat des droits perçus au profit de la ferme des traites pendant la première années du Bail de Forceville pour voir si en ajoutant 2 sols ou 3 sols par livre des produits des différents droits qui se perçoivent à l'entrée et à la sortie du Royaume on ne pourrait pas parvenir à supprimer les droits locaux de l'intérieur. Ces états contiennent les noms, situations, et produits des bureaux qu'on propose de conserver et des bureaux à supprimer.

40. Cartes géographiques enluminées pour l'intelligence des états ci-dessus. On y a distingué par couleurs les différents départements en quoi les bureaux des traites sont divisés.

41. Sortie des fers.

Etat des quantités, prix, et valeur des fers entrés et sortis du Royaume pendant une année commune du Bail de Manis pour juger des demandes réitérées des maîtres de forges de favoriser la sortie de leurs fers.

42. Manufactures et droits qu'elles payent.

Etat de toutes les marchandises manufacturées en France sorties pendant une année commune du Bail de Manis. Cet état contient les quantités, le prix, et valeur desdites marchandises, et les droits qu'elles ont acquittés. Il a été fait dans la vue de montrer l'objet du commerce des manufactures et ce qu'elles rapportent à la ferme des traites et pour voir s'il serait possible de les exempter des droits de sortie en tout ou en partie.

43. Droits de sortie sur les étoffes, bonneteries, et toiles. Etat des tissus de laine, lin, chanvre, soie, poil, fil d'or et d'argent, et autres manufactures

semblables, sorties du Royaume pendant une année commune du Bail de Manis. Cet état extrait du précédent a servi à la discussion des motifs des arrêts des 13, et 15 octobre, 1743, qui déchargent de tous droits à la sortie les étoffes, bonneteries, tapisseries, et toiles des fabriques du Royaume.

44. Projet de l'établissement d'une foire à Cette.

Etat de comparaison servant à faire connaître la différence résultante des droits qui se perçoivent actuellement dans le port de Cette, Direction de Montpellier, tant sur les marchandises et denrées venant de l'étranger dans le Royaume que sur celles du crû de ladite province sortantes pour l'étranger, aux droits d'un projet de tarif pendant le temps des foires qu'on propose d'établir dans ce port.

BIBLIOGRAPHY

Note: Library reference numbers given in brackets are those of the *Bibliothèque nationale* in Paris unless otherwise stated. They indicate the actual volumes used.

1. Manuscript

Archives nationales

AB XIX 327, Registre de documents relatifs à la gestion de Monsieur Dufresne comme Directeur du Trésor public (1789–91), 649 fol.

AD IX 488, 489 and 551, Section administrative, collection Rondonneau (papers on financial administration)

AD XVIII^c 65 and 66, Bibliothèque administrative Rondonneau (collection of printed reports and speeches on customs matters at the Constituent Assembly)

AF IV 1318, Secrétairerie d'Etat impériale (reports and projects from the offices of customs and commerce)

29 AP 81 to 86, papers of Pierre-Louis Roederer

BB^1 72 (plaquet 9), and 84 (plaquet 8), Ministère de la Justice

B^3 348 (Marine), B^7 546 (Marine), Archives de la Marine

C 2, 9 (p. 278), 92 (79), and 98 (136), Procès-verbaux et pièces annexes de l'Assemblée des Notables

DX 1, 2 and 3, Assemblée constituante, Comité des pensions

F^{1a} 566, Administration générale, pensions civiles, 1763–1816

F^4 70 and 71, Administration générale, comptabilité générale

F^4 1032^2, 1040, 1938 and 2678, Administration générale, comptabilité générale

F^{12} 51, 54, 107, 114 to 120, 131, 152, 157, 171, 84 and 203

F^{12} 565, 641, 650, 652, 655^A, 658^A, 660, 693, 694, 713, 714, 716, 724, 726^A, 726^B, 827, 828, 830, 831, 1315^B, 1903, 1094, 1905, 1908, 1909, 1910 and 2427, Commerce et industrie

F^{30} 110^1 and 111, Administration générale des finances

G 134 (Marine), Archives de la Marine

G^1 1–2, 3–5, 6, 13, 63 and 79, Ferme générale

G^1 46, Ferme générale

G^7 1176, 1686, 1687, 1699 and 1704, Contrôle général

H 123–126, 500, 1428 and 1448, Administration locale

H^4 2967^1, *péages*

K 677 and 885, monuments historiques (memoirs on finance, &c.)

O^3 747, Maison du Roi (requests for pensions, &c.)

Bibliothèque nationale

ms. fr. 4701, 6682, 6683, 6799, 7728, 7729, 7771, 7772, 7773, 8038, 8292, 8360, 8370, 8371, 11097, 11098, 11150, 11166 to 11178, 12305 and 14294

ms. fr. 11166 to 11178, *Dictionnaire alphabétique des traites*, 13 vols. in ms., written by Duclos (secretary to the Farmer General de la Borde) between 1726 and 1738, revised shortly after 1754 (A.N., G¹ 79)

nouv. acq. fr. 995, 2721, 7903 and 22253

Collection Fontanieu, portefeuilles 709 to 712

Collection Joly de Fleury, 1038 to 1040

Collection Moreau, 1088

Bibliothèque de l'Arsenal

ms. 4023, Mémoire de Monsieur Daguesseau sur la douane de Lyon et la douane de Valence 1688

ms. 4395 and 4396 (memoirs of the Deputies of Commerce)

ms. 4905

Bibliothèque mazarine

ms. 2406, 2778, 2779 and 2840

Archives de l'Administration de l'Assistance Publique

Papers of Antoine-Jean-Baptiste-Robert Auget de Montyon, of which there are more than fifty unclassified boxes

Bibliothèque de l'Ecole nationale des Ponts et Chaussées

ms. 1045, Le Tarif général du droit unique (1737), 16 vols. in fol., pagination continuous throughout with 8185 fols. Prepared by Michel-Joseph Hyacinth Lallemant de Betz

2. Books, Pamphlets and Articles

ALLARDE, Pierre-Gilbert Le Roi, baron d', *Motion sur un nouveau régime de finances*, 2 October 1789, 42 pp. (A.N., AD IX 551)

—— *Motifs et précis de la motion de Monsieur le baron d'Allarde sur un nouveau régime des finances*, Versailles (Baudouin), 1789, 8 pp. and 142 pp. and 12 pièces justificatives (Le²⁹ 1920)

ALMANACH ROYAL, Paris, 1699 ff., a vol. for each year

AMÉ, Léon, *Etude économique sur les tarifs de douanes*, Paris (Guillaumin), 1859

—— *Etude sur les tarifs de douanes et sur les traités de commerce* Paris (Imp. nat.), 1876, 2 vols.

ANQUETIN, Jean-Charles, 'Les observations sur un ouvrage de Monsieur le maréchal de Vauban intitulé Dixme Royale' (April 1709), *R.h.d.é.s.*, 1910

Aperçu sur le reculement des barrières jusqu'au Rhin (1789), 32 pp. (Lf⁸⁹ 17)

ARNAUNÉ, Auguste, *Le commerce extérieur et les tarifs de douane*, Paris (Alcan), 1911

—— 'Les tarifs douaniers de 1791', *R.h.d.e.s.*, 1911

ARNOULD, Ambroise-Marie, *De la balance du commerce et des relations commerciales extérieures de la France.* . . . , Paris (Buisson), 1791, 2 vols. in 8° and 1 vol. in 4° (V. 30756–30757)

—— *Histoire générale des finances de la France depuis le commencement de la monarchie.* . . . , Paris (Imp. ordinaire du corps législatif), 1806

AUGÉARD, Jacques-Mathieu, *Mémoires secrets*, Paris (Plon), 1866

Avis aux négociants de Lyon sur cette question importante : n'est-il pas plus nuisible qu'avantageux à la ville de Lyon d'avoir une douane sous quelque dénomination qu'on puisse la considérer ? présenté à la société des amis de la constitution. . . . , Lyon (Faucheux), 1790, 16 pp. in 12°, signed 8 December 1790

BACALAN, Isaac de, 'Observations faites par Monsieur de Bacalan dans son voyage en Picardie, Artois, Haynaut et Flandre, l'an 1768', *R.h.d.e.s.*, 1908

BACHAUMONT, Louis and successors, *Mémoires secrets pour servir à l'histoire de la république des lettres en France, depuis 1762 jusqu'à nos jours ou journal d'un observateur.* . . . , London (Adamson), 1784–9, 36 vols. See also, *Table alphabétique des auteurs et personnages cités dans les mémoires secrets pour servir.* . . . , Brussels (Mertens & fils), 1866

BACQUÈS, Henri, *Essai historique sur les douanes françaises*, Paris (Bonaventure & Ducessois), 1852

BACQUIÉ, Franc, *Les Inspecteurs des Manufactures sous l'ancien régime, 1669–1792* (*Mémoires et documents pour servir à l'histoire du commerce et de l'industrie de la France*, ed. Julien Hayem, 11e série), Paris (Hachette), 1927

Bayonne, Chambre de Commerce, Mémoire sur l'ancien état de cette ville et les révolutions arrivées à son commerce, Bayonne, 1738, 64 pp. (V. 5330)

Bayonne, Chambre de Commerce, Réfutation par Messieurs les président et directeurs de la Chambre de commerce et commissaires de la commune de Bayonne, du rapport fait à l'Assemblée nationale sur la franchise de Bayonne, par M. Lasnier de Vaussenay, vice-président de son Comité d'Agriculture et du Commerce . . . , Paris (Roland), 1790, 19 pp. in 4° (B.M., 936 c 4)

BERTHOLON, abbé Pierre, *Du commerce et des manufactures distinctives de la ville de Lyon*, Montpellier (Jean Martel), 1787, 220 pp. and tables (B.M., 8235 ee 9)

BESENVAL, Pierre-Victor, baron de, *Mémoires écrits par lui-même*, Paris (Buisson), 1805, 3 vols.

BIOLLAY, Léon, *Le pacte de famine : l'Administration du commerce*, Paris (Guillaumin), 1885

BLOCH, Camille, ed., *Comité des finances de l'Assemblée constituante* (*Collection de documents inédits sur l'histoire économique de la Révolution française publiés par le Ministère de l'Instruction publique*), Rennes (Oberthur), 1922

BOESNIER DE l'ORME, *De l'esprit du gouvernement économique*, Paris, 1775

BOISGUILLEBERT, Pierre le Pesant de, *La France ruinée sous le règne de Louis XIV par qui et comment, avec les moyens de la rétablir en peu de tems*, Cologne (Pierre Marteau), 1696, 214 pp.

—— *Le détail de la France sous le règne présent augmenté en cette nouvelle édition de plusieurs mémoires et traitez sur la même matière*, 1707, 2 vols.

BOISLANDRY Louis, *Vues impartiales sur l'établissement des assemblées provinciales, sur leur formation, sur l'impôt territorial et sur les traites*, London and Paris (Duplain), 1787, 90 pp.

—— *Opinion sur le projet de tarif du Comité d'Agriculture et de Commerce*, Paris (Baudouin), 1790, 33 pp. (delivered on 30 November 1790)

BOISLISLE, A.-M. de, *Correspondance des Contrôleurs généraux des finances avec les Intendants des provinces*, Paris (Imp. nat.), 1874–97, 3 vols.

BONNASSIEUX, Pierre, and LELONG, *Conseil de commerce et Bureau du commerce, 1700 à 1791, inventaire analytique de procès-verbaux*, Paris (Imp. nat.), 1900, with a biographical appendix

BOULAINVILLIERS, comte de, *Etat de la France*, London (T. Wood), 1727, 2 vols. in fol. (Fol. L¹ 3)

—— *Mémoires présentés à Monseigneur le duc d'Orléans*, The Hague, 1727 (R. 29725–29726)

BOUTEIL, Jeanne, *Le rachat des péages au dix-huitième siècle d'après les papiers du Bureau des péages*, Paris (Univ. of Paris), 1925 (8° F 31025)

BOYETET, Edouard, *Recueil de divers mémoires relatifs au traité de commerce avec l'Angleterre fait avant, pendant et après cette négotiation*, Versailles (Baudouin), 1789, 1 vol. in 8°, 162 pp. and 23 pp. and 18: pp.

—— *Nouveau recueil de mémoires présentés à divers ministres rélativement aux Finances et à l'administration du Commerce*, 1789, 180 pp.

BOYETET DES BORDES, Deputy of Commerce for Bayonne, *Précis sur la franchise de la ville de Bayonne et du pays de Labourd*, Bayonne (Roland), 1790, 27 pp. (Vp 6482)

BRESSON, Louis, *Rèponse d'un citoyen*, Nancy (Thomas), 1762, 132 pp. in 8° (V. 22243)

BRIENNE, le comte de, et Etienne-Charles de Loménie de, *Journal de l'Assemblée des Notables de 1787*, ed. Pierre Chevallier, Paris (Klincksieck), 1960

BROGLIE, duc de, ed., *Mémoires du prince de Talleyrand-Périgord*, Paris, 1891, 5 vols.

BUTENVAL, comte His de, *Précis historique et économique du traité de commerce entre la France et la Grande Bretagne signé à Versailles le 26 septembre 1786*, Paris (Dentu, Sauton), 1869

—— *Des transactions commerciales entre la France et la Grande-Bretagne, étude d'histoire comparée*, Paris (Guillaumin), 1872

—— *Etablissement en France du premier tarif général de douanes*, Paris (Guillaumin), 1876 (L.S.E., W 8411)

CAHEN, Léon, 'Une nouvelle interpretation du traité franco-anglais de 1786–87', *Rev. hist.*, 1939

CALLÉRY, Alphonse, 'Les douanes avant Colbert et l'ordonnance de 1664', *Rev. hist.*, 1882

CALONNE, Charles-Alexandre de, *Mémoires concernant la navigation des rivières de la province des Trois-Evêchés et le commerce de la ville de Metz; lus dans l'Assemblée publique de la société royale des sciences et des arts de*

Metz, tenue le 18 novembre 1772, Metz (Pierre Marchal), 1773, 424 pp. in 4°, pp. 31–54

—— *Réponse de Monsieur de Calonne à l'écrit de Monsieur Necker, publié en avril 1787 contenant l'examen des comptes de la situation des finances rendues...*, London (Spilsbury), January 1788, 424 pp. and 90 pp. and 62 pp. (Lb³⁹ 513 B)

—— *Précis d'un plan d'amélioration des finances présenté au Roi août 1786* (contained in the preceding volume, appendices, pp. 42–62)

CHARLTÉTY, S., 'Le régime douanier de Lyon au XVII siècle', *Rev. d'hist. de Lyon*, 1902

CHASTELLUX, L. E., *Coup d'oeil sur le régime des douanes intérieures en France au dix-huitième siècle (Extrait des mémoires de l'Académie impériale de Metz)*, Metz (Blanc), 1854

CHINAULT, Jules, *La Chambre de commerce de Toulouse du XVIIIᵉ siècle, 1703–1791 (Mémoires de l'Académie de Législation)*, Toulouse, 1956

CLAVIÈRE, Etienne, *Mémoire lu par... Ministre des Contributions publiques à la Convention nationale le 5 octobre 1792*, Paris, 1792 (B.M., F 27*)

CLÉMENT, Pierre, *Histoire du système protecteur en France depuis le ministère de Colbert jusqu'a la Révolution de 1848*, Paris (Guillaumin), 1854

CLIQUOT-BLERVACHE, Simon, *Le Réformateur*, Amsterdam (Arkstée), 1756, 240 pp. and 268 pp.

—— and VINCENT DE GOURNAY, *Considérations sur le commerce et en particulier sur les compagnies, sociétés et maîtrises*, Amsterdam, 1758

Collection des mémoires présentés à l'Assemblée des Notables, première et seconde division, Versailles (Ph. D. Pierres), 1787, see second division, first memoir, *Mémoire sur la réformation des droits de traite, l'abolition des barrières intérieures, l'établissement d'un tarif uniforme aux frontières, et la suppression de plusieurs droits d'aides nuisible au commerce*, 33 pp. and tables.

Compte général des revenus et des dépenses fixes, au premier mai, 1789, Paris (Imp. roy.), 1789, in 4°, 201 pp, 'remis par le premier ministre des finances à MM. du Comité des Finances de l'Assemblée nationale' (A.N., DX 3)

CONDORCET, Antoine-Nicolas, marquis de, *Mémoires sur le règne de Louis XVI et la Révolution extraits de sa correspondance et de celles de ses amis*, vols. vii and viii de *Œuvres choisies de Monsieur le marquis de la Rochefoucault-Liancourt*, Paris (Morris), 1862

Considérations sur l'impôt des gabelles et sur celui du tabac, 1789, 45 pp. (B.M., R 488)

Convention nationale, rapport général sur les contributions de 1793 et projets qui doivent en précéder la fixation, présentés au nom du comité des finances, section contributions directes et indirectes, Paris (Imp. nat.), 1793 (B.M., F.R. 525)

Convention nationale, premier registre des dépenses secrètes de la Cour connu sous le nom de livre rouge, apporté par des députés des corps administratifs de Versailles le 28 février 1793, l'an deuxième de la République, déposé aux archives et imprimé par ordre de la Convention nationale, Paris (Imp. nat.), 1793, 190 pp.; also the deuxième registre (170 pp.), and the troisième registre (63 pp.) (Le³⁸ 200)

COQUELIN and GUILLAUMIN, *Dictionnaire de l'économie politique*, Paris (Guillaumin), 1852, 2 vols. in 8°

CORMERÉ, Guillaume-François Mahy de, *Recherches et considérations nouvelles sur les finances ou mémoire sur leur situation actuelle cause du déficit.* ..., London, 1789, 2 vols. in 8°

—— *Mémoire sur les finances et sur le crédit*, Paris (Moutard & Desenne), 1789, 176 pp. in 8°

—— *Recherches et considérations sur l'impôt ou nouveau régime d'impositions proportionelles aux besoins de l'Etat*, Paris, 1790

—— *Observations à Messieurs les électeurs de la ville et vicomté de Paris par ... sur les réformes utiles et nécessaires dans l'administration des finances*, 1789, 17 pp.

—— *Situation exacte des finances à l'époque du premier janvier 1792: ou lettre de Guillaume-François Mahy de Cormeré à Monsieur le Président et à MM. les Députés composant le Comité des Contributions publiques de l'Assemblée nationale (27 December 1792)*, Nantes (Forest & Hérault), 1792, 59 pp. N.B. for writings in manuscript by Cormeré see *supra* chapter V *passim* and pp. 136 and 147.

COSTER, Joseph-François, *Lettres d'un citoyen à un magistrat sur les raisons qui doivent affranchir le commerce des duchés de Lorraine et de Bar du Tarif général projetté pour le Royaume de France*, 1762, 420 pp. in 8° (V 35455)

—— *Eloge de Jean-Baptiste Colbert*, Paris (Brunet), 1773, 60 pp. in 8° (Ln27 4515)

COURTOY, Ferdinand, *Inventaire des archives de la famille de Gaiffier de Levignen* (at Namur), Brussels, 1949

COYECQUE, Ernest, *L'Inventaire de la collection Anisson sur L'histoire de l'imprimerie et la librairie principalement à Paris*, Paris (Léroux), 1900, 2 vols.

DAIRE, Eugene, ed., *Physiocrates, Quesnay, Dupont de Nemours ... avec une introduction.* ..., Paris (Guillaumin), 1846

DAKIN, Douglas, *Turgot and the Ancien Régime in France*, London (Methuen), 1939

DARIGRAND, avocat au Parlement, *L'Anti-financier ou relevé de quelques-unes des malversations dont se rendent journellement coupables les Fermiers-généraux ...*, Amsterdam, 1764, 57 pp. and 66 pp. in 8° (B.M., 113 n 52)

DELAHANTE, Adrien, *Une famille de finance au dix-huitième siècle*, Paris (Hetzel), 1880, 2 vols.

Département de la Loire inférieure. District de Nantes. Douanes nationales (Extrait de registre des délibérations), 21 December 1790 (B.M., R 496)

Des effets du transport des bureaux des traites aux frontières et autres vues politiques, Metz (Antoine), December 1790, 34 pp. in 8° (Lf89 21)

Dialogue entre Monsieur A ..., Député à l'Assemblée nationale, Monsieur B ..., Fermier Général, et Monsieur le Baron de C [ormeré] sur les impositions indirectes (1790), 76 pp. in 8° (Lb39 3039)

DION, Roger, *Histoire de la vigne et du vin en France*, Paris, 1959

DUBOIS, A., 'Un rapport d'Isaac de Bacalan, Intendant du commerce', *R.h.d.e.s.*, 1908

DUCHESNE DE VOIRON, Louis-Henri, *Projet d'administration remis à Monsieur Turgot quand il fut nommé Contrôleur général et présenté dans l'Assemblée des Notables en 1787 (remis le premier février 1787)* (1789), 16 pp. in 12º (Rp. 8060)

—— *Projet d'imposition juste et facile propre à suppléer.* . . . , Paris, 1789, 34 pp. (B.M., F.R. 519)

DU FRESNE DE FRANCHEVILLE, Joseph, *Histoire du Tarif de 1664 contenant l'origine de ce tarif.* . . , Paris (De Bure l'aîné), 1746, 2 vols. in 4º (G.L., XVIII 40 (2))

DUMAS, François, *La réglementation industrielle après Colbert*, Toulouse, 1908

—— *Etude sur le traité de commerce de 1786 entre la France et l'Angleterre*, Toulouse, 1904

DUPIN, Claude, *Œconomiques*, Carlsruhe, 1745, 3 vols. in 4º (B.N., rés., R 1.347–9); vol. i published with an introduction by Marc Aucuy, Paris (Marcel Rivière), 1913, 300 pp.; for a second edition of 1747 see *Mémoires sur les domaines, le commerce, les droits d'entrées et de sorties du royaume, les droits de péages, les grands chemins, la banque de Law et le crédit public.* . . . , (Lf⁸² 3)

—— *Observations sur un livre intitulé de l'Esprit des Loix, Divisée en trois parties*, Paris 1757–8, 3 vols. (B.N., rés. E 502)

DUPONT (de Nemours), Pierre-Samuel, *Mémoires sur la vie et les ouvrages de Monsieur Turgot (1782)*, new ed., Philadelphia, 1788, 224 pp.

—— *Considérations sur la position politique de la France, de l'Angleterre et de l'Espagne*, Paris, 30 pp. in 8º

—— *Procès-verbal de l'assemblée baillivale de Nemours pour la convocation des Etats généraux*, Paris, 1789

—— *Lettre à la chambre du commerce de Normandie sur le mémoire qu'elle a publié relativement au traité de commerce avec l'Angleterre*, Rouen and Paris (Moutard), 1788, 221 pp.

—— *Tableau comparatif des demandes contenues dans les cahiers des trois ordres, remis à MM. les Députés aux Etats-généraux*, Paris, 1789, 196 pp.

DUPRÉ DE SAINT-MAUR, *Mémoire sur la décadence du commerce de Bayonne et Saint-Jean-de-Luz et sur les moyens de le rétablir*, Bordeaux, 1783, 64 pp. in 4º (V. 14213)

DURAND, *Observations et réflexions politiques sur le commerce et les finances du Royaume, avec un exposé des différents moyens qui peuvent atténuer ou détruire les inconvénients résultants de la perception des impôts actuels précédé de reflexions* . . . , 2nd ed., Paris (Godefroy), 1789, in 12º, 100 pp. and 84 pp. (Lb³⁹ 11391). The first edition was issued anonymously under the title, *Considérations politiques sur le commerce du royaume avec des observations sur les impôts qui nuisent à son activité et dont on propose la suppression ainsi que le remplacement.* . . , (R 32297 and L.S.E. R/OU 1789/3/ 221913)

DUTIL, Léon, *L'état économique du Languedoc à la fin de l'ancien régime, 1750–1789*, Paris (Hachette), 1911

—— 'Un homme de '89. Pierre Roussillou, Député de Toulouse à la Constituante,' *Mémoires de l'Académie des Sciences, Inscriptions et Belles-lettres de Toulouse*, 1939 and 1940

O

Encore deux mots sur le tarif des traites relativement aux toiles étrangères nécessaires aux pauvres, Paris (Vézard & Le Normant), 1790, 8 pp. (Lf[89] 25)

Encyclopédie ou Dictionnaire raisonné des sciences, des arts et métiers, Paris, 1751–65, 17 vols.

Ephémérides du citoyen ou Chronique de l'esprit national et Bibliothèque raisonée des Sciences morales et politiques, 1765–72, 66 vols.

Etat actuel des travaux du Comité de l'Imposition présentée à l'Assemblée nationale, Paris (Imp. nat.), 1790 (B.M., F.R. 519)

Etat des régisseurs des douanes de la République et des employées au bureau de leur administration au premier août 1793, imprimé d'après les décrets des 20 mars et 8 avril 1793, l'an deuxième de la République une et indivisible, Paris (Imp. des régies nationales), 1793, 13 pp. (Lf[130] 5)

Etats de comptant de l'année et des restes de l'année 1783; avec la table alphabétique des personnes qui y sont employés, et quelques notes, Paris (Imp. nat.), 1790, 63 pp. and 108 pp. (B.M., F.R. 551)

Etats présentés à la Commission des douanes par les régisseurs, imprimés par ordre de la Convention nationale le 2 Frimaire an II, Paris (Imp. nat.) (Lf[130] 6)

Expilly, *Dictionnaire géographique, historique, et politique des Gaules et de la France*, Amsterdam, 1768, 5 vols. in fol.

Extrait de la lettre écrite par le Receveur de la Régie générale à Ingrande, direction d'Angers, du 3 juillet 1790 (B.M., R 628)

FALBAIRE DE QUINGEY, Charles-Georges Fenouillot de, *Lettre adressée le 3 septembre 1790 à Monsieur Necker . . . et suivie de quelques réflexions tant sur sa retraite que sur la continuation de l'existence ministérielle de Monsieur Lambert . . .*, Paris (Demonville), 1790, 51 pp. in 8º (Lb[39] 4046)

—— *Œuvres*, Paris (Veuve Duchesne), 1787, 2 vols. in 8º

—— *Mémoires adressés au Roi et à l'Assemblée nationale sur quelques abus et particulièrement contre une vexation de Monsieur Douët de la Boullaye, 1789 (15 August)*, 199 pp.; part two in ms. signed 24 October 1789, 114 fol. in A.N., C 92 (79)

FLEUREAU, *Essai sur les moyens de rendre quelques impositions moins onéreuses, par Monsieur F . . .*, Brussels and Paris (N.F. Valleyre jeune), 1775, 52 pp. in 8º (R 35352)

FLEURY, Gabriel, *François Véron de Fortbonnais, sa famille, sa vie, ses actes, ses œuvres, 1722–1800*, Le Mans (A. de Saint-Denis), 1915

FORTBONNAIS, François Véron Duvergner de, *Recherches et considérations sur les finances de France depuis l'année 1595 jusqu'à l'année 1721*, Basle (Frères Cramer), 1758, 2 vols. in 4º (B.M., 714 g 5 and 6)

FRÉVILLE, Henri, *L'intendance de Bretagne, 1689–1790*, Rennes (Plihon), 1953, 3 vols.

GALLIANI, L'abbé F., *Lettres* (ed. Asse), Paris, 1831, 2 vols.

GEORGEL, abbé, *Mémoires pour servir à l'histoire des évènements de la fin du 18e siècle depuis 1760 jusqu'au 1806*, Paris (Alexis-Eymery), 1820, 6 vols.

GERBAUX and SCHMIDT, ed., *Procès-verbaux des Comités d'Agriculture et de Commerce de la Constituante de la Législative et de la Convention*, Paris (Imp. nat.), 1906, 4 vols. and 1 vol. of tables

GERLIER, Félix, *Voltaire, Turgot et les franchises du pays de Gex*, Geneva (Jullien), 1883 (Lk² 3380)

GIRARDOT, baron de, *Essai sur les Assemblées provinciales et en particulier sur celle du Berry 1778–1790*, Bourges (Vermeil), 1845

GLANIÈRES, Richard des, *Plan d'impositions économiques et d'administration des finances présenté à Monsieur Turgot*, Paris (Simon), 1774, 35 pp. in 4° (R 7295)

GOMEL, Charles, *Histoire financière de l'Assemblée constituante*, Paris (Guillaumin), 1896–7, 2 vols.

—— *Les causes financières de la Révolution française*, Paris (Guillaumin), 1892–3, 2 vols.

GOMIEN, Georges, *La politique douanière de Colbert*, Paris (Rousseau), 1903

GONNARD, René, *Histoire des doctrines économiques*, Paris (Pichon & Durand-Auzias), 1943 (4e éd)

GOODWIN, A., 'Calonne, the Assembly of French Notables of 1787 and the origins of the *Révolte Nobiliaire*', *E.H.R.*, 1946

GOUDAR, Ange de, *Testament politique de Louis Mandrin, généralissime des troupes des contrebandiers écrit par lui-même dans sa prison*, Geneva, 1755, 67 pp. (Lf⁸⁹ 6)

GOUDARD, Pierre Louis, *Rapport présenté au nom des comités d'Agriculture et de Commerce et des Contributions publiques sur la nomenclature des bureaux de traites établis aux frontières, et sur la dépense résultant d'établissements formés en vertu des nouveaux décrets*, 1791, 4 pp. (Le²⁹ 1840)

GOUDARD, FONTENAI and ROUSSILLOU, *Rapport fait à l'Assemblée nationale au nom du Comité du Commerce et d'Agriculture sur la suppression des droits de traite perçus dans l'intérieur du royaume, le reculement des douanes aux frontières, et l'établissement d'un tarif uniforme*, Paris (Imp. nat.), 1790, annexed to the *procès-verbal* of the session of the Constituent Assembly of 27 August 1790, 49 pp.

—— *Rapport sur l'organisation générale de l'administration des douanes nationales, et sur la dépense qu'elle exige, présenté à l'Assemblée nationale au nom des comités réunis des Domaines, Contributions publiques, Finances, et Agriculture et Commerce, par un membre de ce dernier comité* (Decree of 23 April 1791), 31 pp. and tables (A.N., AD XVIIIᶜ 66)

GOURNAY and CLICQUOT DE BLERVACHE, *Considérations sur le commerce et en particulier sur les compagnies, sociétés et maîtrises*, Amsterdam, 1758, 180 pp. in 12° (R 31893)

GROUBER DE GROUBENTALL, *La finance politique réduite en principe et en pratique*, Paris (J. F. Bastien), 1775, 174 pp. in 12° (E 4424)

—— *Théorie de l'administration politique des finances*, Paris, 1788, 2 vols. in 8° (B.M., 1140 c 42)

GUIMBAUD, Louis, *Auget de Montyon, 1733–1820*, Paris (Emile-Paul), 1909

HARDY, Simon-Prospère, *Mes loisirs*, B.N., ms. fr. 6680–6685, published in part by Tourneux and Vitrac, Paris, 1912

HARSIN, Paul, *Les doctrines monétaires et financières en France du XVI au XVIII siècles*, Paris (Alcan), 1928

HESSELN, Robert de, *Dictionnaire universel de la France, contenant la description géographique et historique des provinces, villes, bourgs et lieux remarquables du royaume.* ..., Paris (Desaint), 1771, 6 vols. in 12° (B.M., 575 e 16–21)

HEURTAULT DE LAMERVILLE, J.-L.-T., comte de, *De l'impôt territorial combiné avec les principes de l'administration de Sully, et de Colbert adaptés à la situation actuelle de la France*, Strasbourg (Rolland & Jacob), 1788, 215 pp. in 4°

HIGGS, Henry, *Bibliography of Economics, 1751–75*, London, 1935

HYSLOP, Beatrice Fry, *French Nationalism in 1789 according to the General Cahiers*, New York (Columbia Univ. Press), 1934

Institut national d'études démographiques, *Économie et population. Les doctrines françaises avant 1800. Bibliographie générale commentée.* (Travaux et documents, cahier no. 28), Paris (P.U.F.), 1956

JOHNSON, E. A. J., *Predecessors of Adam Smith*, London, 1937

JOLLY, Pierre, *Calonne, 1734–1802*, Paris (Plon), 1949

—— *Dupont de Nemours, soldat de la liberté*, Paris (P.U.F.), 1956

Journal d'agriculture, du commerce, et des finances, July 1765 to December 1774, 114 tomes in 48 vols.

Journal de commerce, Brussels, 1759 to 1762, 24 vols.

Journal économique, 1751 to 1757, 28 vols., and 1758 to 1772, 15 vols.

LABROUSSE, C.-E., *La Crise de l'économie française à la fin de l'ancien régime et au début de la Révolution*, Paris, 1944, 664 pp.

LACOMBE DE PRÉZEL, Honoré, *Les progrès du commerce*, Amsterdam and Paris (Lottin), 1760, 335 pp. in 12° (Vz 1964)

LA MARE, Nicolas de, *Traité de la Police.* ..., Paris (Michel Brunet), 1713–1738, 4 vols. in fol. (B.M., 25 h 8–11)

LANNOY, de, *Comité des finances, analyse des observations de Monsieur Roederer, conseiller au Parlement de Metz, pour servir de réponse aux questions proposées par la Commission intermédiaire de l'Assemblée provinciale de Lorraine en 1787 sur le Tarif, par un citoyen de la province de Lorraine, de Lannoy, ingénieur du Roi, ci-devant attaché au corps de la gendarmerie*, 7 pp. in 4° (Lf⁸⁹ 22)

LA ROCHEFOUCAULD-LIANCOURT, François-Alexandre-Frédéric de, *Lettre à un membre de l'Assemblée nationale législative sur l'état du travail des contributions publiques lors de la clôture de l'Assemblée nationale constituante par un membre du Comité des Contributions publiques*, Paris (Du Pont), 18 October 1791, 15 pp. (B.M., F.R. 523)

LASNIER DE VAUSSENAY, *Rapport à l'Assemblée nationale sur la franchise de Bayonne*, Paris (Imp. Nat.), 1790, 10 pp. (Le²⁹ 1123 and B.M., F.R. 542)

LAVIE, Jean-Charles de, *Abrégé de la république de Bodin*, London (Jean Nourse), 1775, 2 vols. in 12° (B.M., 8008 aa 6)

—— *Des corps politiques et de leurs gouvernements*, 2ᵉ éd. augmentée, Lyon (Pierre Duplain), 1766. 3 vols. in 12° (B.M., 232 e 36–38)

LAVOISIER, Antoine-Laurent, *Œuvres*, Paris (Imp. nat.), 1893, 6 vols. in 4° (R 7804ᵗᵉʳ)

LECLERCQ, Dom. H., *Histoire de la Régence pendant la minorité de Louis XV*, Paris (Champion), 1922, 3 vols.

LECOQ, Marcel, *La conspiration du marquis de Favras, 1789–1790*, Paris (Foliguet et Rigot), 1955

LEFÈVRE DE LA MAILLARDIÈRE, *Traité d'économie politique embrassant toutes ses branches* . . . *présenté au Roi en 1782*, 1783 (R 52664)

Le Guide des employés ou instructions pour apprendre à verbaliser sur différentes matières concernant les Fermes générales unies du roy, traites, gabelles, et tabac, Amiens (Veuve Charles Caron-Hubault, imprimeur des fermes du Roi), 1751, 164 pp. in 8°. There are two copies of this volume in A.N., G¹ 63.

LELONG, Jacques, *Bibliothéque historique de la France contenant le catalogue des ouvrages, imprimés et manuscrits qui traitent de l'histoire de ce royaume, ou qui y ont rapport, avec des notes critiques et historiques*, new. ed., Paris (Hérissant), 1768–78, 5 vols. in fol.

LÉON, Pierre, *La naissance de la grande industrie en Dauphiné*, Paris (P.U.F.), 1954, 2 vols.

LEPELLETIER, Jean, *Mémoires pour le rétablissement du commerce en France*, Rouen, 1701, 131 pp. in 12° (V 44.723)

LEROUX, Ernest, ed., *Le commerce* (*Extrait du bulletin trimestriel de la Commission de recherches et de publication des documents relatifs à la vie économique de la Révolution*), Paris (Imp. nat.), 1912

LETACONNOUX, J., 'Le comité des députés extraordinaires des manufactures et du commerce de France et l'œuvre économique de l'Assemblée constituante, 1789–91', *Annales révolutionnaires*, 1913

LE TROSNE, Guillaume-François, *Réflexions politiques sur la guerre actuelle de l'Angleterre avec ses colonies et sur l'état de la Russie*, Orléans, 1777, 16 pp. in 8° (Nc 3158)

——— *De l'administration provinciale et de la réforme de l'impôt* (*1779*), Basle, 1788, 2 vols, in 8° (B.M., 907 f 4)

——— *L'Ordre social, ouvrage suivi d'un traité élémentaire sur la valeur, l'argent, la circulation, le commerce intérieur et extérieur*, Paris, 1777, 728 pp. (R 20878)

Lettre à l'auteur des considérations sur les droits particuliers et le véritable intérêt de la province d'Alsace dans la présente de la France, par un citoyen d'Alsace, Strasbourg (Imp. du Roi, Quartier de la Krautenau, No. 15), 1789, 17 pp. (Lk² 92 and B.M., F.R. (109) (5))

Lettre sur un article du Journal de Commerce imprimé à Bruxelles au mois d'octobre dernier, concernant le Projet de porter toutes les douanes de l'intérieur aux frontières du royaume et de la réforme du Tarif, Paris (Prault), 1762, 49 pp. in 12° (R 41797, and bound with Michau de Montaran, *Mémoire sur les tarifs*)

Lettres et pièces intéressantes pour servir à l'histoire du ministère de Roland, Servan, et Clavière, Paris, 1792 (B.M., R 94)

LEVASSEUR, Emile, *Histoire du commerce de la France*, Paris (Rousseau), 1911, 2 vols.

LISLE, chevalier, seigneur de Brainville, d'Harcourt et Malaincourt, de, *Mémoire sur la constitution actuelle des fermes du Roi pour la perceptions des droits sur le sel, sur le tabac, sur l'entrée, la sortie, la circulation des marchandises, 1782*, 227 pp. in 8° (Lf⁸³ 20)

LOMÉNIE DE BRIENNE, Etienne-Charles de, *Compte rendu au Roi au moi de Mars 1788*, Paris, 1788

MAGNIEN, Vivent, *Recueil alphabétique des droits de traites uniformes, de ceux d'entrée et de sortie des Cinq Grosses Fermes, de Douane de Lyon et de Valence* ..., Avignon (?), 1786, 4 vols. in 12º (F 39313-39316 and B.M., 282 g 24-27). For identification of this work see *supra*, p. 141

—— *Tarif des droits de douane et de navigation*, Paris, *an VIII*, in 4º. (This work, which I was not able to consult, is listed in the printed catalogue of the *Bib. de Genève*.)

—— *Tarif des droits de douane et de navigation de l'Empire français*. . . , Paris (Bailleul), 1808, 107 pp. (F 39317)

—— *Dictionnaire des productions de la nature, et de l'art qui font l'objet du commerce de la France*. . . , Paris (Bailleul), 1809, 3 vols., written in collaboration with Deu (B.M., 1029 g 11)

MARION, Marcel, *Histoire financière de la France depuis 1715* (vols. 1 and 2), Paris (Rousseau), 1927

MARTIN, Germain, *Bibliographie critique de l'histoire de l'industrie en France avant 1789*, Paris (Société des études historiques), 1900

—— *Histoire économique et financière*, (tome x of *Histoire de la nation française*, ed. G. Hanotaux), Paris (Plon), 1927

MASSON, Paul, *Ports francs d'autrefois et d'aujourd'hui*, Paris (Hachette), 1904

MASUI, Mitsuzo, *A Bibliography of Finance* (International Finance Seminar in the Kobe University of Commerce), Tokio, 1935

MATHEWS, George T., *The Royal General Farms in Eighteenth Century France*, New York (Columbia Univ. Press), 1958

MEAD, G. J. de C., *The Administrative Noblesse of France during the Eighteenth Century with Special Reference to the Intendants of the Generalities*, London University unpublished Ph.D. thesis, 1954

MELON, Jean-François, *Essai politique sur le commerce (1734)*, new ed., Amsterdam (François Changuion), 1754, 367 pp. in 12º (B.M., 8247 aa 23)

Mémoire de la Chambre de Commerce de Bayonne sur l'ancien état de cette ville; et sur les révolutions arrivées à son commerce, présenté à l'occasion des discussions qui luy ont été suscitées, Bayonne, 1738, 64 pp. (V 5330)

Mémoire et observations pour et contre le reculement des barrières sur la frontière des Trois Evêchés, Metz (Claude Lamort), 1787, 82 pp. in 4º (Lf⁸⁹ 13)

Mémoire historique, critique, et politique sur les droits de souveraineté rélativement aux droits de traite qui se perçoivent en Bretagne, 1765, 116 pp.

MENARD, *Observations sur l'état actuel du commerce de la France*, Paris (Vaufleuri), 1789, 71 pp. in 12º (V 46505)

Mercure de France, 1672 to 1791, 974 vols.

MÉTRA, François, *Correspondance secrète, politique et littéraire . . . depuis la mort de Louis XV*, London, 1787-90, 18 vols.

MICHAU DE MONTARAN, Jacques-Marie-Jérôme (the elder), *Mémoire sur les tarifs des droits de traites en général et en particulier sur le nouveau projet de tarif unique et uniforme*, Paris (Prault), 1762, 196 pp. and three appendices and a map. (F 39.852 and B.M., R 496)

MICHAUD, *Biographie universelle*, New ed., Paris, 1845

MIRABEAU, Victor-Riqueti, marquis de, *Lettres sur le commerce des grains*, Amsterdam and Paris, 1768, 324 pp. in 12° (R 41835)

—— *Lettres sur la législation, ou l'ordre légal dépravé, rétabli et perpétué, par L.D.H.*, Berne, 1775, 3 vols. in 8° (F 24537–39)

MIROT, Léon, *Manuel de géographie historique de la France*, 2ᵉ éd., Paris Picard, 1947, 2 vols.

MOLINARI, Gustave de, *Histoire du tarif*, Paris, 1847

MONGLOND, André, *La France révolutionnaire et impériale. Annales de bibliographie méthodique et descriptive des livres...*, vol. i (for the years 1789 and 1790), Grenoble (Arthaud), 1930

MONTAUDOUIN DE LA TOUCHE, Jean-Gabriel, *Suite des considérations sur les finances et le commerce en France* (1762), 26 pp., bound with Michau de Montaran, *op. cit.*, first published as an article in the Journal de Commerce, Octobre 1761; see *supra*, p. 56.

MOREAU, Jacob-Nicolas, *Mes souvenirs* (ed. Camille Hermelin), Paris, (Plon), 1901, 2 vols.

MOREAU DE BEAUMONT, Jean-Louis, *Mémoires concernant les impositions et droits en Europe* (1768), New Ed. with supplements by Poullin de Vieuville, Paris (Desaint), 1787, 3 vols. in 4ᵉ (B.M., 713 g 1)

MORELLET, abbé André, *Mémoire des fabriquants de Lorraine et de Bar, présenté à Monseigneur l'Intendant de la Province*, 1762, 67 pp., bound with Michau de Montaran, *op. cit.*

—— *Mémoires de l'abbé Morellet suivies de sa correspondance*, Paris, 1823, 2 vols.

NAVEAU, J.-B., *Le Financier citoyen*, 1757, 2 vols. in 12° (B.M., 8228 b 10)

NECKER, Jacques, *Compte rendu au Roi*, 1781 (B.M., 804 e 9)

—— *De l'administration des finances de la France*, 1784, 3 vols., in 8° (Lf⁷⁶ 7)

—— *Eloge de Jean-Baptiste Colbert*, Paris (Brunet), 1773, 135 pp. in 8° (Ln²⁷ 4514)

NIO, Joseph, *Turgot et la liberté du commerce*, Bordeaux (Bière), 1928

Nouvelles éphémérides économiques ou Bibliothèque raisonnée de l'histoire de la morale et de la politique, December 1774 to February 1776

Observations des maîtres crocheteurs et affâneurs commissionnés de l'adjudicataire général des Fermes unies de France, pour le service de la Douane de Lyon, Lyon (Martin), 1789, 4 pp. in 4° (Lf⁸⁹ 27)

Observations du Parlement de Nancy, sur le projet de réunir la province de Lorraine aux Cinq Grosses Fermes, 1780, 'Fait et arrêté en Parlement, les chambres assemblées, le 12 décembre 1778'. (I found only a manuscript copy of the printed brochure in Ass. Pub., papers of Auget de Montyon.)

Observations sommaires pour la ville de Strasbourg sur le reculement des barrières jusqu'au Rhin, présentées par son Député à l'Assemblée nationale, Paris (Moutard), 10 pp. (Lf⁸⁹ 18)

Ordre de travail pour les gardes et employés dans les brigades de la Ferme générale du 5 novembre 1758 (Imp. des Fermes, Lamesle), 15 pp. (A.N., G¹ 63)

PAGANUCCI, Jean, *Manuel historique, géographique et politique des négotiants, ou Encyclopédie portative de la théorie et de la pratique de commerce...*, Lyon (J.-M. Bruysot), 1762, 3 vols. in 8° (G 26280–82)

PAPON, *Histoire du gouvernement français depuis l'assemblée des notables tenue le 22 février 1787 jusqu'à la fin de décembre de la même année*, London, 1788, in 12°

PARISOT, Robert, *Histoire de Lorraine*, Paris (Picard), 1922, 3 vols.

PELLISSERY, Roch-Antoine de, *Eloge politique de Colbert qui n'a point été présenté à l'Académie française pour le prix de la Saint Louis*, 1773, London, 1777, 214 pp. and 132 pp. (Ln^{27} 4519 (1–2))

Petition des citoyens chargés de l'administration des Douanes nationales à l'Assemblée nationale, Paris (Imp. nat.) (1791), 3 pp. in 4^c (Lf^{130} 4)

Pigeonneau et de Foville, *L'Administration de l'agriculture au Contrôle général des finances de 1787*, Paris (Guillaumin), 1882

Plan des travaux du Comité d'Agriculture et de Commerce, présenté à l'Assemblée nationale le 8 mai 1790, 8 pp. (B.N., R. 54449)

Précis pour les Trois-Etats du Pays Messin au sujet du reculement des barrières sur la frontière, Metz (Veuve Antoine), 9 février 1787, 8 pp. in 4° (Lf^{89} 12; copy in A.N., F^{30} 111)

Précis des opérations de la Commission intermédiaire provinciale d'Alsace jusqu'au quinze février 1789, Strasbourg (Levrault), 1789, 121 pp. in 4° (Lf^{15} 9)

Premier rapport fait au nom du Comité de l'Imposition, le 18 août 1790, ordre du travail, 11 pp. (B.M., FR 519)

Procès-verbal et observations présentés au Roi par les bureaux de l'Assemblée des Notables, sur les mémoires remis à l'Assemblée ouverte par le Roi à Versailles, le 23 février 1787 (see mémoire entitled *Traites*, 67 pp.) (B.M., R 36(8))

Procès-verbal de l'Assemblée nationale, Paris (Baudouin)

Procès-verbal des séances de l'Assemblée provinciale d'Auvergne tenue à Clermont-Ferrand dans le mois d'août 1787, Clermont-Ferrand, 1787, 2 vols. (Lk^{88} 13)

Procès-verbal des séances de l'Assemblée provinciale de Dauphiné tenue à Grenoble le premier octobre 1787, Grenoble (Cuchet), 1787, 63 pp. in 4° (Lk^{15} 22)

Procès-verbal des séances de l'Assemblée provinciale de Haute-Guienne, tenue à Villefranche dans le mois de septembre et d'octobre 1779, avec le permission du Roi, Paris (Graport), 1787, 2 vols. in 4° (vol. i for the years 1779, 1780 and 1782; vol. ii for 1784 and 1786)

Procès-verbal des séances de l'Assemblée provinciale des duchés de Lorraine et de Bar, ouverte à Nancy au mois de novembre 1787, Nancy (Haener), 1788, in 4°, 495 pp. (B.M., 180 d 11)

Procès-verbal de l'Assemblée baillivale de Nemours pour la convocation des Etats-généraux avec les cahiers des trois ordres, Paris (Duplain), 1789, 2 vols. (by P.-S. Dupont de Nemours)

Procès-verbal des séances de l'Assemblée provinciale des Trois-Evêchés et du Clermontois, tenue à Metz dans les mois de novembre et décembre 1787, Metz (Antoine), 1787, in 4° (Lk^{15} 53)

Programme, fait et arrêté par la Commission intermédiaire provinciale d'Alsace, à Strasbourg, le 19 novembre 1788 (signed, 'Mathieu'), Strasbourg (Levrault) 1788, 3 pp. in 4° (Lk^{15} 7)

Projet de réforme des différentes compagnies de finance chargées du recouvrement des impôts indirects, dans lequel on indique le danger qu'il y aurait de confier l'exécution du reculement des barrières à la compagnie de la Ferme générale, dans son organization actuelle, 1790, B.M., F.R. 568

Projet pour la suppression des douanes dans l'intérieur du royaume, avec des anecdotes curieuses et intéressantes, Avignon (aux dépenses de l'auteur), 131 pp. and tables in 8° 1763 (Lf⁸⁹ 9)

PRUGNON, *Apperçu des motifs qui s'opposent à ce que les Duchés de Lorraine et de Bar soient compris dans le projet du reculement des barrières,* 1787, 119 pp. in 8° (Lf⁸⁹ 16)

PUGH, Wilma J., 'Calonne's New Deal', *The Journal of Modern History,* 1939

QUÉRARD, J.-M., *La France littéraire ou Dictionnaire bibliographique,* Paris (Didot), 1833

QUESNAY, François, 'Hommes' (1757), *R.h.d.e.s.,* 1908, pp. 3 and 88

—— *Physiocratie, ou Constitution naturelle du gouvernement le plus avantageux au genre humain, par François Quesnay, recueil publié par Du Pont,* Leyde and Paris (Merlin), 1768–69, 2 vols. in 8° (R 21037–38)

RABBE, *Biographie universelle et portative des contemporains,* Paris, (Levrault), 1834, 5 vols.

Rapport sur l'organisation générale de l'administration des Douanes nationales, et sur la dépense qu'elle exige. . . . ; cf. a table compiled by the Committee on Taxation and published 22 June 1791 (B.M., F.R. 524).

RÉBILLON, Armand, *Les Etats de Bretagne de 1661 à 1789, leur organisation, l'évolution de leurs pouvoirs, leur administration financière,* Rennes (Imp. Rennes), 1932

Recueil des tarifs et règlements des droits d'entrée et sortie qui se perçoivent présentement sur toutes sortes de marchandises et denrées dans toutes les douanes et romaines du royaume. . . , Rouen, 1703, 26 pp. and 574 pp. in 16° (G.L. XVIII 03 (4))

Réflexions d'un solitaire sur le projet de priver la province de Lorraine de la liberté de commercer avec l'étranger, pour l'assimiler aux provinces de France, dites des Cinq Grosses Fermes (1786), 56 pp. (Lf⁸⁹ 15)

Réflexions sur la nécessité de l'existence des douanes dans les Pays-Bas Autrichien et sur leur influence sur le commerce en général des mêmes pays, Brussels (Emmanuel Flon), 1788, 122 pp. in 8° (F 3560)

Réimpression de l'Ancien Moniteur, Paris, 1863, 31 vols.

RÉMOND, André, *John Holker, manufacturier et grand fonctionnaire en France au dix-huitième siècle,* Paris (Rivière), 1946

—— *Etudes sur la circulation marchande en France aux XVIII et XIX siècles,* Paris (Rivère), 1956

RENOUARD, A.-A., *Essai sur les moyens de rendre le reculement des barrières véritablement avantageux au commerce tant intérieur qu'extérieur,* Paris (Chalon), September 1790, 32 pp. in 8° (Lf⁸⁹ 20)

—— *Réflexions sur les fabriques nationales et sur celles de gazes en particulier par Monsieur R. . . . , fabriquant de gazes,* Paris, January 1790 (B.M., R 510)

RENOUVIN, Pierre, *Les Assemblées provinciales de 1787,* Paris (Picard), 1921

ROEDERER, Pierre-Louis, *Œuvres*, Paris (Didot), 1853, 8 vols.

—— *Observations sur les intérêts des Trois Evêchés et de la Lorraine relativement au reculement des barrières des traites*, 1787, 24 pp. in 8° (Lf⁸⁹ 11)

—— *Questions proposées par la commission intermédiaire de l'Assemblée provinciale de Lorraine, concernant le reculement des barrières, et Observations pour servir de réponse à ces questions*, 1787, 222 pp. in 12° (Lf⁸⁹ 10)

—— *Réflexions sur le rapport fait à l'Assemblée provinciale de Metz au sujet du reculement des barrières des traites au-delà des provinces dites étrangères*, 1788, 37 pp. in 8° (Lf⁸⁹ 14)

ROQUE, comte de la, *Observations sur les droits de traite en général, et en particulier sur les vins du Périgord et du Quercy, présentés à l'Assemblée nationale. . .* , 13 pp. (Lf⁸⁹ 24)

ROUSSELOT DE SURGY, Jacques-Philibert, *Encyclopédie méthodique, partie finances*, Paris (Panckoucke), 1784–87, 3 vols.

ROUX, Pierre, *Les fermes d'impôt sous l'ancien régime*, Paris (Rousseau), 1916

SAGNAC, Philippe, *La formation de la société française moderne*, Paris, 1946, 2 vols.

—— 'La politique commerciale de la France avec l'étranger de la paix de Ryswick à la paix d'Utrecht, 1697–1713', *Rev. hist.*, 1910

SAINT-SIMON, Louis de Rouvroy, duc de, *Mémoires*, Paris (Gallimard 'Pléiade'), 1953–61, 7 vols.

SAULNIER, Anatole, *Recherches historiques sur le droit de douane. . .* , *jusqu'à la Révolution de 1789*, Paris (Martellon), 1839

SAUVAIRE-JOURDAN, 'Isaac de Bacalan et les idées libre-échangistes en France vers le milieu de XVIIIᵉ siècle', *Rev. d'économie politique*, 1903

SAVARY DES BRUSLONS, Jacques, *Dictionnaire universel du commerce*, new ed., Geneva (Philibert), 1742, 4 vols. in fol.

SCHATZ, Albert, and CAILLEMAR, Robert, 'Le mercantilisme libéral à la fin du XVIIᵉ siècle. Les idées économiques et politiques de M. de Belesbat', *Revue d'économie politique*, 1906

SCHELLE, Gustave, *Du Pont de Nemours et l'école physiocratique*, Paris (Guillaumin), 1888

SÉE, Henri, *Histoire économique de la France*, Paris (Colin), 1939, 2 vols.

—— 'The Normandy Chamber of Commerce and the Commercial Treaty of 1786', *Ec. Hist. Rev.*, 1930

SÉMICHON, E., *Les réformes sous Louis XVI, assemblées provinciales et parlements*, Paris (Didier), 1876

SERANE, J.-F., *Opinion de Monsieur Sérane, député de l'Hérault sur la suppression des douanes, présentée aux deux comités de Marine et de Commerce, réunis, et imprimée par ordre de ces deux comités pour y être discutée* (1790), 39 pp. in 8° (Le³³ 3 F.19)

SÈZE, comte R. de, *Mémoire et consultation pour les Fabricans de toiles peintes dans l'intérieur du Royaume en réponse au mémoire des fabricans de toiles peintes en Alsace* (Signed, 'Ticquet, Sallé, Quesnel, Heutte, députés des manufactures de l'intérieur: délibéré à Paris le 1 avril 1788'), 39 pp. (F 14330–51)

STOURM, René, *Les finances de l'ancien régime et de la Révolution origine du système financier actuel*, Paris (Guillaumin), 1885, 2 vols.

—— *Bibliographie historique des finances de la France au dix-huitième siècle*, Paris (Guillaumin), 1895, 341 pp.

SUSANE, G., *La tactique financière de Calonne*, Paris (Rousseau), 1901

Tarif de la Traite d'Arzac, Dax (Roger Leclercq, imp. des Fermes du Roy), 1783, 34 pp. (A.N., G¹ 3–5)

Tarif des droits d'entrée et de sortie des Cinq Grosses Fermes ordonnés être perçus par l'édit de 1664 sur toutes les marchandises, augmenté de notes et observations sur les mutations des droits depuis ledit Tarif, New Ed., Rouen (Libraires associés), 1758, 2 vols. in 4° (F 23100 à 23101)

Tarif général des droits de sorties et entrées du royaume et des provinces esquelles les Bureaux ne sont établis, ordonnéz estre levez sur toutes les marchandises et denrées, arrêté au Conseil royal le 18 septembre 1664, avec l'édit du Roy du même mois et an, Paris (Libraires associés pour l'impression des Ordonnances des Fermes), 1748, 168 pp. (F 40820)

TOLOZAN, Jean-François de, *Mémoire sur le commerce de la France et de ses colonies, par de Tolosan, Intendant du commerce*, Paris (Moutard), 1789, 122 pp. in 4° (V 17731)

Traite par Terre et Imposition Foraine, Angers, 1765, 35 pp. (A.N., G¹ 79)

TURGOT, A.-R.-J., *Œuvres*, ed. G. Schelle, Paris, 1913–23, 5 vols.

UZEREAU, F., 'Le Trépas de Loire', *Andegaviana*, 13ᵉ série, Angers and Paris, 1913 (8° Lk² 5205)

VAUBAN, Sebastien Le Prestre, marquis de, *Dîme royal*, ed. Michel, Paris (Guillaumin), 1888, 208 pp. in 8° (R 8660 (17))

VERNIER, Théodore, *Nouveau plan de finances et d'impositions formé d'après les décrets de l'Assemblée nationale*, Paris (Imp. nat.), 1790, 46 pp. (B.M., F.R. 521)

VIALAY, Amédée, *Les cahiers de doléances du tiers état aux Etats généraux de 1789*, Paris (Perrin), 1911

VIDAL, Pierre, *Histoire de la Révolution française dans le département des Pyrénées orientales...*, Perpignan, 1885–9, 3 vols.

VIEILH, *Essai sur les finances présenté en 1775 à Monsieur Turgot, Ministre d'Etat et Contrôleur général, par l'auteur du Secret des Finances, imprimé en 1763*, 1789, 104 pp. in 12° (Lb³⁹ 1327)

VIGNES, J.-B. Mauriac, 'Les observations sur un ouvrage de Monsieur le Maréchal de Vauban intitulé Dixme royale', *R.h.d.e.s.*, 1910

VIVENS, François de, *Observations sur divers moyens de soutenir et d'encourager l'agriculture principalement dans la Guyenne*, 1756, 225 pp. and 171 pp. (B.M., 234 c 8)

WEULERSSE, Georges, 'Le mouvement pré-physiocratique en France, 1748–1755', *R.h.d.e.s.*, 1931

WEULERSSE, Georges, *Le mouvement physiocratique en France de 1756 à 1770*, Paris (Alcan), 1910, 2 vols.

—— *La physiocratie sous les ministères de Turgot et de Necker (1774–81)*, Paris (P.U.F.) 1950

WYBO, Bernard, *Le Conseil de Commerce et le commerce intérieur de la France au XVIIIᵉ siècle*, Paris (Domat-Montchrestien), 1936 (L.S.E., HF (44) E2)

INDEX

P